The Musical Language of Rock

THE MUSICAL LANGUAGE OF ROCK

David Temperley

OXFORD
UNIVERSITY PRESS

OXFORD
UNIVERSITY PRESS

Oxford University Press is a department of the University of Oxford. It furthers the University's objective of excellence in research, scholarship, and education by publishing worldwide. Oxford is a registered trade mark of Oxford University Press in the UK and certain other countries.

Published in the United States of America by Oxford University Press 198 Madison Avenue, New York, NY 10016, United States of America.

Library of Congress Cataloging-in-Publication Data
Names: Temperley, David, author.
Title: The musical language of rock / David Temperley.
Description: New York, NY : Oxford University Press, [2018] |
Includes bibliographical references and index.
Identifiers: LCCN 2017047909 | ISBN 9780190653774 (hardcover) |
ISBN 9780190870522 (pbk.) | ISBN 9780190653804 (oxford scholarly online) |
ISBN 9780190653811 (companion website)
Subjects: LCSH: Rock music—Analysis, appreciation.
Classification: LCC MT146 .T44 2018 | DDC 781.66/117—dc23
LC record available at https://lccn.loc.gov/2017047909

This volume is published with the generous support of the Manfred Bukofzer Endowment of the American Musicological Society, funded in part by the National Endowment for the Humanities and the Andrew W. Mellon Foundation.

9 8 7 6 5 4 3 2 1

Paperback printed by Webcom, Inc., Canada
Hardback printed by Bridgeport National Bindery, Inc., United States of America

For Maya

CONTENTS

PREFACE

My interest in the study of popular music goes back to high school, when I made graphs of songs going up and down on the Top 40 charts. When I entered the field of music theory in the mid-1990s, I had no idea that I might be able to pursue this interest further. Yet this was precisely the time that the theoretical/analytical study of popular music was becoming respectable, thanks to the pioneering efforts of Walter Everett, Allan Moore, John Covach, and others. In the early years of my career, I published several articles about harmony and rhythm in rock; in 2008, with my student Trevor de Clercq, I embarked on a corpus project which gave me a valuable new perspective on rock harmony and melody. Over time, ideas from these various strands of research began to connect with each other; it seemed to me that it might be useful to bring it all together in one place. This book is the result.

This book is written for people with a serious interest in rock music. There are no colorful anecdotes about the drug habits, sexual adventures, and lavish lifestyles of rock musicians (many other books have explored that territory!). The book also requires some musical background: an understanding of music notation and of basic theoretical concepts like major/minor triads and Roman-numeral chord symbols. In some ways, it could be considered a scholarly book. It is not an overview of the current state of the field; much of the conceptual material is new and speculative (presented only in my earlier articles, or not even there). Part of my reason for writing the book is to present my ideas for consideration by other scholars.

Having said all this, I hope and believe that the book will be of interest to an audience beyond professional music theorists. Any reader with the interest and basic musical background described above should be able to get something out of it. While I touch here and there on concepts from psychology, statistics, and computational research, no background is needed in any of these areas to understand the book. (The statistics in the book are mostly of a very simple sort: counting things and taking averages.) Nearly every musical example is accompanied by a sound clip from the original song (at the book's website, www.oup.com/us/themusicallanguageofrock); this may be useful to readers who have limited experience with music notation. In addition, chords in the musical examples are identified in both relative terms (Roman numerals) and absolute terms (lead-sheet symbols). While a relative understanding of harmony is crucial for many of the points that I make, the lead-sheet symbols may be helpful for readers less fluent with Roman numerals.

I hope, also, that the book may be useful as a course text in certain situations. It would *not* be suitable in a rock course for non-music-majors, as I have already made clear. But it could well be used in an upper-level undergraduate theory or analysis course (on rock, or of a more general nature), or in a graduate music theory seminar. Some of the earlier chapters in the book—especially chapters 2 and 3—are among the most technical, dealing with issues of pitch organization that may seem "nerdy" to some readers. In the later chapters of the book, I address issues of emotion and meaning which may have broader appeal. But my treatment of these latter topics relies heavily on concepts presented earlier; so I would not recommend, for example, reading the chapters on emotion and form without reading earlier chapters. However, students should be encouraged to skim over any section that, for any reason, they find too difficult; they should try to get the gist and then move on. Instructors might wish to supplement the book with a more historically-oriented text such as Covach & Flory (2015) or George-Warren et al. (2001), or with readings in a more sociocultural vein such as those in Dettmar & Richey (1999).

At the end of each chapter I have provided several "Questions." Roughly speaking, these are of three types: (1) essentially factual questions, testing the reader's understanding of concepts such as diatonic modes; (2) analytical questions requiring some musical thought and judgment, such as analyzing the form of an unusual song; and (3) questions about more general issues, such as the adequacy of the circumplex model for representing emotion in rock. (Each chapter's questions are roughly ordered in this way—from more specific/factual to more general/analytical—though I did not try to categorize them, and not all chapters include all three question types.) Questions of the first type might well be suitable for homework assignments. Questions of the second and third types are clearly more open-ended, lacking a single "right" answer (in some cases I am not sure what the best answer is myself). Indeed, some of these questions are presented partly as a way of indicating issues that I think are unresolved or neglected in the current book and deserve further study. But of course, questions of this kind can be useful in course situations as well—as topics for discussion, or for essay assignments—as long as the instructor is aware of their open-ended nature. Most of the questions of types 1 and 2 involve the close study of individual songs, and music notation of some kind will often be needed to answer them (conventional notation of the melody and/ or other parts, along with harmonic symbols). In such cases, transcribing the necessary information could be part of the assignment; if this is too challenging, a transcription could be provided to the student, either done by the instructor or obtained from the internet (but beware of inaccurate transcriptions!).

This book has benefited from the help of many people, both directly and indirectly. To my wonderful colleagues at the Eastman School of Music, I am grateful for many conversations that I am sure have shaped my thinking about rock in profound ways. (It was Bill Marvin who pointed out to me the ♭VII chord in "Not Fade Away.") A seminar on rock with eight terrific Eastman graduate students in 2015 was also extremely helpful. My former student and collaborator Trevor de Clercq has been an invaluable "second opinion" on countless matters, from large theoretical issues to small details of analysis and transcription. Thanks are also due to several collaborators on projects cited in the book: Adam Waller provided great help on creating the corpus of post-2000 songs, Iris Ren and Zhiyao Duan worked with me on the "blue note" project (Iris also created Example 10.4), and Ethan Lustig and Ivan Tan created the lyric and stress components of the *Rolling Stone* corpus. Ken Stephenson and Christopher White gave me excellent feedback on chapters from the book. In the later stages of the project, Ivan Tan created the sound files for the website and checked the musical examples, and Chanmi Na helped me with the reference list. Suzanne Ryan, Jamie Kim, Ed Robinson, and Lauralee Yeary at Oxford University Press were consistently helpful and professional. I am of course solely responsible for any errors in any aspects of the book.

On a personal note, thanks go to my sisters, Lucy and Sylvie, for many happy occasions of playing/singing rock music together and talking about it. Thanks to my amazing children, Asha and Roshan, for taking breaks from their computer games to allow me to write the book, and for being a constant source of wonder and amusement. To my wife, Maya, I am grateful for her putting up with my obsession with this book over the last two years, and for her unwavering support and understanding.

ABOUT THE COMPANION WEBSITE

URL: www.oup.com/us/themusicallanguageofrock

Oxford University Press has created an open website to accompany *The Musical Language of Rock*. Recordings of many of the musical excerpts referenced in the book may be streamed at this site. (Examples available online are indicated in the text with Oxford's symbol ▶.) The website also contains some other supplementary materials relevant to the book. The reader is encouraged to take advantage of these additional resources.

The Musical Language of Rock

CHAPTER 1

Introduction

1.1 THE MUSIC OF ROCK

This is a book about rock—specifically, about the *music* of rock. There is no shortage of books about rock; in a book store or university library, they will typically fill several shelves. Many of these books are biographical studies of individual artists and bands, or historical surveys of subgenres such as Motown or punk rock. Other books on rock have taken a sociological perspective—focusing on its role in social and cultural identity, its implications for issues of race and gender, and its political and economic aspects.[1] But relatively few books have focused on the purely *musical* dimensions of the style: dimensions of harmony and melody, tonality and scale, rhythm and meter, phrase structure and form.

This is not to say that the musical aspects of rock have been completely neglected; and research in this area has contributed greatly to our understanding of the style. However, this literature, too, has been limited in a fundamental way. For the most part, it has been what I would call *analysis* rather than *theory*. By "analysis," I mean an intensive study of a particular song (or perhaps album or artist). By "theory," I mean the study of the general features and principles of a musical style. Of course, analysis and theory inform each other; we cannot understand a style without closely examining individual works. But we also cannot appreciate individual works without understanding the norms and regularities of the

---

1. See, for example, Frith (1981), DeCurtis (1992), Friedlander (1996), Dettmar & Richey (1999), Gracyk (2001), and Kearney (2006).

style. Most of the books and articles on rock music have been analytical in character (though there have been some important contributions to the theory of rock, which I will discuss below).[2] I believe that, in order to better understand individual rock pieces, we need to come to a better understanding of the style itself. In this book, I offer an investigation of the musical language of rock.

My choice of title—the *musical language* of rock—may seem provocative; for the issue of whether, or how, music is a language is complex and contentious.[3] However, I only wish to assert certain basic parallels between music and language that I hope will be uncontroversial. Like language, music is a system of human communication, in which symbolic patterns are conveyed from the producer to the perceiver via the medium of sound. In language, these patterns are words and the higher-level (syntactic and semantic) representations that are inferred from them; in music, they include notes and chords, more abstract elements such as phrases, scales, and metrical frameworks, and larger structures formed by combinations of these elements. A language distinguishes grammatical sentences (those that follow the rules of the language) from ungrammatical ones; in a musical style, similarly, certain combinations of elements are normative within the style and others are not. (In music, these norms tend to be of a fuzzy, gradient nature rather than hard-and-fast grammatical "rules.") To say that musical elements and patterns are "symbolic" is simply to say that they in some way imply or signify other things. The nature of this signification is a matter of debate—in particular, whether it corresponds to "meaning" in language. To a large extent, musical elements seem to point to other musical elements (in the way that a motive points to an earlier occurrence of itself, or a certain chord progression establishes a key or indicates the end of a section); in other ways, they can carry undeniable "extramusical" significance.[4] But however one comes down on the issue of meaning, the basic parallel between music and language as systems of symbolic communication seems beyond dispute.

A second parallel between music and language is that the production and perception of music—like language—relies on knowledge that is not

---

2. Among the many recent analytical studies of rock are the essays in Covach & Boone (1997), Holm-Hudson (2002), Everett (2008a), and Spicer & Covach (2010), as well as many articles, some of which will be cited below. The distinction between "analytical" and "theoretical" studies is of course an oversimplification—analytical studies may have some theoretical content, and vice versa; but the distinction is still a useful one.

3. See Swain (1997) and Patel (2008) for discussions of this issue.

4. See Meyer (1956), for a classic discussion of the issue of meaning in music; see also Coker (1972) and Swain (1997).

easily articulated and, to some extent, unconscious. Anyone who can speak and understand English has some kind of knowledge of the rules of English grammar, but few such people are able to state exactly what those rules are. Similarly, I will argue, creators and listeners of rock music have knowledge about the norms and regularities of rock, but largely at an unconscious level. In large part, my goal in this book is to articulate this tacit knowledge, to uncover the mental processes and representations involved in musical creation and perception. In this way, the current book follows in the tradition of "cognitive" music theory, seen most famously in the work of Lerdahl and Jackendoff (1983). This approach might also allow us to *explain* aspects of the listener's experience—why it is, for example, that a particular moment in a song is especially satisfying or creates an effect of tension or sadness. In other cases, my analyses may reveal aspects of a song that were not part of the reader's listening experience at all, but perhaps enrich and expand that experience in some way; this, too, is a common—and perfectly valid—goal of music theory and analysis. For the most part, I will remain noncommittal between these two goals.[5] But the hope is that, one way or the other, the book will be relevant to the reader's experience of rock music, either by explaining it or enriching it; if the book does not achieve either of these goals, it will have missed its mark.

In developing my ideas about rock music, I have largely employed the conventional methodology of music theory—relying on my intuitive knowledge of the style, coupled with close study of a large number of individual songs. I have also employed another kind of evidence, however, namely, statistical corpus data. My colleague Trevor de Clercq and I have created a corpus of 200 rock songs, annotated with melodic transcriptions and harmonic analyses (the details are discussed further in section 1.4). If the goal is to uncover the stylistic knowledge that guides the creation of rock songs, corpus evidence provides a direct reflection of this. For example, if one is arguing that a certain harmonic progression is normative in the minds of rock musicians, showing that the progression actually occurs frequently will greatly strengthen the claim. In an indirect way, a corpus approach can also give insight into listeners' knowledge of rock music.

---

5. Much work in music theory and analysis is similar in this respect. In an earlier article (Temperley, 1999a), I was critical of this noncommittal stance with regard to the goals of music theory and analysis. Over the years, I have come to see that it is defensible and often productive. Still, I believe it is important to recognize that the two goals are, in principle, distinct.

Presumably, knowledge of a musical style comes from exposure to a large number of pieces in the style; deriving conclusions from corpus data mirrors this learning process.[6] Corpus data has been helpful to me in testing my own intuitions about the stylistic norms of rock, and it has sometimes yielded interesting new insights as well; I refer to it frequently in the following chapters.

Following this introductory chapter, chapters 2 through 6 of the book are organized around a series of musical topics: scales and key (ch. 2), harmony (ch. 3), rhythm and meter (ch. 4), melody (ch. 5), and timbre and instrumentation (ch. 6). In the remaining five chapters, I attempt to unify these musical dimensions and to bring them to bear on larger issues. Chapter 7 considers two aspects of musical experience, emotion and tension, exploring how they are shaped by the musical parameters discussed earlier. Chapter 8 addresses the topic of form—large-scale structure—which, again, relies heavily on the local features explored in previous chapters. In chapter 9, I consider several strategies that are used to shape songs and song sections in pursuit of aesthetic goals; these goals include the balance between closure and continuity, and the creation of trajectories of tension, energy, and emotional valence. In chapter 10, I present in-depth analytical discussions of six songs, hopefully substantiating my earlier claim that a better theory of rock can inform and improve our analyses. Finally, in chapter 11, I consider rock from a broader stylistic perspective, examining its musical roots, historical evolution, and recent development.

I have made clear that my focus in this study will be on music rather than lyrics. However, it might seem bizarre, in a study of rock, to ignore lyrics entirely; the lyrics of a song are, after all, part of the song. Here, the distinction between analysis and theory is important. In an analysis—an intensive exploration of a song in all of its aspects—consideration of lyrics would seem essential. In a theoretical study, however, where one is exploring the general musical features of a style, the relevance of lyrics is less clear. For example, in discussing a particular harmonic progression or formal pattern, it would seem unnecessary—indeed, cumbersome and distracting—to refer constantly to the lyrical content of every song that is mentioned. I will touch on lyrics, however, in cases where they seem to correlate in consistent ways with the musical dimensions under discussion—for example, in my treatment of the emotional connotations of scales. And

6. This reasoning invokes the concept of statistical learning, an important principle in recent music cognition research (Huron, 2006) and in cognitive science more generally (Saffran et al., 1996).

of course, in the analytical discussions in chapter 10, lyrics will receive due consideration.

1.2 WHAT IS ROCK?

What is rock—and what is not? With any category of musical style, boundaries are blurred and gray areas arise. Probably everyone would consider groups like the Rolling Stones, the Police, and Nirvana to be rock; but what about Aretha Franklin, the Bee Gees, and Joni Mitchell? These are probably not the first artists that the term brings to mind; they would probably not be played on a "rock" radio station, for example. There is, however, a broader definition of rock, also widely used, that does include these artists, and it is this broader definition that I will assume here, for reasons that I will explain.

If we assume the broader understanding of rock, what exactly does this category include? One source of evidence is what might be called "greatest" lists: lists of the greatest songs in rock (and other styles) compiled by music media outlets (magazines, radio stations, and cable channels). If a song is included on a list of the "greatest rock songs," this presumably indicates that it is considered to be rock. (Whether or not the songs on the list are in fact the *greatest* rock songs is not important for present purposes.) Table 1.1 shows part of one such list—*Rolling Stone* magazine's "500 Greatest Songs of All Time" (2004). (Only the top 20 songs are shown; the complete list can be seen at this book's website.) The list was based on a poll of 172 "rock stars and leading authorities" who were asked to list the 50 top songs "of the rock & roll era," and these song selections were combined using a "numerical weighting system." It can be seen that the list reflects a fairly broad spectrum of late 20th-century popular styles—1950s rock & roll (Chuck Berry and Elvis Presley), "British Invasion" bands (the Beatles and the Rolling Stones), soul and Motown (Aretha Franklin, Marvin Gaye), punk rock (the Clash), and 1990s grunge (Nirvana). A bit further down the list we have disco (Donna Summer's "Hot Stuff"), soft rock (Elton John's "Your Song"), heavy metal (AC/DC's "Back In Black"), 1980s pop (Michael Jackson's "Billie Jean"), and a wide range of other artists—the Eagles, Simon & Garfunkel, U2, Stevie Wonder.

The *Rolling Stone* list provides an indication of the genres that are generally included in a broad definition of rock, and it roughly corresponds to the scope of the term that is assumed in this book. (The *Rolling Stone* list is also the basis for the corpus of harmonic and melodic data that will be used here, discussed later in this chapter.) A similar understanding of "rock" can be found in many other places as well. For example, in the cable

Table 1.1 THE TOP 20 SONGS FROM *ROLLING STONE* MAGAZINE'S LIST OF THE "500 GREATEST SONGS OF ALL TIME" (2004)

Rank	Title	Year	Artist
1	Like a Rolling Stone	1965	Bob Dylan
2	Satisfaction	1965	The Rolling Stones
3	Imagine	1971	John Lennon
4	What's Going On	1971	Marvin Gaye
5	Respect	1967	Aretha Franklin
6	Good Vibrations	1966	The Beach Boys
7	Johnny B. Goode	1958	Chuck Berry
8	Hey Jude	1968	The Beatles
9	Smells Like Teen Spirit	1991	Nirvana
10	What'd I Say	1959	Ray Charles
11	My Generation	1965	The Who
12	A Change Is Gonna Come	1964	Sam Cooke
13	Yesterday	1965	The Beatles
14	Blowin' in the Wind	1963	Bob Dylan
15	London Calling	1980	The Clash
16	I Want to Hold Your Hand	1963	The Beatles
17	Purple Haze	1967	The Jimi Hendrix Experience
18	Maybellene	1955	Chuck Berry
19	Hound Dog	1956	Elvis Presley
20	Let It Be	1970	The Beatles

channel VH1's list of the "100 Greatest Songs of Rock & Roll" (2003), six of the top ten songs on the list are also in *Rolling Stone*'s top ten (those by Bob Dylan, the Rolling Stones, John Lennon, Aretha Franklin, the Beach Boys, and the Beatles). The list of inductees in the Rock and Roll Hall of Fame reflects a similar stylistic range, as do many books about rock.[7] Note that this broad definition of rock does not include all late-20th-century Anglo-American popular music. Country music is generally excluded, as is rap music; the relationships between rock and these genres will be considered in chapter 11.[8]

7. See for example George-Warren et al. (2001), Larkin (2003), and Covach & Flory (2015).

8. I know of no source that considers country music a subgenre of rock. The case of rap is more complex. The *Rolling Stone* 500-song list contains a handful of rap songs; the Rock and Roll Hall of Fame has also inducted several rap artists. My reasons for excluding rap are musical: in particular, the absence of vocal melody in rap, and frequently of harmony as well, makes it fundamentally different from all the genres of rock.

While there are undoubtedly significant differences between the sub-genres of rock—a Motown song sounds very different from a punk song—I will try to show that there are strong similarities across them that justify the broad definition of rock assumed here. Historically, too, I will argue that the musical language of rock has remained rather consistent—despite certain passing fashions and gradual evolutionary changes—over a period of some 40 years, from the early 1960s to the turn of the century. (The very early years of the rock era—the 1950s—are stylistically somewhat distinct from the later period, as I will discuss.) Part of my aim in this book is to show that there is enough internal consistency in this broad conception of rock to make it historically and theoretically useful.

It is also important to recognize the very profound commonalities between rock and other kinds of Western music—earlier and concurrent popular styles (Tin Pan Alley, blues, swing-era jazz, country) as well as music of the European common-practice tradition. At the same time, rock is not merely a hodgepodge of earlier styles; indeed, some aspects of its musical language are quite distinctive. In the final chapter of the book, I will consider the broader stylistic context of rock and offer some thoughts about its musical heritage. The final chapter will also consider the stylistic evolution of rock over the last decade and a half (i.e., since 2000). Many would argue that the cultural importance of rock has declined during that time, partly due to the rise of other genres, especially rap; but it lives on, though it has evolved in some interesting and surprising ways.

Two other stylistic terms deserve mention. The term "pop" is often encountered as a stylistic category, distinct from rock; for example, Michael Jackson is sometimes called the "King of Pop." In practice, pop seems to refer to artists who have had extensive commercial success with singles (especially on the Billboard "Hot 100" chart); thus the Supremes (who have had many number one hits) are pop and Led Zeppelin (who have had none) are not.[9] Construed in this way, most pop falls under the broad category of rock assumed here.[10] It is difficult to find any specific musical features that

9. The Billboard Hot 100 is the industry standard for measuring the commercial success of individual songs. In the early years of rock, the Hot 100 was based mainly on sales of singles; as this declined, however, the chart gave more weight to radio airplay and other sales media such as digital downloads.

10. Some have defined the rock/pop distinction in terms of the attitude of the performer, and in particular, in terms of *authenticity*: rock is an authentic expression, while pop is mere entertainment (e.g., Frith, 1987). But this approach is controversial (Middleton, 2001; Keightley, 2001), and even its defenders (e.g., Moore, 2002a) acknowledge that it is subjective and does not correlate with musical features in any consistent way.

distinguish pop in general from other rock. With respect to certain eras, however, the term denotes bodies of music with fairly consistent characteristics (e.g., "1980s pop"), and it can be useful in that way. ("Pop" is not the same as "popular music," a term with a much more general meaning; see Middleton, 1990.) The term "rock & roll" also deserves mention. This is sometimes taken to be synonymous with rock; I take it this way in *Rolling Stone*'s polling instructions, which use both "rock & roll" and "rock," and also in the Rock and Roll Hall of Fame. But it is also used to refer specifically to very early (1950s) rock, and I will sometimes use it that way here.[11]

1.3 CONTROVERSIAL ISSUES

This book, then, is an attempt to characterize the general features of the rock style, broadly defined, focusing on musical parameters. This is not the first such study to be attempted. In particular, three earlier books, by Allan Moore (2001), Ken Stephenson (2002), and Walter Everett (2009), have laid the groundwork for the current study, both in their general approach and in their insights about specific issues; I will refer to them frequently. A number of recent articles have also made important contributions, as later citations will show. Despite these precedents, the whole project of studying the music of rock remains controversial. A book such as this may be met with skepticism and objections in some quarters, and it seems prudent here to address some of the concerns that may arise.

One issue that arises in the study of rock concerns the use of theoretical concepts borrowed from "common-practice" music. This term generally refers to Western art music of the eighteenth and nineteenth centuries— what is often referred to as "classical" music—though the basic principles of this style are shared with a much wider range of music, including hymns, Christmas carols, marches, children's songs, many folk songs, and much music in movies, TV, and advertising. Many of the terms and concepts I use in the following chapters do indeed come from common-practice music theory—terms such as "cadence," "modulation," and "phrase overlap." In taking this approach, there is a danger of imposing theoretical constructs on rock that are alien and inappropriate to it. I believe I have avoided this

11. Even more problematic is the term "rhythm and blues" (or "R & B"—which may or may not be the same thing). In some contexts this refers to a subgenre of the blues that preceded and influenced rock; in other cases, it may refer to later, predominantly African-American genres (included in "rock" as defined here) or to still other genres, such as the blues-influenced British rock of the 1960s. Given this range of meanings, the term seems best avoided altogether.

trap, and I hope the reader will agree. I do sometimes take common-practice theory as a starting point for my discussions, since it is well understood and probably familiar to many readers. But I often conclude that the differences between rock and common-practice music are more striking than the similarities. For example—to use two examples just mentioned—the reader will see that the role I propose for cadences and modulation in rock is quite different from anything found in common-practice music.

In some ways, the differences between rock and common-practice music are as profound as they could be—extending to the very processes of creation and dissemination and the nature of the musical work. A common-practice piece is (or was) created by a composer, and initially encoded in the form of music notation; it is conveyed to performers in this form, and then transmitted to listeners through a multitude of performances. A rock song, by contrast, is often composed by more than one person (that is, there may be more than one nominal "songwriter"). During the rehearsal of the song, the musicians (who may or may not include the songwriters) may contribute to the composition in important ways: the bass player may compose the bass line, and the drummer the drum part. The distinction between composer and performer is therefore blurred (and notation frequently plays no part in the process). The song is then recorded—sometimes essentially "live" but often subjected to considerable studio post-processing—and it is normally a particular recording of the song that most listeners hear and that essentially defines the song.[12]

These differences between rock and common-practice music raise a further methodological issue: the use of music notation. As can be seen, I use notation quite extensively in the book, although I also employ a variety of other representations, such as harmonic analyses and metrical grids. The use of music notation in studies of rock has sometimes been criticized, as it neglects certain important musical parameters—in particular, timbre and pitch nuance (Tagg, 1982, 41–42; Middleton, 1990, 104–5). This is a point well taken—though I do, in fact, give some attention to timbre (chapter 6) and non-notatable aspects of pitch such as "blue notes" (chapter 5). We should remember also—as noted above—that notation plays a very different role in rock than in common-practice music: it is an analytical

12. This is somewhat oversimplified; a song can also have an identity apart from a particular recording. This is evident when we speak of multiple versions of a song, such as live and recorded versions by the same artist, or one artist's "cover" of a song by another artist. See section 6.1 for discussion of one such case; see also Plasketes (2010) and Rings (2013). A complication of a different kind is where a song functions as part of a larger musical work; this is seen in concept albums such as Pink Floyd's *The Wall*. But the vast majority of rock songs can be understood as self-contained musical forms.

representation created after the fact, rather than a definition of the work. Transcription of rock melodies requires that the notes be assigned to conventional chromatic and rhythmic categories; such decisions can sometimes be subjective and open to debate. Still, as long as we are cognizant of these issues, the tremendous value of music notation—as a communicative device, and as a way of "freezing" the musical object to allow careful study—outweighs its limitations.

Another objection that I anticipate to the current project is that it is misguided, or even illegitimate, to examine the musical aspects of rock without consideration of their context and sociocultural meaning. This argument has been raised on a number of occasions with regard to what is sometimes called "formalist" analysis of rock. In John Shepherd's view, such analysis misses "the central question of how music articulates from within its very structure social and cultural meaning" (1982, 148). Philip Tagg voices a similar view:

> No analysis of musical discourse can be considered complete without consideration of social, psychological, visual, gestural, ritual, technical, historical, economic and linguistic aspects relevant to the genre, function, style, (re-)performance situation and listening attitude connected with the sound event being studied. (1982, 40)

Others have suggested that it is impossible to understand even the "purely musical" aspects of music without consideration of meaning. In Robert Walser's words, "musical details and structures are intelligible only as traces, provocations, and enactments of power relationships" (1993, 30); Stan Hawkins argues that harmonic analysis of popular music must involve "an investigation related to social causes and programmatic effects" (1992, 334). While these views have more recently been challenged by a number of authors who defend the legitimacy of purely musical analysis, they remain widespread and deserve discussion.

In response to this objection, I should emphasize first that I do not claim that purely musical analysis can provide a "complete" understanding of rock. Social context and cultural meanings are of undeniable importance—as important with rock as with any other kind of music. At their best, analyses of the social meanings in rock are highly persuasive and illuminating. Richard Middleton (1990, 18–19) is convincing when he argues that Elvis's fusion of boogie and Tin Pan Alley elements in "Heartbreak Hotel" mirrors the conflicted attitudes toward adolescent sexuality in American culture of the time. Lori Burns (2005) makes a compelling case for Sarah McLachlan's "Ice" as a depiction of ambivalent attitudes toward an abusive relationship and—at a broader level—a commentary on prostitution and sexual subordination. Walser (1993) argues persuasively that appropriations of classical virtuosity in heavy metal express ambitions of prestige, potency, and individuality, and he shows how metal's attitudes toward women—ranging through misogyny, androgyny, exclusion, and romance—reflect the contradictions of contemporary social attitudes. These analyses, and others, raise important issues about rock, and I do not in any way wish to deny or downplay their significance.

But here is the point: to exclude something from consideration in a book is not to deny its importance—as long as its exclusion is warranted by the book's purported scope and subject matter. Again, the parallel with language comes to mind: surely linguists can study syntax and phonology, disregarding meaning for the time being, without being accused of denying its reality and importance. Actually, at some points in the book I *will* discuss what could be considered musical "meanings" of various kinds, though perhaps more abstract meanings than those discussed above—meanings relating to the expression of emotional states, and such notions as unity/individuality, tension, and closure/continuity. But I would defend on principle the validity of a study such as this one, even without these relatively limited explorations of meaning. One cannot study everything, and in a subject of great complexity, the way to make progress is often to focus at least temporarily on one part of it.

As for the relative importance of the social and purely musical aspects of rock: this is obviously a highly subjective matter. For me—and, I suspect, for most other authors on rock as well—the central issue is really this: What is it about listening to rock that gives so many people so much satisfaction and reward, so that they are willing to devote so much of their time and disposable income toward it? In answering this question, we are all, no doubt, greatly influenced by our own personal experiences. When I first started listening to rock radio at the age of 12 or so, it was because my friends were doing it and I wanted to be cool; at that stage, then, social considerations were admittedly paramount. But soon after that, I found myself becoming much more interested in the music itself—songs and moments in songs that had a mysterious appeal (and it was the music rather than the lyrics having this effect, for at that time I was almost completely unable to make out the lyrics). My sense, from talking to other rock listeners about their preferences and priorities, is that this kind of experience is widely shared. I believe that, ultimately, the explanation for the enjoyment of rock lies largely in its purely musical aspects. It is here, I submit, that we will find answers to the really big questions: why some songs are pleasing and effective while others are not, and why the rock style "works" as a whole and is capable of yielding so much pleasure and satisfaction. I hasten to add that I do not offer any conclusive answers to these questions; I certainly offer no formula for creating or identifying a successful rock song. But I do offer some tentative, partial answers as to how certain musical configurations achieve certain aesthetic goals. By focusing on the musical dimensions of rock, I believe we can make progress toward an explanation of why it has so much value to so many people.

As I have noted, it is only in the context of the *norms* of rock that its special moments can be appreciated. Much of this book is concerned with establishing these norms, sometimes with the help of statistical evidence; inevitably, these sections may sometimes seem dry and formalistic. The payoff will come—I hope—in my discussion of individual songs, where I show how their engagement and "play" with stylistic norms can help to explain their appeal. My hope is that the reader will sometimes experience moments of "aha" recognition: yes, this *is* an effective song (or an effective moment), and I now understand better why it works so well. Through this approach, I hope that this book will make a contribution to the question of why listening to rock music is a compelling, enjoyable, and worthwhile experience.

1.4 THE CORPUS

As noted earlier, the current study makes extensive use of a corpus of rock songs compiled by me and Trevor de Clercq from *Rolling Stone* magazine's list of the "500 Greatest Songs of All Time."[13] Some general comments about the corpus are appropriate here. Our goal in developing the corpus was to facilitate the statistical investigation of harmony, melody, and other musical issues in rock. We had several reasons for choosing the *Rolling Stone* list as the basis for the corpus. First of all, we wanted the corpus to contain songs that are generally considered to be rock; the polling method used to create the *Rolling Stone* list (described above) seemed to ensure this. (The broad definition of rock implied by the *Rolling Stone* list is similar to that found in many other sources, as discussed earlier.) We also thought it was desirable for the corpus to contain well-known songs. This allows the stylistic content of the corpus to be more easily judged; and if the individual analyses and transcriptions are to be useful (as we hope

13. The corpus is publicly available, with extensive documentation, at http://rockcorpus. midside.com/. Further investigations of the corpus, including some not reported here, can be found in de Clercq & Temperley (2011) and Temperley & de Clercq (2013).

they will), it is clearly advantageous to analyze songs that people know and care about.

The original *Rolling Stone* list spans roughly from 1954 to 1999 (with just a few songs from earlier and later years), but is strongly biased toward the earlier decades of this period. To make the corpus more chronologically balanced, we took the top 20 songs from each decade, the 1950s through the 1990s (excluding one song that contained no melody or harmony). At a later stage, we added the 101 highest-ranked songs on the list that were not already in this 99-song set, creating a set of 200 songs. This 200-song set still has more songs from the early decades than the later ones: there are 35 songs from the 1950s, 86 from the 1960s, 38 from the 1970s, 19 from the 1980s, and 20 from the 1990s.[14] The complete list of songs can be seen at the book's website.

To create harmonic analyses of the songs, we could have used the analyses (chord symbols) in published lead sheets. However, the harmonic analysis in a lead sheet represents just one opinion (not usually that of the songwriter), and we saw no reason to take it as authoritative. In addition, lead sheet analyses typically lack some important harmonic information, such as key and modulations. For these reasons, we decided to analyze the harmony ourselves. We developed a system for encoding Roman numeral analyses that allows repeated patterns to be represented in a succinct way. Example 1.1 shows my analysis of the Beatles' "Hey Jude." The system is recursive, meaning that symbols expand to other symbols. The top-level symbol, S (at the left end of the last line), represents the entire song; this expands to a series of section symbols, which in turn expand to other section symbols or to actual chord sequences. The top-level analysis can be taken as a kind of formal analysis of the song. (We use abbreviations like "Vr" for verse or verse-refrain, "Br" for bridge, and so on.) We wrote a computer program to take such an analysis and expand it into a complete harmonic sequence for the entire song; the beginning of the expanded analysis of "Hey Jude" is shown in Example 1.2.

We also transcribed the melodies of all 200 songs (except for six songs that contained no melodic data, e.g., rap songs). Here we used a "scale-degree" notation, representing each note by its pitch in relation to the key. (In the key of F, F is 1, G is 2, and so on.) The beginning of my transcription of "Hey Jude" is shown in Example 1.3.

14. The 200-song set also contains one song from before 1954, Hank Williams's "I'm So Lonesome I Could Cry" (1949), and one from after 1999, Eminem's "Lose Yourself" (2002). Since these are the only songs from these decades, however, it seems reasonable to describe the corpus as representing the years 1954–1999.

Example 1.1. My harmonic analysis of the Beatles' "Hey Jude" (part of the *Rolling Stone* corpus). "S" (the last line) is the top-level definition of the entire song, which can then be expanded recursively to produce a chord sequence. "F" indicates the tonal center; vertical bars indicate bar lines; "R" indicates a measure of rest; [2/4] and [4/4] indicate changes in time signature. (The time signature is 4/4 unless otherwise stated.) Symbols preceded by "$" are section symbols that are defined on other lines. "CP*18" means that the CP section is repeated 18 times.

```
Vr: I | V | | I | IV | I | V | I |
BrP: V7/IV | IV I6 | ii vi6 | V6 V | I |
Br: $BrP $BrP [2/4] I | [4/4] V | |
CP: I | bVII | IV | I |
Fadeout: $CP*18
S: [F] R | $Vr $Vr $Br $Vr $Br $Vr I | $Fadeout
```

Example 1.2. The expanded chord progression generated from my analysis of "Hey Jude."

```
[F] R | I | V | | I | IV | I | V | I | | V | | I | IV | I | V |
I | V7/IV | IV I6 | ii vi6 | V6 V | I | (etc.)
```

Example 1.3. My melodic transcription of the opening of "Hey Jude." Each measure is divided equally into a number of equal rhythmic units (the number of units may vary from one measure to the next, e.g., 4, 8, or 16). A unit with no note is marked by a dot. (Only the onsets of notes are shown, not the durations.) "OCT=4" indicates the octave of the first note ("4" is the octave starting at middle C). Each subsequent note is the closest representative of that scale degree to the previous note, unless it is an octave higher or lower, in which case it is preceded by ^ or v, respectively.

```
[F] [OCT=4] ...5 | 3....356 | v2.....23 | 4.^1..175 |
6.543.........5. (etc.)
```

De Clercq and I both analyzed the harmony of all 200 songs; for the melodies, we each transcribed half of them, although we both transcribed a small set of melodies to allow comparison between our transcriptions. Both harmonic analysis and melodic transcription are somewhat subjective. It may be unclear what chord is represented by a certain combination of notes, or what key it is in. (In "Hey Jude," for example, de Clercq analyzed the bridge section as modulating to B♭ major.) Similarly, melodic transcriptions involve judgment calls with regard to both pitch and rhythm. However, comparison of our analyses and melodic transcriptions showed a high level of agreement between us: 93.3% of the time, our harmonic analyses were in agreement on both the root and the key; 89.3% of the time, our melodic transcriptions were in agreement. (See Temperley & de Clercq [2013] for explanation of how these figures were calculated.) The statistical tests reported in this book are based on 200 harmonic analyses and 194 melodic transcriptions, half by me and half by de Clercq.

It should be noted that our project is only one of several to gather statistical data about rock. The McGill Billboard Corpus (Burgoyne et al., 2011) is somewhat similar to ours, containing harmonic analyses as well as sectional labels; one difference is that chords are labeled in absolute terms (e.g., "G7") rather than in relation to the key (though the initial key of each song is also indicated). Also noteworthy is a corpus of harmonic analyses created at the Center for Digital Music (CDM) at the University of London, containing songs by selected artists such as the Beatles, Queen, and Carole King (Mauch et al., 2009). A very different kind of corpus is the Million-Song Dataset (Bertin-Mahieux et al., 2011). This corpus contains features automatically extracted from audio recordings regarding tempo, pitch content, key, meter, loudness, and other things.[15] The crowd-sourced project hooktheory.com, in which statistical data is extracted from harmonic analyses contributed by users, is also of interest. Each of these corpora has advantages and disadvantages. As far as I know, our corpus is the only one that contains melodic transcriptions of rock songs, which will be of great value to us here. The issue of style arises as well. The McGill corpus is based on songs taken from the Billboard "Hot 100" list; while many songs on that list certainly qualify as rock, its stylistic range is somewhat broader than that of the *Rolling Stone* list. Certainly, though, the statistical analyses presented in the following chapters should not be taken as the final word on any issue. Future analyses—using these corpora and perhaps others not yet created—will no doubt shed further light on many of the topics examined here.

1.5 QUESTIONS

At the end of each chapter, I present several questions. Some are of a factual nature; others are more open-ended, perhaps suitable for a class discussion. More factual questions tend to be listed first. The questions for this chapter (shown below) are all fairly open-ended.

1. Some lists of the "greatest rock songs" (or the like) define rock more narrowly than the *Rolling Stone* and VH1 lists mentioned here. Consider the list presented by Planet Rock (a British radio station), at http://www.planetrock.com/music/backstage/the-rock-lists/the-greatest-ever-rock-song/. How would you characterize the differences between this and

---

15. Other research on rock has also made use of statistical information, such as that reported in Everett (2009), Summach (2011), and Schellenberg & von Scheve (2012). In these cases, however, the corpus data has not been made publicly available.

the *Rolling Stone* list? Which list corresponds more closely to your own understanding of "rock"?

2. I say in section 1.3 that "it is normally a particular recording of [a rock song] . . . that essentially defines the song." As I acknowledge in a footnote, this is oversimplified. Sometimes an artist records a song initially recorded by someone else (a "cover"); the fact that we describe the situation in this way suggests that a rock song can also have a more general identity apart from a particular recording. Think about cover songs (choose your own examples): When two artists record different versions of the same song, what are the aspects that tend to be maintained from one version to another?

3. Examine the *Rolling Stone* corpus (the harmonic analyses and melodic transcriptions), as well as one of the other corpora mentioned in section 1.4, such as the McGill Billboard corpus or the Million-Song Dataset. Compare the corpora with regard to the kinds of information that they represent. Do they differ in their stylistic range (the kinds of music that are included)? What are their pros and cons, as tools for the study of popular music? Would they be suitable for exploring different kinds of questions?

4. Philip Tagg (1982, 41–42) has argued that the study of popular music requires a fundamentally different approach from that used for classical music. He writes, "Popular music cannot be analysed using only the traditional tools of musicology. . . . It is impossible to 'evaluate' popular music along some sort of Platonic ideal scale of aesthetic values" (p41). Allan Moore notes the particular importance of "meaning" in the study of popular music (2012, 1–4). Read these two passages and discuss. Do you think popular and classical musics require different analytical approaches, with regard to issues of aesthetics and meaning?

CHAPTER 2

Scales and Key

By general agreement, rock is *tonal* in the broadest sense. By this I mean that in each rock song, there is a single pitch class which serves as a *tonal center*—a tonic or "home" pitch, a point of focus and stability.[1] Other pitches and chords within the song are then understood in relation to this tonal center. Consider the opening of the Beatles' "She Loves You" (Example 2.1). We could describe the chord progression here as E minor–A major–C major–G major; this is correct as far as it goes, but it tells us little about the *function* of the chords. Once we recognize that the tonal center of the song is G, we can appreciate the (unusual) fact that the song begins on a non-tonic chord (vi) and only reaches a point of tonal stability with the arrival on G major (I) in the seventh measure.[2] Clearly, then, identifying the tonal center of a song is an essential part of understanding it. How tonal centers are established and identified in rock is an interesting question that we will return to later in the chapter.

1. A *pitch class* is a category of pitches one or more octaves apart; for example, all B♭s are members of the same pitch class.
2. Following convention, I label chords with Roman numerals, indicating the root of the chord in relation to the key: in G, a G major chord is I, A minor is ii, and so on. Uppercase indicates major triads, and lowercase indicates minor triads. (Lead-sheet symbols—"G" for G major, "Em" for E minor, etc.—are shown above the Roman numerals, or occasionally next to them for reasons of space.) Roman numerals always refer to degrees of the major scale (whether or not the song uses that scale) unless indicated by a flat or sharp sign; so given a tonic of G, ♭III would be B♭ major. The same convention is used for scale-degrees, indicated with Arabic numerals (e.g., ♭$\hat{3}$). Major and minor key signatures are used in an ad hoc fashion to minimize the need for accidentals; they should not be taken to imply major and minor keys, as will be discussed below. Melodies are sometimes transposed an octave up for convenience.

Example 2.1. The Beatles, "She Loves You." (Note: All musical examples are from the beginning of the vocal, unless otherwise indicated.)

It is commonplace to equate tonal center with *key*; we might say that "She Loves You" is in the key of G, for example. In common-practice music, a key is not only defined by a tonal center (a pitch class) but is additionally specified as major or minor. In rock, however, this is a controversial issue. While major/minor key labels are often used in discussions of rock songs, some authors have challenged the validity of this distinction (Covach, 1997; Stephenson, 2002). One of my aims in this chapter is to address this issue in a more systematic way than has been done before, partly based on corpus evidence.

In common-practice theory, each key is associated with a *scale*—a set of pitch classes from which the notes of the piece are (mostly) drawn. A natural way to approach questions about tonality and key in rock, then, is by examining the scales that are used. In what follows, I survey some previous authors' views about scales in rock, and present some statistical evidence that bears on this issue. I then turn to the related topic of key identification.

2.1 SCALES IN ROCK: PREVIOUS VIEWS

The topic of scales in rock has been quite widely discussed, and a variety of viewpoints have been presented. Some discussions of rock use major/minor key labels, thus invoking the classical system of major and minor scales. Many rock songs do employ the major scale; "She Loves You" is an example. (This does not imply that *every* note in the song is from the G major scale—for example, the A major chord of the third measure contains a C♯; there may be occasional "chromatic" notes, just as there are in common-practice music.) The classical minor scale takes several forms; the harmonic minor, $\hat{1}$–$\hat{2}$–♭$\hat{3}$–$\hat{4}$–$\hat{5}$–♭$\hat{6}$–$\hat{7}$, is generally treated as the primary form of the scale. The use of this scale—in particular, the combination of a minor tonic triad ($\hat{1}$–♭$\hat{3}$–$\hat{5}$) and a major dominant one ($\hat{5}$–$\hat{7}$–$\hat{2}$)—is relatively rare in rock, and it does not *sound* very characteristic of the style. Example 2.2 is illustrative;

Example 2.2. The Rolling Stones, "Paint It Black"

I see a red___door and I want___ it paint-ed black

Example 2.3. Scales (always assuming C as tonal center)

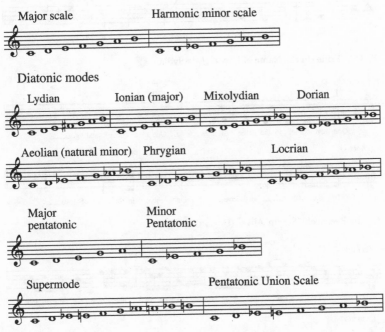

Major scale   Harmonic minor scale

Diatonic modes

Lydian   Ionian (major)   Mixolydian   Dorian

Aeolian (natural minor) Phrygian   Locrian

Major   Minor
pentatonic   Pentatonic

Supermode   Pentatonic Union Scale

the repeated i–V progression (combined with the exotic-sounding sitar) creates a sound that is quite atypical of rock.

Another scale system often invoked in discussions of rock is *diatonic modality*. In this system, a diatonic (i.e., major) scale is used, but the tonic can be at varying positions in the scale, yielding different modes. The modes can also be generated by raising or lowering scale degrees in relation to a fixed tonic (see Example 2.3). Moore (1992, 2001) has advocated diatonic modality as the primary system of pitch organization in rock; he notes that Ionian (equivalent to the major scale), Mixolydian, Dorian, and Aeolian (the "natural minor" scale) are the most commonly used modes (see also Biamonte, 2010). Example 2.4 shows melodies from well-known rock songs in each of these modes. Each mode has specific stylistic associations. Mixolydian was fashionable in the mid-1960s (e.g., the Vogues' "Five O'Clock World," the Monkees' "Last Train to Clarksville");

Example 2.4. Songs in the common rock modes (transposed to C for comparison)

A. The Who, "The Kids Are Alright" (Ionian)

Dorian appears in 1960s music as well (Jefferson Airplane's "Somebody To Love," Steppenwolf's "Born To Be Wild"), but is most common in late 1970s funk and disco (Stevie Wonder's "I Wish," Chic's "Le Freak"). Aeolian is often used in harder varieties of rock (Blue Öyster Cult's "Don't Fear the Reaper" and the Scorpions' "Rock You Like A Hurricane"), and is also favored by 1980s "new wave" bands like Depeche Mode and the

Cure. Ionian (major mode) seems to be an option in nearly all subgenres of rock, though more so in some than others. Each of the four modes has a distinctive sound, defined in part by the forms of the tonic, dominant, and subdominant triads: in Ionian mode, all three triads are major (I, IV, V), while in Aeolian they are all minor (i, iv, v); Mixolydian combines I and IV with v, while Dorian combines i and v with IV. Lydian, Phrygian, and Locrian are generally rare in rock, though it has been suggested that Phrygian and Locrian are common in heavy metal; I will say more about this topic in chapter 7.

Pentatonic scales also play a prominent role in rock, particularly in melodies. Both the major ($\hat{1}$–$\hat{2}$–$\hat{3}$–$\hat{5}$–$\hat{6}$) and minor ($\hat{1}$–$\flat\hat{3}$–$\hat{4}$–$\hat{5}$–$\flat\hat{7}$) pentatonic scales are widely used, especially the minor form; Example 2.5 shows one melody using each scale. Many rock songs feature pentatonic melodies over harmonic progressions that employ other scalar frameworks (see section 5.3). One occasionally also sees "modes" of the pentatonic scale other than major and minor: the passage in Led Zeppelin's "No Quarter" shown in Example 2.5C might be said to employ the Dorian pentatonic mode, $\hat{1}$–$\hat{2}$–$\hat{4}$–$\hat{5}$–$\flat\hat{7}$; the Police's "Voices inside My Head" could be described as Mixolydian pentatonic, $\hat{1}$–$\hat{2}$–$\hat{4}$–$\hat{5}$–$\hat{6}$. And some melodies can convincingly be analyzed as mixtures of the major and minor pentatonic scales, as I discuss further below. "Hexatonic" scales (with six pitches) have also been mentioned, notably the "diatonic hexachord," $\hat{1}$–$\hat{2}$–$\hat{3}$–$\hat{4}$–$\hat{5}$–$\hat{6}$ (Stephenson, 2002).

Still other songs employ pitch collections that have no conventional label. For example, the chord progression of the chorus of the Rolling Stones' "Jumpin' Jack Flash" is D♭–A♭–E♭–B♭; these four major triads do not fit into any diatonic mode. In such cases, one might argue that the scale simply arises from the harmony rather than having any independent reality. Similarly, the verse of the Beatles' "Can't Buy Me Love" features $\flat\hat{3}$ in the melody over a tonic dominant-seventh chord (with $\hat{3}$) in the accompaniment (Example 2.6); no conventional scale contains both $\flat\hat{3}$ and $\hat{3}$. Such phenomena have often been attributed to the influence of the blues. Stephenson (2002) sees the use of $\flat\hat{3}$ in a major-mode context as representing a blues-influenced "alteration" of an underlying diatonic or pentatonic scale. Wagner (2003) suggests that many early Beatles songs involve the combination of major-mode diatonic harmonies with the minor pentatonic scale (widely used in the blues); the "blue notes," $\flat\hat{3}$ and $\flat\hat{7}$, can then generate triads underneath them such as ♭VII, ♭III, and ♭VI.[3]

3. Some might include the "blues scale" as a scalar structure for rock, but there is no consensus as to the definition of this term. See Titon (1994), Levine (1995), and Robinson (2002) for three quite different conceptions of the blues scale.

Example 2.5. Pentatonic melodies

A. Whitney Houston, "How Will I Know" (major)

B. Deep Purple, "Smoke on the Water" (minor)

C. Led Zeppelin, "No Quarter"

Example 2.6. The Beatles, "Can't Buy Me Love"

This survey suggests that the situation with regard to scales in rock is complex: songs use a variety of scale-degree frameworks, including many for which we do not have conventional names. This diversity is recognized by Everett (2004), who rejects the view of rock as a single unified harmonic language. Everett posits six distinct tonal systems for rock, characterized by varying degrees of adherence to the norms of common-practice tonality. (We will say more about Everett's viewpoint in chapter 3.) I would agree with Everett and others that the use of scales in rock cannot be reduced to anything as neat and tidy as the classical major/minor system. However, there are some general observations that can be made about scale structures in rock that can help us make sense of this complex situation.

In what follows, it will be helpful to employ a graphic representation of scales, which I have called the "line of fifths" (Example 2.7). This resembles the well-known "circle of fifths"—pitch classes a fifth apart are adjacent—but it is stretched out in either direction, so that differences in spelling are

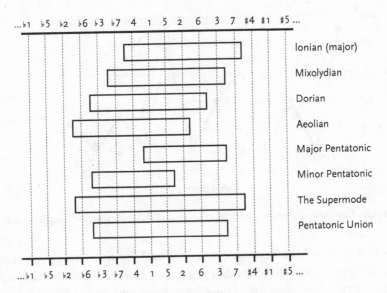

Example 2.7. Scales represented on the line of fifths

represented (such as G♯ versus A♭); it can also be used to represent scale degrees, as shown in the diagram. It can be seen that both diatonic modes and pentatonic scales form sets of scale degrees that are *compact*—adjacent to one another with no gaps in between. The figure also shows two other scalar structures that will be discussed below.

2.2 A CORPUS APPROACH TO SCALES IN ROCK

In classical music, corpus studies have found that the statistical distribution of scale degrees accords well with theoretical assumptions about scales. In major-key pieces, the degrees of the major scale are more frequently used than any others; in minor-key pieces, the harmonic-minor scale degrees are the most frequent (see Example 2.8).[4] In light of this, perhaps examining the distribution of scale degrees in a corpus will shed light on the use of scales in rock. For this purpose, we employ the *Rolling Stone* corpus, described earlier in section 1.4.

As a first step, we can examine the overall scale-degree distribution of the entire corpus (Temperley & de Clercq, 2013). We do this separately for

---

4. These distributions were generated from a corpus of classical excerpts in a theory textbook—the "Kostka-Payne corpus" (Temperley, 2007b).

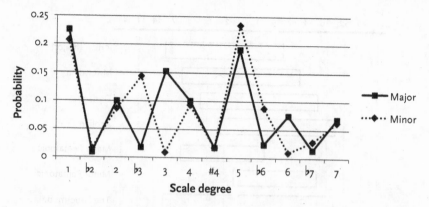

Example 2.8. Scale-degree distributions in a corpus of classical excerpts (Temperley, 2007b)

the melodies and the harmonic progressions.[5] For the harmonic progressions, we take each chord symbol to represent one instance of each scale degree that it contains; for example, a I chord contains one $\hat{1}$, one $\hat{3}$, and one $\hat{5}$. The results are shown in Example 2.9. It can be seen that the harmonic and melodic distributions (or "profiles") are very similar; perhaps the most notable difference is that $\hat{7}$ is more common than $\flat\hat{7}$ in the harmonic distribution, whereas in the melodic distribution the reverse is true. Not surprisingly, $\hat{1}$ is the most commonly used degree in both distributions, followed by $\hat{5}$. In both distributions, also, the least common scale degrees are $\sharp\hat{4}$ and $\flat\hat{2}$ (though $\flat\hat{6}$ is also quite infrequent in the melodic distribution). Notably, these are the two degrees that do not occur in any of the four common diatonic modes noted by Moore (Ionian, Mixolydian, Dorian, and Aeolian). This suggests that there is a "global" scale for rock, including all twelve pitch classes except for $\sharp\hat{4}$ and $\flat\hat{2}$, from which smaller scales are then selected for individual songs; elsewhere I have called this scale the "supermode" (Temperley, 2001). The supermode also excludes more remote spellings of basic scale degrees, such as $\sharp\hat{5}$ (=$\flat\hat{6}$) and $\sharp\hat{2}$ (=$\flat\hat{3}$).[6] Like other scales discussed previously, the supermode forms a compact set of scale degrees on the line of fifths, as shown in Example 2.7.

5. Of course, melody and harmony are not independent (though this is a complex issue—see section 5.3), and our judgments about harmony were often influenced by the melody. But the harmonic analyses also consider accompaniment notes, and the melodic transcriptions include notes (non–chord tones) that are not reflected in the harmony. So in this sense, the two distributions are complementary: each one captures something that the other does not.
6. Our melodic transcriptions observe such spelling distinctions—for example, distinguishing $\flat\hat{6}$ from $\sharp\hat{5}$. In Example 2.9, enharmonically equivalent degrees (such as $\sharp\hat{5}$ and $\flat\hat{6}$) are collapsed together, but since "remote" spellings such as $\sharp\hat{5}$ are quite

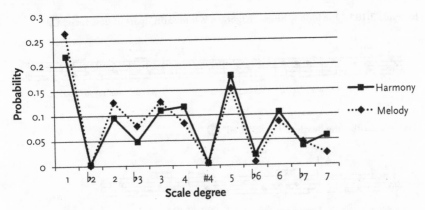

Example 2.9. Harmonic and melodic scale-degree distributions from the *Rolling Stone* corpus (Temperley & de Clercq, 2013)

Since ♭$\hat{2}$ and ♯$\hat{4}$ are not included in the supermode under any spelling, they are unavoidably "chromatic." This is an important aspect of rock's pitch organization. The claim is not that ♭$\hat{2}$ and ♯$\hat{4}$ are *never* used in rock; but when they are used, they tend to have a surprising and destabilizing effect. Consider, for example, the dramatic use of the ♭II chord in the Moody Blues' "Nights in White Satin" (Example 2.10A). Even a ♯$\hat{4}$ such as that found in m. 3 of "She Loves You" (Example 2.1)—part of a major II chord—tends to steer us away from the tonic of G more than toward it. (Some heavy metal uses the ♭$\hat{2}$ and ♯$\hat{4}$/♭$\hat{5}$ degrees much more extensively, as will be discussed in section 7.1.) The same applies to spellings of other degrees that fall outside the supermode, such as ♯$\hat{5}$ and ♯$\hat{2}$. For example, the VII chord (not ♭VII!) in the Beatles' "I'm So Tired" (Example 2.10B) introduces the ♯$\hat{2}$ degree (B♯) as well as ♯$\hat{4}$ (D♯); this has a comic effect, like someone pouring orange juice on their cereal.

Sometimes chromatic scale degrees are best understood as implying tonicizations—brief suggestions of other keys; I will say more about tonicization in chapter 3. Chromatic scale degrees may also occur unobtrusively as passing or neighbor notes (moving by step to another note), just as they do in classical music; Example 2.11A contains ♯$\hat{5}$ (A) and ♯$\hat{6}$ (B) used in this

rare, they make little difference to the totals. One might ask how pitch spellings are chosen; how do we *know* whether a note is ♭$\hat{6}$ or ♯$\hat{5}$? This depends mainly on line-of-fifths proximity to other nearby notes; e.g., we prefer to spell a chord as $\hat{4}$–♭$\hat{6}$–$\hat{1}$ rather than $\hat{4}$–♯$\hat{5}$–$\hat{1}$, since the former spelling locates the notes closer together on the line. There is also a preference to spell chromatic notes on a different staff line from the following note: For example, ♯$\hat{4}$/♭$\hat{5}$ is usually spelled as ♯$\hat{4}$ if it moves to $\hat{5}$, but ♭$\hat{5}$ if it moves to $\hat{4}$ (see Example 2.11B). For more on this topic, see Temperley (2001).

Example 2.10A. The Moody Blues, "Nights in White Satin" (part of first verse)

Let-ters I've__ writt-en_____ Nev-er mean-ing to send__

Example 2.10B. The Beatles, "I'm So Tired"

I'm so_____ tired I have-n't slept a wink

Example 2.11A. Prince, "Little Red Corvette"

I guess I should 've known by the way you parked your car side-ways that it would-n't last

Example 2.11B. Aerosmith, "Walk This Way" (guitar solo)

way. An important special case of this is $\#\hat{4}/\flat\hat{5}$, which is often used in blues-influenced genres of rock, almost always moving by step to $\hat{4}$ or $\hat{5}$. In the guitar solo to Aerosmith's "Walk This Way" shown Example 2.11B, $\#\hat{4}/\flat\hat{5}$ (F#/G♭) occurs several times—twice in the excerpt shown, and three more times in the following two measures. Such uses of $\#\hat{4}/\flat\hat{5}$ are fairly common, but because of their consistent stepwise resolution and the overall rarity of $\#\hat{4}/\flat\hat{5}$, I would not consider them to be part of the scale.

Not many songs make use of the entire supermode; rather, they usually use smaller scales formed by subsets of this "global" scale. A number of scale structures have been proposed for rock, as discussed in the previous section; one might wonder which of these scales are used most frequently in practice. This proves to be a difficult question to answer statistically. One could define the "scale" of a song as the set of all the scale degrees that are ever used in the song; this does not give very satisfactory results, since it takes no account of how often each scale degree is used. The five most common scales in the melodies of the *Rolling Stone* corpus, by this definition, are shown in Table 2.1. Two of these scales use the $\sharp\hat{4}$ degree; however, closer inspection shows that in many of these songs, $\sharp\hat{4}$ occurs only once or twice. Alternatively, we could define the scale of a song as those scale degrees that occur more than a certain number of times; Table 2.2 shows the results for the *Rolling Stone* melodies, with a "cutoff" of three (admittedly an arbitrary number). Now we get somewhat more intelligible results. The most common scale is the major scale, occurring in 30 of the 194 melodies; second most common is the scale $\hat{1}$–$\hat{2}$–$\flat\hat{3}$–$\hat{3}$–$\hat{4}$–$\hat{5}$–$\hat{6}$–$\flat\hat{7}$ (an interesting scale that I will discuss further below); third is $\hat{1}$–$\hat{2}$–$\hat{3}$–$\hat{4}$–$\hat{5}$–$\hat{6}$, the "diatonic hexachord"; the fourth scale includes all the degrees of the supermode except $\flat\hat{6}$; the fifth scale, $\hat{1}$–$\hat{2}$–$\flat\hat{3}$–$\hat{3}$–$\hat{4}$–$\hat{5}$–$\hat{6}$, is like the second, but without $\flat\hat{7}$. It is notable that these scales mostly form compact regions on the line of fifths, like the conventional scales discussed earlier. (The only exception is the fifth one, which has a "gap" at $\flat\hat{7}$.) Beyond that, however, it is difficult to find any meaningful generalization about them. In

Table 2.1 THE FIVE MOST COMMON
SCALES IN THE MELODIES IN
THE *ROLLING STONE* CORPUS

Scale	Number of occurrences
1 2 3 4 5 6 7	24
1 ♭3 3 4 5 6 ♭7	18
1 ♭3 3 4 ♯4 5 6 ♭7	13
1 ♭3 3 4 ♯4 5 6 ♭7 7	12
1 ♭3 3 4 5 6 7	8

Table 2.2 THE FIVE MOST COMMON
SCALES IN THE MELODIES IN THE
ROLLING STONE CORPUS, INCLUDING
ONLY SCALE DEGREES THAT OCCUR
MORE THAN THREE TIMES

Scale	Number of occurrences
1 2 3 4 5 6 7	30
1 ♭3 3 4 5 6 ♭7	17
1 2 3 4 5 6	13
1 ♭3 3 4 5 6 ♭7 7	8
1 ♭3 3 4 5 6	7

addition, the five scales together account for less than half of the melodies in the corpus; the remaining songs feature a large number of other scales, each one occurring no more than a few times. (Some songs also shift in scale from one section to another, maintaining the same tonal center—a topic we will explore in section 9.5.)

Earlier I raised the controversial issue of the major/minor key system and its validity with regard to rock. Let us consider this issue from a statistical perspective: Do the scale structures in the *Rolling Stone* corpus reflect anything like the major/minor distinction of common-practice music? Suppose we simply define a "major" melody as one in which $\hat{3}$ occurs more often than $\flat\hat{3}$, and a "minor" melody as one in which $\flat\hat{3}$ occurs more often. We can then examine the overall scale-degree distributions for all major and minor melodies in the corpus; we can do the same procedure for the harmonic analyses.[7] The major and minor melodic profiles are shown in Example 2.12A. The major profile reflects the major scale: the seven major degrees have much higher values than the other five (though $\hat{7}$ is only slightly more common than $\flat\hat{7}$). Within the major scale, the five degrees of the major pentatonic scale ($\hat{1}$–$\hat{2}$–$\hat{3}$–$\hat{5}$–$\hat{6}$) have the highest values. The minor melodic profile is more difficult to interpret. In this profile, $\hat{6}$ is much more common than $\flat\hat{6}$, and $\flat\hat{7}$ is much more common than $\hat{7}$; in classical minor the reverse is true in both cases (see Example 2.8). It is notable also that the value for $\hat{3}$ is fairly high in the minor rock profile. If one were to interpret this distribution as implying a scale, the closest approximation would appear to be the eight-note scale $\hat{1}$–$\hat{2}$–$\flat\hat{3}$–$\hat{3}$–$\hat{4}$–$\hat{5}$–$\hat{6}$–$\flat\hat{7}$; these eight degrees have much higher values than the remaining four. This scale can be viewed as the union (combination) of the major and minor pentatonic scales, containing all the scale degrees that are in either scale; de Clercq and I (Temperley & de Clercq, 2013) have called it the *pentatonic union scale* for this reason (it is shown in music notation in Example 2.3). Like diatonic modes and pentatonic scales, the pentatonic union scale occupies a compact region of scale degrees on the line of fifths (see Example 2.7).

---

7. This method might seem to be *imposing* a major/minor distinction on the corpus. However, a more objective "clustering" method, which simply groups songs together according to the overall similarity between their scale-degree distributions, yields very similar results (Temperley & de Clercq, 2013): 90.2% of the melodies in the *Rolling Stone* corpus are classified in the same way in the "clustering" method as they are in the "imposed" method reported here, and the resulting profiles are very similar as well. I use the "imposed" method here because it is easier to explain and reproduce. It should also be kept in mind that some songs shift in scale, or even in tonal center (31 songs in our corpus contain modulations); the current method is insensitive to such shifts.

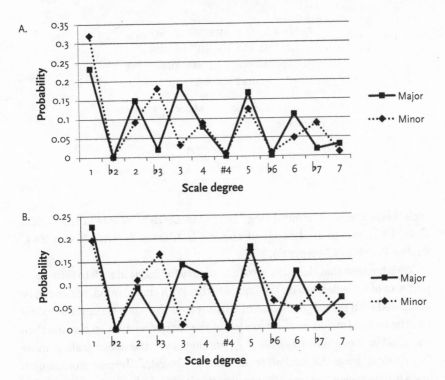

Example 2.12. "Major" and "minor" profiles for the *Rolling Stone* corpus, for the melodies (A) and the harmonic progressions (B).

The major and minor profiles extracted from the harmonic data are shown in Example 2.12B. Here again, the major category strongly reflects the major scale. In the minor category, $\flat\hat{7}$ is far more common than $\hat{7}$ (as in the minor profile generated from the melodies), but $\flat\hat{6}$ is somewhat more common than $\hat{6}$; one could say this reflects the Aeolian mode (or "natural minor" scale) more than anything else.

One might ask how well the melodic and harmonic classification schemes align with each other: Do harmonically major songs tend to be melodically major as well? This is shown in Table 2.3. Not surprisingly, the melodic and harmonic category systems are indeed strongly correlated; 153 of the 194 songs are either major in both the melodic and harmonic systems or minor in both systems. Interestingly, the vast majority of the remaining songs (all but one) are minor in the melodic system and major in the harmonic one, rather than vice versa. This seems to reflect a phenomenon observed earlier (and noted by several previous authors): many songs feature $\flat\hat{3}$ in the melody but $\hat{3}$ in the harmony. I offered "Can't Buy Me Love" as an example of this; the pattern is also widely seen in 1950s

Table 2.3 THE NUMBER OF SONGS
IN THE MAJOR AND MINOR
HARMONIC AND MELODIC
CATEGORIES

Harmonic	Melodic	Major	Minor
Major		121	40
Minor		1	32

rock (Elvis Presley's "Hound Dog," Jerry Lee Lewis's "Whole Lotta Shakin' Goin' On") and in soul songs of the 1960s (James Brown's "I Got You," Aretha Franklin's "Respect").

We have seen that there is a strong tendency for scales in rock to form compact sets of scale degrees on the line of fifths. With this in mind, scales can be compared with regard to the line-of-fifths region that they occupy. For example, the Ionian (major) mode is further in the sharp direction on the line than the Aeolian mode (see Example 2.7); we might say the major scale is more "sharp-side," while the Aeolian scale is more "flat-side." The pentatonic union scale is in between the two. We can also think of an individual *song* as having a position on the line of fifths, which is the average position of all the scale degrees used in the song. To make this measure a bit more nuanced, we can weight scale degrees to reflect their frequency; for example, if two songs both used the pentatonic union scale but one used $\hat{3}$ more and the other used $\flat\hat{3}$ more, the first song would be further in the sharp direction. (This is an important motivation for the "line of fifths" model; on a circle, it is not clear how the "mean position" of a scale or a song would be calculated.) Example 2.13 shows the scale-degree distributions of two well-known melodies projected onto the line of fifths, along with their mean positions. "(I Can't Get No) Satisfaction" employs the pentatonic union scale, with a strong presence of $\flat\hat{3}$ and $\flat\hat{7}$; "She Loves You" does not adhere strictly to any conventional scale (and occasionally uses flat-side degrees), but it is predominantly major, and its mean position is further in the sharp direction as a result.

The possibility of mapping each melody onto the line of fifths suggests a further investigation. If there is a clear-cut division between major and minor songs, this should be reflected in a two-peaked or "bimodal" distribution of songs on the line of fifths. This is not what we observe, however (see Example 2.14). There is a strong peak of songs toward the "sharp" end of the distribution, but no comparable peak toward the "flat" end. This suggests that the distinction between major and minor songs is more of a

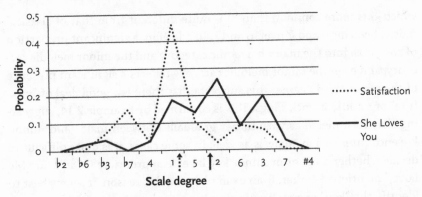

Example 2.13. Melodic scale-degree distributions of two songs, the Rolling Stones' "(I Can't Get No) Satisfaction" and the Beatles' "She Loves You," projected onto the line of fifths. The mean positions of the two distributions are shown with arrows.

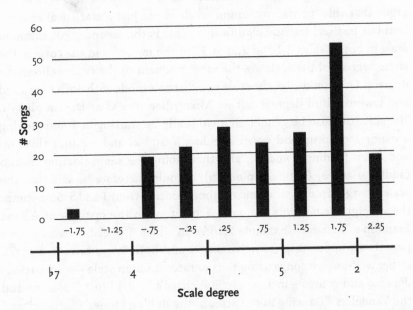

Example 2.14. Melodies in the *Rolling Stone* corpus represented by their mean positions on the line of fifths (assuming scale-degree 1 is zero, as shown below the graph). Songs are grouped into ranges of 0.5 in the line; numbers below the bars indicate the center point of each range.

continuum than a clear-cut division. We will return to this idea in the next chapter.

Based on all of this evidence, one could say that rock reflects something like the major/minor distinction of common-practice music, but with several important differences. The melodic profile of "minor" melodies (in which ♭3̂ is more common than 3̂) is quite different from that of classical music, favoring 6̂ and ♭7̂ over ♭6̂ and 7̂. In addition, a significant proportion of songs fall into the major harmonic category and the minor melodic category, and even the minor melodic category reflects a significant presence of the major third degree. This suggests that there is a good deal of "mixture" of 3̂ and ♭3̂ in rock songs. This is confirmed by Example 2.14, suggesting that rock melodies vary rather gradually between major and minor. We encounter this in analysis as well; in some cases, it is quite difficult to decide whether a major or minor key label is appropriate ("Can't Buy Me Love," mentioned earlier, is an example). For this reason, it seems best to identify the "key" of a rock song simply as its tonal center, without specifying it as major or minor, and I will generally do so here.

As noted earlier, the melodically generated minor profile could be interpreted as implying an eight-note scale: 1̂–2̂–♭3̂–3̂–4̂–5̂–6̂–♭7̂. I would argue that this "pentatonic union" scale is not just a statistical abstraction but has real musical significance. This is the second-most common scale in both Tables 2.1 and 2.2; in 37 of the melodies in the corpus, the eight degrees of the scale are the most frequent of the twelve chromatic degrees. One could view the scale as a diatonic mode with both the raised and lowered third degrees (either Mixolydian plus ♭3̂ or Dorian plus 3̂). The scale can also be generated melodically by starting at 1̂ and moving a major second up and down (yielding ♭7̂ and 2̂) and a minor third up and down (adding 6̂ and ♭3̂), and then doing the same starting from 5̂ (adding 4̂ and 3̂) (see Example 2.15). It could therefore be said that the scale emerges from pentatonic neighbor motion from 1̂ and 5̂. Sometimes these neighbor motions are quite explicit, as in the opening of Aretha Franklin's "Respect" (Example 2.16A), in which 1̂ is elaborated by both pentatonic upper neighbors (♭3̂ and 2̂) and both lower ones (6̂ and ♭7̂). Other well-known songs using the pentatonic union scale—from various decades and genres—include Little Richard's "Tutti Frutti," Martha and the Vandellas' "Dancing in the Street," the Rolling Stones' "Satisfaction," Guns N' Roses' "Sweet Child O' Mine," and Prince's "Purple Rain." Of particular interest in these songs is the way that 3̂ and ♭3̂ are combined, often within a single section or even a single phrase. For example, the opening of "Satisfaction" (Example 2.16B) uses both 3̂ and ♭3̂ within the space of

Example 2.15. The pentatonic union scale arising from neighbors of 1̂ and 5̂. (Slurs above show major pentatonic neighbors; slurs below show minor pentatonic neighbors.)

Example 2.16A. Aretha Franklin, "Respect"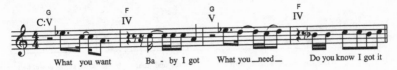

What you want   Ba - by I got   What you __need__   Do you know I got it

Example 2.16B. The Rolling Stones, "Satisfaction"

I __ can't get no ____   sat - is - fac - tion   I can't get no

a few measures; ♭3̂ then returns at the beginning of the second section (after the double bar), though the underlying tonic harmony is major. This is an important and distinctive aspect of rock melody, as I will discuss in chapter 5.

On the whole, this investigation confirms the conclusions reached by Everett (2004) and others: scale structures in rock are highly complex and cannot be reduced to two or a few simple categories. Even the scales of individual songs are frequently of a "fuzzy" nature: For example, a song may use the Mixolydian mode but with 7̂ at certain strategic places, or major mode with occasional ♭7̂s. It seems likely that the fuzzy character of scales in rock grew out of a fusion of the European musical tradition (common-practice music and related styles such as Tin Pan Alley and country) with the blues (see Moore, 1995). Many rock melodies show some adherence to the minor pentatonic scale favored by the blues, but adjusting it to adhere more closely to the harmony, or elaborating pentatonic degrees with diatonic whole steps and half steps—either filling in pentatonic intervals (1̂–2̂–♭3̂ or 5̂–6̂–♭7̂) or adding neighbor tones (as discussed in the previous paragraph). This is already seen in the very earliest rock—a song like "Rock Around the Clock" (Example 2.17). The melody first outlines a major triad (rather than using ♭3̂ as a blues melody typically would); it then moves up to ♭7̂, part of the minor pentatonic, but fills this in with 6̂; in the fourth measure, 1̂ is elaborated with 2̂ as an upper neighbor; in the following measures, ♭3̂ of the minor pentatonic is used, which also fits with the harmonic move to IV (as the chordal seventh). Stylistic compromises of this kind may give rise to diatonic modes (Dorian or Mixolydian), the pentatonic union scale, hexatonic scales, or fuzzier mixtures of

Example 2.17. Bill Haley & His Comets, "Rock Around the Clock" (second verse)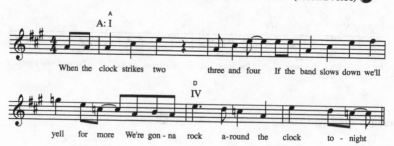

these.[8] Different songs make these compromises in different ways, yielding a variety of scale structures in individual songs, each one a part of that song's distinctive sound.

2.3 KEY-FINDING

How do listeners determine the key of a song as they hear it? (As noted earlier, the "key" of a song simply means its tonal center.) There is reason to believe that listeners in general are sensitive to key: for example, they can judge how well a note "fits" with a previously established key (Krumhansl, 1990). The problem of "key-finding," as it is sometimes called, has received great attention in music psychology (for a review, see Temperley, 2012). Most key-finding models have employed what is known as a *distributional* approach. Each key is associated with an ideal distribution of pitch classes, known as a "key profile." Key profiles for each key can be generated from scale-degree distributions like those in Example 2.9, by shifting them along the chromatic scale. (For the C major profile, $\hat{1}$ is C and $\flat\hat{2}$ is Db; for Db major, $\hat{1}$ is Db and $\flat\hat{2}$ is D; and so on.) The key whose profile most closely matches the distribution of notes in the piece is then the chosen key. There are various mathematical ways of doing the matching, but they all involve the same basic idea: a match is good if the frequently occurring pitch classes in the song have high values in the key profile. The distributional method of key-finding works remarkably well in common-practice

---

8. Diatonic "filling in" of the pentatonic scale and harmonic accommodations (e.g., $\hat{3}$ over tonic harmony) are seen in the blues as well, but I would argue that this process is taken much further in rock. Melodic patterns such as the outlined major triad in Example 2.17 and the descending diatonic line $\hat{5}$–$\hat{4}$–$\flat\hat{3}$–$\hat{2}$–$\hat{1}$ in Example 2.6 are not characteristic of the blues. Songs on disc 2 of MCA's *Blues Classics* collection offer a useful sample of the "urban" blues style that most influenced rock.

music; in rock, however, it proves to be less successful. A few examples illustrate some of the complexities that arise in key-finding in rock, and some of the factors that must be considered.

Consider a song such as the Beatles' "Can't Buy Me Love," shown earlier in Example 2.6. There are several possible cues in this phrase that might convey the tonal center of C. The underlying harmony is C major (with an added flat seventh) throughout the phrase. The melody starts and ends on C, and the high point of the melody (and the first downbeat note) is G, another important degree in the key of C. One might also point to the factor of scale—the set of pitches used in the melody and accompaniment—though this is a complicated and murky issue in rock, as discussed earlier. It is hard to know, from a single example, which of these factors is really crucial to the perception of key; things become clearer if we find examples that tease the factors apart.

In Example 2.18, a tonal center of D is implied, but it is not as obvious as in Example 2.6, and some of the factors that were present there are absent here. As a harmonic root, D is barely present (there might be brief first-inversion D major chords in the first and third measures, but even this is debatable); by contrast, G major appears on every downbeat. To use a term suggested by Spicer (2017), this is a song with a "fragile tonic"—a greatly de-emphasized tonic harmony.[9] Melodically, too, D receives little support; the phrase beginnings in the first and third measures emphasize B—part of the underlying G major triad—and the second phrase arguably ends on B as well (the melisma to A seems rather like an afterthought). Given the harmonic and melodic support for G, we might expect this to be the tonal center, but clearly it is not. Here, I would argue, the factor of *scale* is crucial. Recall that, in general, rock melodies and harmonic progressions stay within a set of ten scale degrees—the "supermode"—avoiding $\flat\hat{2}$ and $\sharp\hat{4}$. In this case, the A major chords of the accompaniment contain C♯, which is $\sharp\hat{4}$ of G; this explains why G is ruled out as a tonal center, despite its melodic and harmonic prominence. To put it another way, a tonal center of G would imply Lydian mode, which is extremely rare in rock.[10] But why

9. The chorus of the song establishes D more strongly, with clear IV–V–I progressions in that key. In Spicer's (2017) terms, then, the song as a whole might be better described as having an "emergent" tonic rather than a "fragile" one.

10. Not all authors agree on this point; Clement (2013) argues for Lydian interpretations of a number of songs. We should bear in mind that there is some subjectivity in key analysis. Indeed, one might point to a kind of circularity here: if our key-identification process favors keys that do not entail $\flat\hat{2}$ or $\sharp\hat{4}$, it is not surprising that those degrees turn out to be rare in the data. In most songs, though, multiple cues all point to the same conclusion, as was observed with "Can't Buy Me Love."

Example 2.18. Michael Jackson, "Human Nature"

is D favored? Couldn't the song be in A Mixolydian, or B Aeolian? In general, there appears to be a slight preference for Ionian mode: other things being equal, we will favor a "major" interpretation over other alternatives. Perhaps this is not surprising, when we consider that the seven degrees of the major mode are the most common ones in the harmonic distribution of the *Rolling Stone* corpus (Example 2.9).

The previous discussion has suggested two principles in the perception of key in rock:

1. Prefer a key whose supermode includes all the pitches of the passage. (In other words, try to avoid an interpretation that involves $\flat\hat{2}$ and $\sharp\hat{4}$.)
2. Among the remaining alternatives, prefer a key whose major scale includes all the pitches of the passage.

These principles (and others presented below) might be considered "preference rules" (Lerdahl & Jackendoff, 1983): rules of a flexible nature that combine and interact to determine our preferred interpretation.

While scale plays an important role in rock key-finding, it is not the only factor. Consider these two chord progressions (all major triads):

F B♭ | F C |
C F | B♭ F |

The first one is the main progression of Bruce Springsteen's "Rosalita"; the second is the main progression of the Romantics' "That's What I Like about You" (transposed for comparison). It seems fairly clear, from the chord progressions alone, that the tonal center is F in the first case, C in the second (and this is confirmed by the melodies of the songs and other aspects). Both progressions use the same sequence of harmonies (if we imagine them repeating), and hence the same distribution of pitch classes; what accounts for the difference? The answer, I submit, lies in the metrical placement of the harmonies. If we assume a level of hypermeter in which odd-numbered measures are metrically stronger than even-numbered ones, then the metrically strongest harmony is F major in the first case, C major in the second. (We will return to the topic of hypermeter in chapter 4.) Analysis of the *Rolling Stone* corpus shows that, indeed, there is a much stronger tendency for tonic harmony to occur on odd-numbered downbeats than at other locations.[11] This suggests another preference rule for key-finding in rock:

3. Prefer a tonal interpretation in which the tonic harmony is hypermetrically strong.

There is yet one more factor in rock key-finding. Stephenson (2002) points out that a single harmonic progression—even with the same metrical placement—can have different tonal implications depending on the melody.[12] A case in point is shown in Example 2.19 (again, the second example has been transposed for comparison): though the two passages use the same progression (Em–C–G–D), with E minor hypermetrically strong in both cases, the implied tonal center is E in the first case, G in the second.[13] The crucial difference seems to lie in the way certain melodic degrees are emphasized—through repetition, metrical placement, and location at phrase beginnings and endings: if the emphasized pitches belong to a particular major or minor triad, this favors the corresponding key. Example 2.19A emphasizes E and G, favoring the E minor triad; Example 2.19B emphasizes G and B, which favor the G major triad. (G and B are also part of the E minor triad, but the tonic is absent; also, the general bias towards major mode may favor G.) This leads to our final preference rule for rock key-finding:

11. Among harmonies starting on odd-numbered downbeats, 47.9% are tonic; on even-numbered downbeats, 28.6%; on non-downbeats, 18.2%.
12. Stephenson uses the example of I→♭VII–IV, which can also be interpreted as V–IV–I. My treatment of the topic of key-finding builds on Stephenson's in several ways (2002, 29–47) (and also on my own earlier treatment of the topic in Temperley, 2001). Stephenson suggests that we favor the first chord of the song as tonic; this is related to my rule 3, since the first harmony is usually hypermetrically strong, but my rule better captures cases such as the Beatles' "She Loves You" and "I Want to Hold Your Hand" which do not begin on tonic. Stephenson says we favor a tonic supported by an outlined perfect fourth or fifth in the melody, and beginning and ending on a "structural tone" (37); this is similar to my rule 4. Stephenson generally downplays the role of pitch collection, saying that we can usually identify key before hearing the complete collection (31), but acknowledges that it can sometimes play a role; I believe it is an important factor, as shown by my Example 2.18. Doll (2007) offers another interesting treatment of this topic.
13. Others have also noted the ambiguity of this common progression (Koozin, 2000; Doll, 2011; Osborn, 2013); we will say more about it in section 3.4.

Example 2.19A. The Offspring, "Gotta Get Away" (chorus)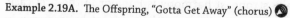

Think I'm on a roll but I think it's kind-a weak Say-ing all I know is I got-ta get a-way from me

Example 2.19B. Boston, "Peace of Mind" (chorus)

I un - der-stand a-bout in-de - ci - sion__But I don't care if I get be - hind

4. Prefer a tonal interpretation such that emphasized notes of the melody are notes of the tonic triad: $\hat{1}$ (especially), $\flat\hat{3}$, $\hat{3}$, or $\hat{5}$.

De Clercq and I (2013) took a computational approach to the key-finding problem; using the *Rolling Stone* corpus, we tried out a number of key-finding models and examined how well each one performed at identifying the keys of the songs in the corpus. (For this test, we split the corpus into two, using half of the songs as a training set—for setting the models' parameters—and the other half as a test set. Songs containing modulations were all put in the training set, so that each song in the test set was in a single key throughout.) The most successful of our models was one that considered two factors. One was the distribution of scale degrees in the melody; we took the usual distributional approach here, comparing the song distribution to key profiles generated from the overall distribution of the training set (similar to that shown in Example 2.9) and favoring the key that yielded the best match. In effect, this incorporates rule 1 above, since the melodic scale degree distribution favors degrees within the supermode. (Within the supermode, one might say it roughly favors the major scale, though $\flat\hat{7}$ is more common than $\hat{7}$.) This method also incorporates rule 4 in a crude way, since the tonic triad degrees have relatively high values in the distribution, though it does not consider the emphasis of these degrees in terms of meter and placement within the phrase. The second factor used in our model is the progression of harmonic roots in the song; again, a distributional approach is used, matching the distribution of roots to an ideal distribution of roots in each key. (More will be said about the distribution of roots in rock in chapter 3.) But the metrical placement of roots is also considered, so that a key is favored that places tonic harmony in metrically

Example 2.20A. Fleetwood Mac, "Dreams"

Example 2.20B. U2, "Beautiful Day"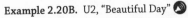

strong positions. Overall, this model identified the correct key in 97% of the songs.[14]

The four key-finding principles proposed above interact in complex ways, sometimes reinforcing each other and sometimes conflicting. In most cases, the four rules together yield a clear and unambiguous key judgment; occasionally, however, they may be indecisive between two possible keys, resulting in an ambiguous situation. Fleetwood Mac's "Dreams" is a famous case in point (Temperley, 2001; Stephenson, 2002; Doll, 2007; Spicer, 2017); see Example 2.20A. As in Example 2.18, the harmony features an alternation between two major triads a whole step apart; by analogy with that example, we might expect the tonal center to be C. In this case, however, the melody strongly outlines an A minor triad, suggesting A as a possible tonal center. From using this example in class, I have found that listeners are divided between A, F, and C as possible keys. In U2's "Beautiful Day" (Example 2.20B), the A major harmony is hypermetrically emphasized, but the pitch content of the song (harmony and melody together) comprises a D major scale, favoring D; the melody is indecisive, with phrases beginning and ending on degrees of the A major triad (A and E), but also emphasizing D and F♯ through repetition. As a result, the song is delicately balanced between the two keys. Another kind of tonal ambiguity occurs when a song establishes different tonal centers in the verse and chorus, a topic we will consider further in chapter 9.

14. Examining the model's errors is instructive. For example, the Clash's "London Calling" is in E, but uses the ♭II chord extensively; because of the rarity of this root, the model chose G as the tonal center. Giving more weight to the melodic distribution and the hypermetrical placement of the harmony would have yielded the correct choice. For more detail, see Temperley & de Clercq (2013).

2.4 QUESTIONS

1. Each of these songs is (predominantly) in a single diatonic mode: Santana, "Evil Ways"; the Rolling Stones, "Start Me Up"; the Cure, "Love Cats"; R.E.M., "Losing My Religion"; Blind Melon, "No Rain." Which mode is used in each song? You should be able to determine this from the first 30 seconds of each song.

2. Choose a song and identify its scale—the set of pitch classes that is used, considering both the melody and the accompaniment. (Remember that pitch classes used only occasionally may be considered "chromatic.") Does the song's scale match (or resemble) any conventional scale? Plot the song's scale onto the line of fifths; you may wish to indicate some pitch classes as being more frequent than others, as shown in Example 2.13. (This can be done in an approximate way, without actually counting notes.)

3. Lynyrd Skynyrd's "Sweet Home Alabama" is a famous case of tonal ambiguity. What are the two possible tonal centers? Which one do you favor, and why? Could one argue that different tonal centers are implied in different parts of the song?

4. Consider these four songs: the Byrds' "So You Want To Be a Rock'n'Roll Star," R.E.M.'s "Man in the Moon," Tom Petty and the Heartbreakers' "Here Comes My Girl," Jane's Addiction's "Jane Says." Analyze the harmony of the introduction and the opening vocal section. All four of these passages have a harmonic pattern that is discussed in the current chapter; what is the pattern? How do you hear the tonality of these passages? Do later events in the song affect how you hear the opening section?

CHAPTER 3

Harmony

Example 3.1 shows one of my favorite moments in rock: the chorus of the Who's "Bargain." When a song has a profound effect on us, we naturally wonder why: What makes this passage so effective, so compelling? No doubt Roger Daltrey's powerful vocals and Keith Moon's unique drumming style have something to do with it. But I would argue that harmony also plays a crucial role. While the harmonic progression of Example 3.1 might at first glance seem quite simple, I will show that it actually combines several conventions of rock harmony—particularly regarding the use of the IV chord—in a unique way, and that this can help to explain the effect of the passage. But it will take us some time to get to that point (we will return to this song in chapter 9). In this chapter, we lay the groundwork for our exploration of harmony, which will be one of our central concerns throughout the book. As we will see, the harmonic progression of a song affects our experience of it in many ways: its phrasal and formal structure, its stylistic associations, and its trajectories of emotion and tension.

As in the previous chapter, common-practice theory offers a useful starting point, since its harmonic logic is familiar and well understood. In common-practice music, the set of available chords in each key is defined by the scale. In a major key, the scale gives us the major triads I, IV, and V, the minor triads ii, iii, and vi, and the diminished triad vii°; seventh chords based on these triads are also used. (In minor keys, one could say that the chords define the scale, since the harmonic minor scale arises from the combination of the basic minor-key triads i, iv, and V.) Chords outside of the scale can usually be explained as tonicizations—brief moves to the scales of other keys. The progression of harmonies within the key is constrained

Example 3.1. The Who, "Bargain" (chorus)

by a few simple and fairly consistent principles: dominant chords (V and vii°) go to tonics; pre-dominants (IV and ii) go to dominants; tonic chords can move to any other chord.[1] In general, certain root motions are strongly favored over others: motions by descending fifth, descending third, and ascending second are generally prescribed as normative (Schoenberg, 1969). These principles are not hard-and-fast rules but rather strong preferences, and corpus studies have shown that they are generally followed; for example, IV goes to V much more often than V goes to IV (Tymoczko, 2003; Temperley, 2009). Very similar principles are operative in jazz harmony as well (Dobbins, 1994). It is natural to wonder if anything similar or analogous to these principles is present in rock, though as always, we must be careful not to impose common-practice norms on rock beyond what is justified by the facts.

3.1 THE CHORDAL VOCABULARY

A few basic observations will get us started. Chords in rock are overwhelmingly triadic. In our harmonic analyses of the *Rolling Stone* corpus, 92.9% of the chords are major or minor triads. Major chords are much more common than minor ones, accounting for 76.4% of all triads. (Diminished and augmented triads are extremely rare.) Besides triads, the remaining chords in the corpus are mostly seventh chords; these account for 5.3% of the chords in our corpus. Extended chords such as ninths, very common in jazz, are mostly very rare in rock. Also occasionally seen are "slash chords," in which a chord is placed over another note in the bass (this is indicated in lead-sheet notation with a slash, e.g., "C/D" for C major over D). Not

1. These principles can be found in any music theory textbook. See, for example, Aldwell et al. (2011) or Laitz (2012).

surprisingly, occurrences of these more complex harmonies in rock tend to be found in jazz-influenced artists such as Stevie Wonder and Steely Dan.

Seventh chords in rock are sometimes used in fairly classical ways— for example, the IV7–V7–I progression in the Beatles' "Yesterday" ("Now I need a place to hide away"), or the I–ii7–V7 progression in the chorus of the Beach Boys' "Don't Worry Baby."[2] In the early years of rock, dominant seventh chords were sometimes treated as tonic harmonies. Chuck Berry's "Johnny B. Goode" ends with such a chord; the Beatles' "I Saw Her Standing There" and Aretha Franklin's "Respect" also have tonic-functioning dominant sevenths. Tonic-functioning minor sevenths and major sevenths also occasionally occur; the tonic-functioning major seventh enjoyed a curious spurt in popularity in around 1971, seen in songs such as Carole King's "It's Too Late" and Chicago's "Color My World." On the whole, though, seventh chords are not common in rock. Also rare are inversions, in which the root of the chord is not in the bass; the vast majority of chords in our rock corpus are in root position (93.9%). Inversions are occasionally used to create a linear pattern in the bass, or an effect of instability; we will revisit this topic in section 6.4. But the meat, potatoes, and vegetables of rock harmony are root-position major and minor triads; other chords add occasional spice.

One distinctive feature of rock harmony is the bare fifth or open fifth chord: just a root and fifth with no third. Bare fifths are often used with a highly sustained and distorted guitar sound (partly because adding a third would create additional distortion); this is known as a "power chord." Example 3.2 shows two uses of bare fifths. In some cases, the context clarifies the harmonies as either major or minor; in Example 3.2B, the melody clearly implies the progression I–V–vi–iii. In Example 3.2A, by contrast, no thirds are present, and bare-fifth labels (e.g., "I5") seem appropriate. Example 3.2A is a good example of a "riff"—a distinctive melodic or chordal pattern, usually in the guitar, that occurs repeatedly throughout a song.

What determines the set of chords that are available in a given song? In common-practice music, as noted earlier, this is dictated by the scale. In rock, however, scales are a thorny issue (as discussed in the previous chapter); many songs do not adhere to any conventional scale. As a first step,

2. By convention, lower-case Roman numerals with 7 are minor seventh chords (minor third, minor seventh); capital ones with 7 are major seventh chords (major third, major seventh), except for V7, which is a dominant seventh (major third, minor seventh). In our corpus we use "d7" to indicate dominant seventh chords on degrees other than $\hat{5}$, e.g., "IVd7."

we can again consider some corpus data. Table 3.1 shows the frequency of the 12 roots in the *Rolling Stone* corpus, represented in relative terms (in relation to the tonic) and grouping major and minor forms of each triad together; I will call these *relative roots*, and I will show them with italicized Roman numerals (to distinguish them from major triads). The table also shows the proportional frequency of each of the 24 major and minor triads

Example 3.2A. Deep Purple, "Smoke on the Water"

Example 3.2B. Green Day, "Basket Case"

Table 3.1 PROPORTIONAL FREQUENCIES OF TRIADS IN THE *ROLLING STONE* CORPUS[A]

Relative roots and proportions		Major triads (as proportion of all triads)		Minor triads (as proportion of all triads)	
I	.335	I	.254	i	.081
bII	.003	bII	.003*	bii	.000*
II	.049	II	.007*	ii	.039
bIII	.021	bIII	.020	biii	.001*
III	.018	III	.004*	iii	.013
IV	.228	IV	.210	iv	.018
#IV	.003	#IV	.001*	#iv	.000*
V	.171	V	.154	v	.018
bVI	.037	bVI	.036	bvi	.000*
VI	.063	VI	.004*	vi	.059
bVII	.070	bVII	.070	bvii	.000*
VII	.003	VII	.001*	vii	.002*

[A]Major and minor triads outside the supermode are marked with an asterisk.

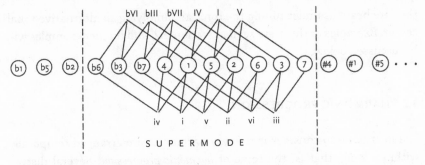

Example 3.3. The common rock triads represented on the line of fifths

(as a proportion of all triads). (In this analysis we group sevenths and other extended chords together with triads, depending on whether the third of the chord is major or minor.) It is probably not surprising that the most common relative roots are *I*, *IV*, and *V*; nor is it surprising that the major forms of these chords are more common than the minor ones, especially given the strong general preference for major triads noted earlier. Also relevant here is the concept of the supermode—a set of ten scale degrees, excluding ♭$\hat{2}$ and ♯$\hat{4}$, which I suggested forms a kind of "global scale" for rock (see section 2.2). In Table 3.1, major and minor triads containing one or more degrees that are not part of the supermode are marked with asterisks. Spelling distinctions are important here: if we think of the supermode arranged on the line of fifths (as in Example 3.3), then ♭6 is in the supermode but ♯$\hat{5}$ is not; thus the III triad ($\hat{3}$–♯$\hat{5}$–$\hat{7}$) contains a degree outside the supermode.[3] It can be seen that, without exception, the triads containing degrees outside the supermode are less common than those entirely within it. (The twelve triads within the supermode are shown in Example 3.3.) This gives further validation to the supermode as defining the basic pitch vocabulary of rock.

The twelve triads within the supermode can be regarded as the common chords of rock. These chords form a logical set: we have the major and minor versions of the tonic, dominant, and subdominant (these are sometimes called *primary* triads); the minor triads ii, vi, and iii on the "sharp" side of the line of fifths (see Example 3.3); and the major triads ♭VII, ♭III, and ♭VI on the "flat" side. Chords outside the supermode set do sometimes occur, but they usually have a surprising or destabilizing effect; frequently

3. In Table 3.1, enharmonic equivalence is assumed: for example, the ♭VI category also includes ♯V. Generally speaking, though, nearly all the occurrences of a triad in the corpus follow one particular spelling; for example, ♭VII chords are always spelled as ♭VII (♭$\hat{7}$–$\hat{2}$–$\hat{4}$) chords rather than ♯VI (♯$\hat{6}$–♯♯$\hat{1}$–♯$\hat{3}$).

they are heard as undermining the tonic and implying an alternative tonal center. Examples of this were seen in section 2.2, and further examples will be discussed below.

3.2 HARMONIC PROGRESSION

The next issue to consider is the way harmonies are arranged temporally within a song: that is, the topic of *harmonic progression*. Several discussions of this topic can be found in the rock literature; here we consider the views of two important rock scholars. Stephenson (2002) argues that the normative harmonic principles of rock constitute a kind of mirror image to those of common-practice music. In contrast to that style, where descending fifths and thirds and ascending seconds are prevalent, the normative motions of rock—according to Stephenson—are precisely the opposite: ascending fifths and thirds and descending seconds. (Stephenson refers to this latter practice as "rock-standard" harmony.) It follows from this that the most natural approach to I is from IV (ascending fifth) rather than from V (descending fifth). Everett (2008b, 2009) offers a very different view. Everett views rock harmony in a hierarchical fashion: events (notes or chords) elaborate other events, which elaborate still other events, forming a complex multileveled structure. (More will be said about this hierarchical view of harmony in section 3.5 below.) In Everett's approach, the normative harmonic motions of classical harmony (such as descending fifths and progressions like IV–V–I) are taken to be normative in rock as well. Chord sequences that go against these norms (such as ♭VII–IV–I and other ascending-fifth patterns) are often analyzed not as true harmonic progressions, but as patterns of linear elaboration.

Everett and Stephenson put forth strongly contrasting perspectives on rock harmony. While both authors acknowledge that many songs go against the harmonic norms of rock (see also Everett, 2004), they have quite different views of what those norms are. Can corpus statistics provide any insight into this matter? Table 3.2 shows a complete "transition table" from the 200 songs of the *Rolling Stone* corpus: the number of times each harmony is followed by each other harmony. (Again, these are relative roots, collapsing together major and minor chords.) For example, the number of times *I* is followed directly by *IV* is 2,419. To help us make sense of this barrage of numbers, Table 3.3 shows some more selective data extracted from the table. The left-hand column shows the proportional frequency of each harmonic root in the corpus; this is like the first column of Table 3.1, except in this case the tonic is excluded. The second column

Table 3.2 TRANSITIONS FROM ONE ROOT ("ANTECEDENT") TO ANOTHER ("CONSEQUENT") IN THE *ROLLING STONE* CORPUS

Cons. Ant.	I	bII	II	bIII	III	IV	#IV	V	bVI	VI	bVII	VII	Totals
I	0	20	391	170	124	2419	7	1282	178	544	793	17	5945
bII	26	0	5	0	0	0	0	0	0	0	0	14	45
II	315	5	0	11	36	110	1	327	2	43	16	7	873
III	59	6	12	0	0	114	5	22	96	0	68	0	382
bIII	8	0	81	7	0	90	0	9	0	128	3	5	331
IV	2379	14	106	109	57	0	8	1128	107	119	94	9	4130
#IV	15	0	1	6	0	16	0	9	1	0	0	1	49
V	1833	1	93	11	30	689	11	0	29	280	98	0	3075
bVI	319	3	2	34	0	25	7	67	0	17	185	0	659
VI	281	0	183	0	64	407	0	173	33	0	5	2	1148
bVII	630	0	0	34	4	276	3	79	219	12	0	0	1257
VII	22	0	2	1	14	0	7	3	0	3	2	0	54

shows the frequency of roots in "pre-tonic" position—directly preceding tonic harmony; the third column shows their frequency in "post-tonic" position. It can be seen that the pre-tonic and post-tonic frequencies of chords are quite similar to their overall frequencies (excluding tonic). The most common chords in pre-tonic and post-tonic position are the same as the most common chords overall: *IV*, then *V*, then ♭*VII*. There are some slight positional preferences for specific chords: *IV*'s pre-tonic and post-tonic frequencies are both higher than its overall frequency; *V* is more common in pre-tonic position, less common in post-tonic position. But these differences are fairly subtle. Similarly, the pre-tonic frequency of *II* (.054) is only slightly lower than its post-tonic frequency (.066). We see nearly symmetrical relationships between other common chord pairs as well (shown in Table 3.2); for example, *V* moves to *IV* 22% of the time (689/3,075), while *IV* moves to *V* 27% of the time (1,128/4,130). All this points to a strong contrast with common-practice harmony, where harmonic motions are highly asymmetrical: *I* often moves to *II* but is rarely approached from *II*, and *IV* moves to *V* much more often than the reverse.

We can also describe harmonic motion in intervallic terms. Table 3.4 shows the frequencies of harmonic motions in the *Rolling Stone* corpus. The left side of the table shows chromatic root motions; the right side groups them into diatonic intervals (e.g., grouping major and minor seconds together). Focusing first on the diatonic intervals, it is of interest to compare ascending and descending versions of the same interval. Descending

Table 3.3 PROPORTIONAL FREQUENCY OF RELATIVE ROOTS OVERALL (EXCLUDING TONIC), IN PRE-TONIC POSITION AND IN POST-TONIC POSITION

Relative root (excluding tonic)	Proportional frequency (excluding tonic)	Proportional frequency in pre-tonic position	Proportional frequency in post-tonic position
bII	.004	.004	.003
II	.073	.054	.066
bIII	.032	.010	.029
III	.027	.001	.021
IV	.342	.404	.407
#IV	.004	.003	.001
V	.258	.311	.216
bVI	.055	.054	.030
VI	.095	.048	.092
bVII	.105	.107	.133
VII	.005	.004	.003

fifths (−P5) are more common than ascending ones (+P5), but the difference is not large; similarly, descending thirds are slightly more common than ascending, and ascending seconds slightly more common than descending. Altogether, one could say there is a preference for "classical" harmonic motions (descending fifths and thirds and ascending seconds), but it is fairly slight. As for chromatic intervals, a rather consistent pattern emerges; Example 3.4 shows the intervals represented on the line of fifths. (Each interval can be represented as a certain number of fifth motions. For example, two descending fifths make a descending major second, e.g., C–(F)–Bb.) The frequency of intervals decreases as line-of-fifths distance increases. Thus, there is a very definite preference for motions that are "close" on the line of fifths. We saw in chapter 2 that common rock scales tend to form compact regions of pitches on the line of fifths; the same principle seems to be at work here, since moving between close roots on the line will generally keep the pitches close together as well. The fact that the most common roots (excluding *I*) are *IV* and *V*—adjacent to *I* on the line of fifths—also reflects this principle.

What does all this tell us about rock harmony? Certainly some triads are more common than others, and there is a general preference for "close" motions on the line of fifths. But we do not see strong, specific constraints analogous to those found in common-practice harmony. Rock does not show strong directional preferences for specific chord pairs (for example, *V* to *IV* is nearly as common as *IV* to *V*); or for particular intervallic motions (e.g., ascending versus descending fifths). There are some specific

Table 3.4 ROOT MOTIONS IN THE *ROLLING STONE* CORPUS[a]

Chromatic interval	Proportional Frequency	Diatonic interval	Proportional frequency
+m2	.012	+M2/m2	.166
+M2	.154		
+m3	.044	+M3/m3	.076
+M3	.033		
+P4 (−P5)	.286	−P5(+P4)	.286
+TT	.002	TT	.002
−P4 (+P5)	.237	+P5(−P4)	.237
−M3	.036	−M3/m3	.083
−m3	.048		
−M2	.134	−M2/m2	.149
−m2	.015		

[a]M = major [e.g., +M2 = ascending major second], m = minor, P = perfect, TT = tritone. Every possible interval within an octave is represented here; for example, an ascending minor seventh is the same as a descending major second.

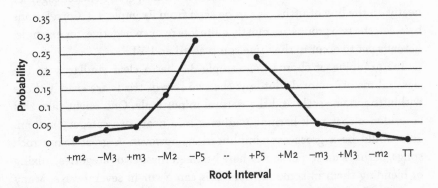

Example 3.4. Root motions in the *Rolling Stone* corpus arranged on the line of fifths

patterns that occur in rock harmony with particular frequency, as we will discuss in a later section. On the whole, however, the relatively unconstrained nature of harmonic progression in rock is an important feature of the style, setting it apart from other harmonic styles such as common-practice music and jazz.

3.3 THE LINE-OF-FIFTHS AXIS

Returning to the twelve common rock triads mentioned in section 3.2, one might wonder if there are particular combinations of these chords that tend to occur together. One way of getting at this is through the technique of correlation. We can calculate the correlation between two chords X and Y by examining the extent to which they occur in the same songs (here we disregard the number of times they occur within a song and their temporal relationship to each other). If chords X and Y occur in exactly the same set of songs, the correlation is perfectly positive (1.0); if the songs containing X are exactly those that do *not* contain Y, the correlation will be perfectly negative (−1.0). I examined the correlations among the twelve common rock triads. A summary of the data is shown in Example 3.5; high correlations (above 0.4) are shown in solid lines, and moderate correlations (between 0.2 and 0.4) are in dotted lines. Some interesting patterns can be seen: the "flat-side" triads, ♭VII, ♭III and ♭VI, emerge as a group in which all three pairs are strongly correlated; the "sharp-side" triads ii, vi, and iii are another such group (except that ii and vi are only moderately correlated). Generally, too, the flat-side triads are more correlated with the minor primary triads (i, iv, and v), and the sharp-side triads with the major primary triads. Overall, the chords form two highly interconnected but separate groups: I/IV/V/ii/vi/iii and i/iv/v/♭VII/♭III/♭VI. The chords within each group cluster together neatly on the line of fifths, as can be seen from Example 3.3. Correlations between the two groups are mostly quite low or even negative; for example, iii tends *not* to occur in the same songs as ♭III and ♭VI.

The grouping of chords in Example 3.5 has a clear similarity to the classical major/minor dichotomy: the two sets of triads are exactly those within the major scale and the natural minor scale. One might take this as evidence that rock harmony adheres to a neat, two-category system. This would be a gross oversimplification, however. A great many rock songs, perhaps most, fall somewhere between these two categories, mixing or blending them in some fashion. This can occur in several ways. Many songs combine flat-side triads with major primary triads, especially I and IV. Progressions like I→♭VII→♭VI→♭VII–I, seen in the Rolling Stones' "Gimme

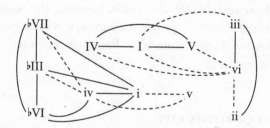

Example 3.5. Correlations between triads in the *Rolling Stone* corpus. Solid lines represent correlations above .35; dotted lines represent correlations between .2 and .35.

Shelter," are not unusual. By contrast, the combination of minor primary triads (i, iv, v) with sharp-side triads (ii, vi, and iii) is rare.[4] Other songs mix major and minor forms of the primary triads, often in a modal context: combining I and v (characteristic of Mixolydian mode) or i and IV (Dorian mode). And in still other songs, major primary triads are combined with a melody using flat-side degrees ($\flat\hat{3}$ and $\flat\hat{7}$), pulling the song as a whole somewhat in the flat direction. Thus, rather than speaking of two separate harmonic practices, I would rather think of pitch organization in rock songs in terms of an *axis*—a span on the line of fifths that includes the entire supermode; individual songs tend to occupy smaller regions within this span, often compact or nearly so. (I prefer to label the ends of this axis as "flat-side/sharp-side," rather than "major/minor," both to capture the gradient nature of the distinction and because the "minor" side of rock is rather different from classical minor, as discussed earlier.)

The idea of mapping songs on to regions on the line-of-fifths axis accords well with findings presented in the previous chapter. Examining data from the *Rolling Stone* corpus (Example 2.12), we found that songs that use more $\flat\hat{3}$ than $\hat{3}$ in their harmonic progressions also tend to use more $\flat\hat{7}$ than $\hat{7}$, and more $\flat\hat{6}$ than $\hat{6}$; for songs that use more $\hat{3}$ than $\flat\hat{3}$, the opposite is true. This is what we would expect if songs tend to stay within fairly compact regions on the line of fifths. The melodic data shows this pattern as well (though somewhat less strongly; the "minor" melodic profile has fairly high values for $\hat{6}$ and $\hat{3}$). The distribution of melodies on the line of fifths (shown in Example 2.14) shows that songs vary quite rather gradually in terms of their line-of-fifths positions, rather than falling neatly into two categories; again, this points to the gradient nature of the sharp-side/flat-side distinction. The idea that rock favors compact sets of scale degrees fits well with conventional ideas about scales in rock (diatonic and pentatonic scales are maximally compact), and also with our data about root motions, which shows that the most favored motions are those that traverse small distances on the line of fifths.

4. Of the 79 songs in the corpus that contain one or more flat-side triads ($\flat$VII, $\flat$III, or $\flat$VI), 53 contain I as well; only 36 contain i. In light of this, it may seem odd that the graph does not show any correlations between major primary triads and flat-side triads; indeed, these correlations are mostly negative. This is because, while major primary triads are frequent in songs with flat-side roots, they are even more frequent in songs *without* flat-side roots. Among the 102 songs containing sharp-side triads, far more contain I (96) than i (18). This asymmetry is perhaps not surprising, given that major primary triads are much more frequent than minor ones overall (Table 3.1). I should note, though, that both de Clercq and I tended to notate bare fifths as major triads in our analyses; for this reason, the frequency of major primary triads may be somewhat overstated.

The line-of-fifths model is also useful in describing stylistic categories within rock. Many of the more "sharp-side" songs in the *Rolling Stone* corpus might be described as "pop" (such as the Ronettes' "Be My Baby" or the Jackson 5's "I Want You Back") or soft rock (such as Elton John's "Your Song"). Many flat-side songs are on the harder side of rock, such as Neil Young's "Rockin' in the Free World," based on the progression i→♭VII→♭VI–(i), and Nirvana's "Smells Like Teen Spirit," with the progression i–iv→♭III→♭VI. Our earlier categorization of songs as "major" or "minor" found, also, that a large group of songs falls into the major harmonic category but the minor melodic one; this includes many blues-influenced songs in genres such as 1950s rock, soul, and early hard rock. The line-of-fifths model will also be helpful to us in exploring the emotional connotations of rock songs, a subject we will address in chapter 7.

Earlier, we considered the controversial issue of the norms of root motion in rock; one might wonder if the line-of-fifths axis can shed any light on this issue. To examine this, I categorized songs in the *Rolling Stone* corpus as sharp-side or flat-side in a rather crude way: sharp-side songs are those that contain either ii, vi, or iii (or some combination), but not ♭VII, ♭III, or ♭VI; flat-side songs are defined as the reverse. (By this criterion, many songs are neither sharp-side or flat-side: those using only primary triads or both flat-side and sharp-side ones.) Example 3.6 shows the distribution of diatonic root motions in the two sets of songs. It can be seen that the sharp-side songs contain more "classical" motions, +M/m2, −M/m3, and −P5; the flat-side ones contain more "anti-classical" ones, with the exception of fifths, where ascending and descending forms are about equal. The samples used in this test are small, and perhaps we should not read too much into it, but I find the results interesting, especially in light of Stephenson's and Everett's views of rock harmony discussed earlier; perhaps these authors' divergent conclusions about the norms of root motion in rock are due partly to differences in the repertoire they were examining.[5] It is also noteworthy that the root motions of flat-side songs feature more seconds (overall) and fewer fifths than sharp-side songs, perhaps representing a departure from classical norms in another way.

The tendency for rock songs to stay within fairly compact regions on the line of fifths is useful to bear in mind, for it brings our attention to moments that do not follow this norm. When a song breaks out of its established

---

5. Everett's 2009 study focuses primarily on songs in the Billboard Hot 100 charts of the 1960s; as noted in chapter 1, this approach may favor the "pop" side of the rock spectrum. Similarly, Burgoyne (2011) presents corpus analyses based on the Hot 100, and also finds a stronger presence of classical norms than that found in the *Rolling Stone* corpus.

line-of-fifths region, this can create an effect of real surprise. Consider the passages shown in Example 3.7. The chorus of Dionne Warwick and the Spinners' "Then Came You" is predominantly in major mode, both the harmony and the melody. The move to ♭VII at the end of the chorus implies a

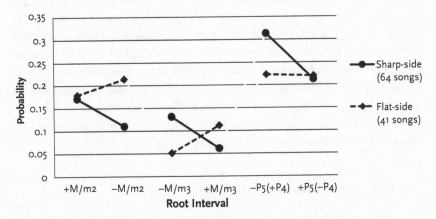

Example 3.6. Diatonic root motions in "sharp-side" songs (those containing sharp-side triads but no flat-side ones) and "flat-side" songs (containing flat-side triads but no sharp-side ones), as a proportion of the total in each set

Example 3.7A. Dionne Warwick and the Spinners, "Then Came You" (end of chorus)

Example 3.7B. Dire Straits, "Money for Nothing" (chorus)

Example 3.7C. The Doors, "Light My Fire"

shift to the flat side (the melody follows this too, with ♭3 and ♭7); perhaps this expresses the change in the singer's situation brought about by the arrival of "you." The opposite pattern is seen in the Dire Straits' "Money for Nothing." In this case the chorus mainly uses flat-side harmonies—♭VI, ♭III, and ♭VII—but ends with a remarkable shift to VI5; though this chord is an open fifth—neither major nor minor—the mere appearance of this *root* is enough to suggest a move to the sharp side. A harmonic oddity of a rather different kind is seen in the verse of the Doors' "Light My Fire." Here we find an alternation between i7 and vi7; combining minor primary chords with sharp-side chords is unusual, as noted earlier, and gives the song a strange, quirky feel. (The minor sevenths in the two chords add color but do not change the fundamental effect.) Other interesting mixtures of sharp-side and flat-side harmonies will be seen in chapter 10.

3.4 COMMON HARMONIC SCHEMATA

Beyond the general points about rock harmony mentioned above, certain harmonic patterns seem to be especially common; some of these are associated with specific periods in rock's history. In the language of contemporary music theory, we might speak of a common harmonic pattern as a *schema* (plural: *schemata*). In this section we consider some important harmonic schemata in rock.

A natural starting point is the twelve-bar blues progression—shown here in its most common form, with variants of the first four measures and the last four measures shown below:

```
    I  |   |   |   | IV |   | I  |      | V | IV | I |   |
  (OR: I  | IV | I |   | )        (OR: | V |    | I |   | )
```

The influence of the blues on rock is well-known. Many of the early songs in our corpus (the 1950s) are based on the blues progression; a number of them do nothing but cycle through it several times, such as Elvis Presley's "Hound Dog" and Little Richard's "Long Tall Sally." Elvis Presley's "Jailhouse Rock" can be viewed as a modified blues progression in which the opening I is extended from four to eight measures. In the 1960s, the progression is most clearly evident in covers of earlier blues songs by bands such as the Rolling Stones and Cream,[6] but a great many other songs also

6. For a penetrating study of the way Cream used and transformed blues materials, see Headlam (1997).

use the progression or variants of it. Many such songs preserve the first eight measures of the pattern—I–I–I–I–IV–IV–I–I—but deviate from it after that; examples include the Beatles' "Day Tripper," Cream's "Sunshine of Your Love," and the Doors' "Love Me Two Times." The progression arises only occasionally in later decades, in songs such as Bruce Springsteen's "Dancing in the Dark." The blues progression may have influenced rock harmony in more subtle ways as well. The final part of the progression (in the first variant), (I)–V–IV–I, reflects "anti-classical" harmonic moves: ascending fifth, descending second, ascending fifth. As suggested by Stephenson (2002), this may have encouraged the use of these motions in rock, counterbalancing the strong norms of classical harmonic motion seen in other genres influencing rock (such as jazz and Tin Pan Alley); this may explain the relatively even distribution of ascending and descending motions that we see in rock as a whole.

In the late 1950s and early 1960s, another very common progression emerged: I–vi–IV–V–(I) (and its variant, I–vi–ii–V). Sometimes known as the "doo-wop" progression, this pattern was employed in innumerable songs of the era, such as the Five Satins' "In the Still of the Nite," the Ronettes' "Be My Baby," the Four Seasons' "Sherry," and the Everly Brothers' "All I Have to Do Is Dream." (See Everett, 2009, 220, for statistics on the rise and fall of this progression.) Note the strongly classical character of the root motions (−3rd, −3rd, +2nd, −5th). Moving into the mid-1960s and beyond, it is difficult to identify any single progression that held sway as strongly as the blues and doo-wop progressions had done in earlier periods. The 1990s saw the rise of another common pattern: I–V–vi–IV. Green Day's "When I Come Around" and Bush's "Glycerine" are well-known examples; since 2000, this progression has become even more popular. It is interesting that this pattern simply reorders the four chords of the doo-wop progression; one could think of it as shifting the V chord from the fourth position to the second, replacing the classical V–I motion with IV–I. The progression is commonly seen in different rotations: it often starts on vi (as in Joan Osborne's "One of Us") and sometimes on V or IV. It is also open to tonal ambiguity, particularly when it starts on vi, sometimes suggesting an interpretation of i–♭VI–♭III–♭VII; an instance of this was given in Example 2.19A.

In some cases, a single progression serves as the basis for multiple sections of a song—not just the introduction, verse, or chorus, but more than one of these (or perhaps all three); this makes us feel that it somehow represents the harmonic essence of the song. In such cases I will call this the "main progression" of the song. Usually these progressions are one, two, or four measures long and involve two to four chords—what Tagg (2009) has called "loops." The common schemata noted above—I–vi–IV–V and I–V–vi–IV—often appear as main progressions. Other harmonic patterns are also used as main progressions in numerous songs, such as I→♭VII–IV (with the IV chord twice the length of the other two) and I–IV–V–IV.[7] It is sometimes unclear whether such patterns are true "schemata" in the minds of rock musicians (and listeners) or whether they simply arise independently on multiple occasions. After all, a progression such as I–IV–V–IV consists entirely of common chords and common harmonic moves; it would be surprising if it did *not* occur.

Moore (2001, 2012) makes a useful distinction between harmonic patterns that are "closed," ending on I, and "open," ending on non-tonic harmony. While open patterns are the norm in rock (the schemata discussed in the previous paragraph could all be described as open patterns), closed patterns are also common, such as I→♭VII | IV–I |.[8] (Vertical bars represent measures or two-bar or four-bar "hypermeasures"—see section 4.4.) Closed and open patterns are quite different in their effect. A closed pattern such as I→♭VII | IV–I | seems like a complete musical thought; there is no doubt that it forms a two-measure (or four- or eight-measure) unit aligned with the meter. But with an open pattern such as I–V | vi–IV | (I), each instance seems to lead into the next one.[9] One could say the open-ended character of such progressions is a virtue, keeping momentum going from one instance of the pattern to the next. This trade-off between closure and continuity arises at larger structural levels as well, as we will see. A repeated pattern could also *begin* on non-tonic harmony; this is less common but does sometimes occur, especially in choruses (see section 8.3).

Moore also discusses what he calls "cyclic" harmonic patterns: those that repeat a single root interval. Gloria Gaynor's "I Will Survive" features seven descending fifths (including one diminished fifth), i–iv→♭VII→♭III→♭VI–ii°–V–i: a very common pattern in classical music. More distinctive to rock

7. Well-known examples of the I→♭VII–IV pattern include Fleetwood Mac's "Don't Stop," AC/DC's "Back in Black," and the J. Geils Band's "Centerfold"; sometimes the I is twice the length of the other two chords, as in Led Zeppelin's "Good Times Bad Times." Examples of I–IV–V–IV include the Rascals' "Good Lovin'," the Rolling Stones' "Get Off of My Cloud," and The Troggs' "Wild Thing."

8. Examples of this particular closed pattern include Who's "I Can't Explain," Bachman-Turner Overdrive's "Takin' Care of Business," and Robert Palmer's "Addicted to Love."

9. In fact there is some ambiguity in the delineation of such patterns. Given a section built on a repeating pattern like I–V | vi–IV | I . . . , does each instance of the pattern end with the IV chord, or does it also contain the following I, overlapping with the next instance? (If it does end on the following I, one might say that is no longer "open.") I find this difficult to decide. The segmentation of harmonic patterns is frequently somewhat ambiguous, as we will discuss in section 5.1.

are patterns of ascending fifths, such as ♭III→♭VII–IV–I, seen in the Rolling Stones' "Jumpin' Jack Flash," or ♭VI→♭III→♭VII–IV–I, in Al Green's "Take Me to the River." Cyclic patterns of seconds are also common, especially using flat-side harmonies, such as I→♭VII→♭VI and ♭VI→♭VII–I (sometimes with i instead of I). In the *Rolling Stone* corpus (Table 3.2), it can be seen that the most common root following ♭*VI* is ♭*VII*: this pattern occurs in 11 songs in the corpus, and in all but one case the ♭*VII* is followed (at least once) by *I*. (This partly accounts for the high frequency of motion by seconds in "flat-side" songs, noted earlier.) Biamonte (2010) refers to ♭VI→♭VII–I as the "Aeolian progression," and offers many examples.

3.5 LINEAR AND COMMON-TONE LOGIC

Consider Example 3.8A, showing the chord progression from the verse of the Eagles' "Hotel California." One way to think of this progression (the first six chords, anyway) is as a repeated pattern of root motions: descending fourth, ascending third. It can be also seen, however, that an inner voice of the progression traces a descending chromatic line, from scale-degree $\hat{1}$ down to $\hat{5}$: B–A♯–A–G♯–G–F♯ (this is shown by lines on the example). Rather than thinking of these chords in terms of root motion, then, we could also think of them as providing harmonic support for the chromatic line. This is a central idea behind the Schenkerian approach to harmony (named after the theorist Heinrich Schenker), reflected especially in the work of Everett (2004, 2008b, 2009) as well as a number of other rock scholars (Brown, 1997; Burns, 2000; Wagner, 2003; Nobile, 2011). Sometimes linear patterns are seen in root motions themselves: common patterns such as I–♭VII→♭VI and ♭VI→♭VII–I, mentioned above, could be explained in this way.

Another essential aspect of Schenkerian theory is a "hierarchical" view of harmony: some harmonies are elaborations of other, more "structural" ones. In "Hotel California," for example, the entire pattern could be reduced to a i–V–(i) progression in which the i–V is filled in with linear motion. Another illustration of this approach is seen in Everett's (2008b) analysis of the progression ♭VII–IV–I (Example 3.8B): he suggests that it emerges from neighbor motions—♭$\hat{7}$–$\hat{6}$ (B♭–A), then $\hat{4}$–$\hat{3}$ (F–E)—supported by triadic harmonies. Similarly, Everett analyzes the common I–IV–V–IV progression as a I–IV alternation in which the IV is elaborated by V through neighbor motion (Example 3.8C).

The Schenkerian view deserves consideration, and is sometimes quite useful; surely no one could deny the linear basis of the progression in "Hotel California." However, it can also be highly subjective. For example,

Example 3.8A. The progression of the verse in the Eagles' "Hotel California"

Example 3.8B.

Example 3.8C.

responding to Everett's analysis of the ♭VII–IV–I progression, Doll (2009) offers another hierarchical analysis, suggesting that it arises from an interpolation of IV between the motion from ♭VII to I. (Spicer [2000] suggests yet another possibility—that the ♭VII substitutes for the V of the blues progression.) Unlike questions about surface harmonic progressions, such questions cannot be resolved in any obvious way by corpus data. My own intuitions about hierarchical relations between chords are often quite weak; I see little reason to favor one hierarchical analysis of ♭VII–IV–I over the other. This is not to say that we can never make structural distinctions among chords; certainly some chords seem more important than others, especially those that are emphasized in some way (e.g., by duration or metrical emphasis) or serve large-scale structural (e.g., cadential) functions. But to incorporate every chord into a reductive hierarchical framework often seems arbitrary. The Schenkerian approach will not play a major role in the remainder of the book, but we will occasionally make use of it, especially with certain harmonic progressions that seem best explained in linear terms.

Another kind of harmonic logic, deserving brief mention, is common-tone logic. Consider Example 3.9, Depeche Mode's "Shake the Disease." The progression here—vi–i–♭VI–IV—presents an unusual mix of sharp-side and flat-side harmonies. But all four chords have something in common: they contain the $\hat{1}$ scale degree, F, which is present in the accompaniment throughout. This gives the passage a weird kind of cohesion. Capuzzo

Example 3.9. Depeche Mode, "Shake the Disease" (chorus)

(2004) discusses this and other examples of common-tone progressions in rock. Common-tone harmonic logic is widely used in late-nineteenth century music; in rock, it is more of an occasional curiosity.

3.6 TONICIZATION, CADENCES, AND PEDAL POINTS

To complete our survey of rock harmony, three concepts deserve brief discussion. All of them are drawn from common-practice theory, but each one takes on quite a different character in the context of rock.

Tonicization. Tonicization refers to a brief suggestion of a key within a larger context of another key. (Larger-scale shifts of key—modulations—will be discussed further in section 9.5.) In common-practice music, tonicization is most often achieved by preceding a chord by its dominant (a "secondary" or "applied" dominant). Tonicization is not common in rock, but it is occasionally seen. Sometimes it is used in quite a classical fashion. The chorus of Elton John's "Goodbye Yellow Brick Road" (Example 3.10A) features a very conventional secondary dominant, V7 of ii ("V7/ii") going to ii. (The chord after the slash indicates the chord being tonicized—*not* the bass note, as in a lead-sheet "slash chord.") The previous V7/vi—if that is what it is—is more unusual, as it does not resolve to vi. More characteristic of rock is where a chord is tonicized by its IV chord. The fifth measure of the "Hotel California" progression (Example 3.8A), though labeled as ♭VI, could also be regarded as IV of ♭III. Consider also the chorus of John Cougar Mellencamp's "Lonely Ol' Night" (Example 3.10B). While one could analyze this as ♭VII–IV, the repetition of the pattern and orientation of the melody around the IV triad are sufficient to suggest IV as a temporary tonal center.

A curious chord that deserves mention here is II. As II contains the ♯$\hat{4}$ degree, it is chromatic—under the current theory at least—and should destabilize the tonic; and it often does. A progression that might be analyzed as alternating between I and II is difficult to hear that way; we tend to search for an alternative interpretation (Example 2.20A is a case in point). But there are also genuine occurrences of II, sometimes even in the main progression of a song. Especially common is the pattern I–II–IV–I

Example 3.10A. Elton John, "Goodbye Yellow Brick Road" (chorus)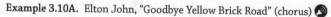

Example 3.10B. John Cougar Mellencamp, "Lonely Ol' Night"

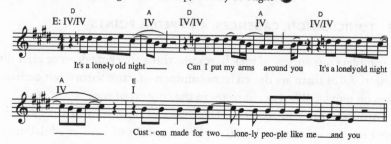

Example 3.11.

(Example 3.11)—a favorite progression of the Beatles, found in "Eight Days a Week" and a number of other songs. Everett (1999) argues that this progression is built on a descending chromatic line, $\hat{5}$–#$\hat{4}$–$\hat{4}$–$\hat{3}$ (G–F♯–F–E in Example 3.11), and perhaps that does explain it in a way. I still maintain, though, that it is mildly destabilizing; the II chord tugs us slightly away from the tonic key, and the IV–I pulls us back again. Normally, chords that challenge the tonic are understood as tonicizing some other key (such as applied dominants in classical music). But what does II tonicize? In classical music, an apparent II most often functions as V/V, but I certainly do not hear the II in Example 3.11 as tonicizing V—nor anything else, really. It seems to undermine the tonic without suggesting any specific alternative.

Cadences. Generally speaking, a cadence is simply a musical gesture that implies the end of a phrase or section; the most famous example is the V–I cadence of common-practice music, which often marks phrase and section endings and which is virtually obligatory at the end of a piece.

Other styles also have cadential patterns, such as medieval music and Indian classical music. In rock, there is no consensus as to what the term "cadence" means; it is clear that there is no mandatory cadential gesture analogous to the perfect cadence of classical music. Elsewhere (Temperley, 2011) I have proposed a definition of cadence which I find useful in the context of rock: *a cadence is a harmonic move to I coinciding with the end of the vocal line of a chorus (or refrain)*. (The distinction between chorus and refrain will be discussed further in section 8.1.) By this criterion, many songs have cadences—59% of the songs in the *Rolling* Stone corpus—but many do not. Example 3.12 shows three songs with cadences (A, B, C) and two without (D, E). In (D), the chorus vocal does not end over I; in (E), the chorus vocal

Example 3.12. The ends of five choruses, three with cadences (A, B, C) and two without (D, E)

A. Carl Perkins, "Blue Suede Shoes"

B. Michael Jackson, "Billie Jean"

C. Guns N' Roses, "Sweet Child O' Mine"

D. AC/DC, "Back in Black"

E. Creedence Clearwater Revival, "Proud Mary"

does not end over a *move* to I (the move to tonic harmony occurred two measures earlier). A chorus that ends with a cadence imparts a sense of closure and completion; a chorus that does not seems more open-ended, leading into the next section. Notably, my definition of a cadence does not require the melody to end on $\hat{1}$ (as would be required in the "perfect cadence" of classical music); in many cases it does not (e.g., Example 3.12B, which ends on $\hat{5}$), and this does not greatly weaken the sense of closure, in my opinion. A harmonic gesture also feels more cadential if it is somehow *distinctive* within the section, not merely a repeat of a pattern that has occurred many times.

It is of interest to examine the pre-tonic chord—the one immediately preceding the tonic—in rock cadences. In cadences in the *Rolling Stone* corpus, the most common pre-tonic root is *V* (occurring in 54% of cadences) followed by *IV* (31%); ♭*VII* is a distant third (6%) (Temperley, 2011). We should also mention one harmony that has not come up so far, the V11 chord (Example 3.13A). This chord can be viewed as a IV triad over $\hat{5}$ in the bass (though sometimes $\hat{2}$ is included as well). V11 nearly always moves to I, and it is especially common at cadences, or at other structurally important points such as the end of a verse or bridge. Example 3.13B shows a typical cadential usage; in Example 3.13C, the chord occurs at the end of the verse. Perhaps the V11 functions so well at cadences because it combines the two most common pre-tonic chords (IV and V). Uses of the chord

Example 3.13A. The V11 chord

Example 3.13B. Billy Joel, "Just the Way You Are" (end of chorus)

Example 3.13C. Carole King, "You've Got a Friend" (end of verse)

in other contexts—such as after the first phrase of the Beatles' "Long and Winding Road"—are exceptional. The V11 is especially characteristic of the softer genres of rock; it is seen also in many pop ballads, such as Diana Ross and Lionel Richie's "Endless Love."

In common-practice music, a *half-cadence* is a harmonic move to V at the end of a phrase or section, creating a sense of partial closure. I cannot find any common convention analogous to this in rock, though I will occasionally use the term half-cadence in an ad hoc way. Often, when a section in a rock song ends on non-tonic harmony (again, in a distinctive gesture that is not part of a repeating pattern), the effect is not so much of closure but of an increase in tension and anticipation for the move to tonic (often reinforced by a textural buildup and other means). This is common at the ends of verses and bridges; Example 3.13C is a case in point. When the section-ending chord functions to steer the song back toward the main key after a move away from it, we could call it *retransitional*, following Everett (2009). Dominant harmony seems to be the preferred choice for such half-cadential and retransitional moments, though by no means the only possibility.

Pedal Points. A pedal point, or just a pedal, refers to a situation in which harmonies change over a sustained or repeated bass note. This is not infrequent in rock; two instances are shown in Examples 3.14A and B. In most cases, the bass note is the tonic (making it a "tonic pedal"), though pedals on other bass notes are occasionally seen (the bridge to the Beatles' "Day Tripper" features a dominant pedal). There is no standard way of labeling pedal points; Example 3.14 shows one possible notation.[10] Pedal points can give rise to ambiguities: In "Jumpin' Jack Flash," are the A♭s and E♭s really harmonic, or just non-chord tones—large-scale "neighbor-tones" of the underlying B♭ harmony? Pedals occur more often in verses than in choruses. Some rock verses consist entirely of a repeating progression over a tonic pedal; "Jumpin' Jack Flash" fits this description, as do Stevie Wonder's "Living for the City" and Prince's "1999."

Sometimes in rock, we encounter a repeated pitch or pitch pattern in an upper register, with changing harmonies beneath—sometimes known as an "upper-voice pedal" (or "inverted pedal"). As with bass pedals, $\hat{1}$ and $\hat{5}$ are the scale degrees most commonly used in this way. In the Supremes' "You Keep Me Hangin' On" (Example 3.15), a rhythm guitar plays octave E♭s ($\hat{5}$) throughout the chorus, sometimes clashing with the underlying

---

10. One can also notate pedal points using "slash chords" (see section 3.1), e.g., "A♭5/B♭" in "Jumpin' Jack Flash." This would seem to have much the same meaning, but using slashes with Roman numerals is confusing since a slash is also used for applied chords.

Example 3.14A. The Rolling Stones, "Jumpin' Jack Flash"

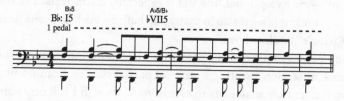

Example 3.14B. Pink Floyd, "Run Like Hell"

Example 3.15. The Supremes, "You Keep Me Hangin' On"

harmonies. The synthesizer pattern in the Alan Parsons Project's "Games People Play," alternating between $\hat{1}$ and $\hat{5}$ (across two octaves), is another nice example. In U2's "With or Without You," one could argue that the arpeggiated tonic triad in the guitar, heard in the background throughout much of the song, acts as a kind of upper-voice pedal pattern.

3.7 QUESTIONS

1. Each of these four songs features a harmonic progression that is (arguably) built on a linear pattern: Bob Dylan, "Like a Rolling Stone" (verse); Bob Dylan, "Lay Lady Lay" (chorus); Duran Duran, "Rio" (chorus); Stone Temple Pilots, "Plush" (verse). Analyze the harmony in each case and

identify the linear pattern. Is it in the melody, the bass, or an inner voice? Ascending or descending? Chromatic or diatonic?

2. Each of these three song sections uses one of the common harmonic schemata discussed in section 3.4: Elton John, "Crocodile Rock" (intro); the Rolling Stones, "Beast of Burden" (verse); Michael Jackson, "Black or White" (verse and refrain). Identify which schema is used in each song. In each case, the song is outside the historical period in which the schema was most commonly used; explain.

3. These three song sections all use chordal inversion (i.e., chords not in root position) in interesting ways: the Supremes, "Stop! In the Name of Love" (chorus); the Spinners, "Could It Be I'm Falling in Love" (introduction); Elton John, "Someone Saved My Life Tonight" (introduction and first two vocal lines, "When I . . . electric chair"). Analyze the harmony, showing the inversions. What is the function of the inversions; how would the effect be different if only root-position chords were used?

4. Harmonic analysis involves many judgment calls. We may wish to say that a chord is "implied" even when not all of its notes are literally present. The opening two lines of Billy Joel's "It's Still Rock and Roll To Me" (What's the matter . . . tie's too wide") feature just a melody and bass line; transcribe them. How would you analyze this passage harmonically? Could events later in the song affect our analysis of the passage?

5. Some authors have suggested that chords in rock can be grouped into categories according to their harmonic *function*—an idea borrowed from common-practice theory. In particular, Doll (2007, 16–27) suggests that the ♭VII chord can often serve a dominant function, similar to V; this is due partly to the shared scale degrees between the two chords, $\hat{2}$ and $\hat{7}$ (though $\hat{7}$ is flattened in ♭VII). What do you think? What kinds of evidence could be brought to bear on this issue?

CHAPTER 4

Rhythm and Meter

4.1 METER AND "THE BEAT"

"Calling out around the world, are you ready for a brand new beat?" sings Martha Reeves in Martha and the Vandellas' classic 1964 song "Dancing in the Street." "The beat" has long been an essential and familiar concept in rock music. The term appears in names of groups (the Beatles, the English Beat—known in the UK as the Beat), song titles ("The Beat Goes On," "We Got the Beat") and iconic lyrics like the one above—or Janet Jackson's "Gimme a beat!" at the beginning of "Nasty." In TV shows of the 1960s like "American Bandstand," where audience members rated new hit songs, the quality of the beat was often decisive: "It's got a good beat" was a standard comment. The exact meaning of the term in such contexts is difficult to define, but it clearly has something to do with a song's underlying rhythmic feel or "groove"—a concept that we will explore later in the book (section 7.4).

In music theory, the term "beat" has a somewhat different meaning, though related. A beat is a point in time that is perceived as accented—though it may not receive any explicit accentuation and may indeed even be silent. Beats form a regular, multileveled pattern—a metrical structure, or simply a *meter*. Levels of beats are sometimes represented by rows of dots, as in Example 4.1: each row corresponds to a rhythmic value (whole note, half note, quarter note, eighth note). The relationships between these levels define the time signature of the piece; the structures in Example 4.1 correspond to 4/4, 3/4, and 12/8. Beats that are present in higher levels are called "strong" beats—a relative term; in 4/4 time, for example, the third quarter-note beat (which is also a half-note beat) is stronger than the second

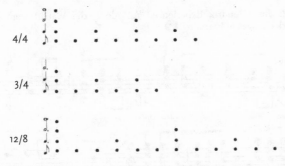

Example 4.1. Metrical grids

(which is not), but weaker than the first (which is a half-note beat and also a whole-note beat, or "downbeat"). There may be lower levels of beats (e.g., sixteenth notes); there may also be higher ("hypermetrical") levels, so that, for example, odd-numbered downbeats are stronger than even-numbered ones. One level of beats is generally heard as the main beat or "tactus"— the level at which one naturally moves or taps; this is normally the quarter note in the case of 4/4 and 3/4 ("simple" meters) and the dotted quarter in the case of 12/8 ("compound" meter). A meter is "duple" if tactus beats are grouped in twos (like 4/4 or 12/8) or "triple" if they are grouped in threes (like 3/4). The *tempo* of a song is essentially the speed of the tactus level— defined as the number of tactus beats per minute (BPM); in rock, this is most often in a range of 80 to 140 or so, but it can also be faster or slower.

The meter of a piece is established by the sounds of the piece; but once it is established, the music need not constantly reinforce it and may even go against it. Thus, meter must be *inferred* from the music and then maintained in the mind of the listener. In rock, this is usually a fairly straightforward process, and relies largely on the standard rock drum pattern: By convention, the bass (or "kick") drum marks beats 1 and 3 of a 4/4 measure (by far the most common meter in rock) and the snare drum marks beats 2 and 4. (There are many variants on this pattern, as we will discuss in section 6.3.) For this reason, cases of metrical confusion or ambiguity—where the meter is unclear—very rarely occur in rock. When they do arise, it is usually at the very beginning of a song, before the drums have entered. One example is shown in Example 4.2. The meter is clearly 4/4, given the repeated pattern in the guitar; the issue is the "phase" of the meter, that is, how it is aligned with the music. The changes of harmony on the points marked with asterisks favor these points as quarter-note beats, out of phase with the "correct" meter. The drums are ambiguous at first; the snare hits in the fourth full measure suggest the correct meter, but we are thrown off once again by the off-beat cymbal crash at the end of

Example 4.2. Jimi Hendrix Experience, "All Along the Watchtower" (introduction). Asterisks mark changes of harmony.

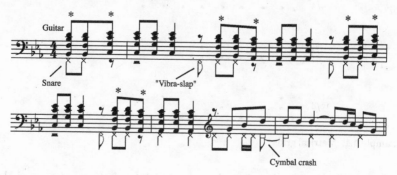

that measure. It is only after that, with the snare's consistent marking of quarter-note beats, that we infer the correct meter with certainty.[1]

The vast majority of rock songs are in 4/4. However, other metrical structures have also played a role, in ways that have evolved over rock's history. Many songs from the very early years of rock (the 1950s) are in 4/4 but with a "swing" feel—borrowed from jazz and Tin Pan Alley—in which the quarter note is unevenly divided, the first half slightly longer than the second; Bill Haley & his Comets' "Rock around the Clock" and Elvis Presley's "All Shook Up" are examples. In the doo-wop style of the late 1950s and early 1960s, a slow compound meter was popular, seen in songs such as the Five Satins' "In the Still of the Nite." By the time of the British Invasion in 1964, a "straight" (not swung) 4/4 feel had become predominant. But throughout the decade, a number of important groups showed an interest in a moderate compound meter: this is seen in a large number of songs by the Beatles ("Penny Lane," "With a Little Help from My Friends," and at least a dozen others), the Beach Boys ("California Girls," "Good Vibrations"), the Doors ("Love Street," "People Are Strange"), and the Supremes ("Where Did Our Love Go").

Moving into the late 1960s and early 1970s, compound meter waned in popularity and simple duple meter took over almost completely. Two other important developments in rock meter also occurred in the 1960s. One was a substantial slowing of the tempo. Example 4.3 shows the average tempo for songs in the *Rolling Stone* corpus (considering only songs that are entirely in 4/4), broken down by decade. It can be seen that the tempo drops significantly from the 1950s to the 1960s and then remains fairly

1. London (n.d.) provides a useful list of such metric "fake outs"; see also Hesselink (2014).

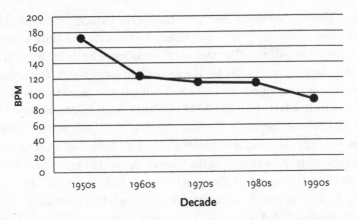

Example 4.3. Average tempo for songs in the *Rolling Stone* corpus (in BPM), for songs in 4/4 only, broken down by decade

stable for the next two decades after that. A second development in the 1960s is the rise of the sixteenth-note level (that is, division of the quarter note beat into four rather than two). This seems to have emerged first in mid-1960s soul music; it is reflected, for example, in Aretha Franklin's "Respect" and James Brown's "Papa's Got a Brand New Bag." No doubt these two developments were related: the slowing of the tactus allowed rhythmic patterns that might have been cognitively taxing at a faster tempo (for both performers and listeners). In the 1990s, we see another significant decrease in tempo; I suspect this may be due partly to the influence of rap, which favors a dense, sixteenth-note syllabic rhythm and thus benefits from a somewhat slower tempo.[2]

I noted earlier that one particular level in a metrical structure is generally assumed to have privileged status—the tactus. Generally, it is very obvious which level is the tactus in rock, due to the conventional drum pattern, but sometimes it is not. For one thing, some songs have no drums at all (the Beatles' "Yesterday," for example). In other songs, the drums do not play the conventional pattern; in "Satisfaction," for example, both the snare

2. The dataset used in Example 4.3 is fairly small (135 songs), but I believe the trends are real. Schellenberg & Van Scheve (2012), using a much larger corpus of songs from the Billboard Hot 100 from the 1960s to the 2000s, also found a significant drop in tempo going into the 1990s. This is not to deny that there is considerable variation in each decade. Late-1970s punk and new wave often has a fast tempo—partly inspired by the simple, energetic rock of the 1950s—and this is often retained in punk-influenced music in later decades, such as Green Day's "Basket Case." Every era also has its slow songs—ballads and the like—which bring down the mean somewhat, but only a small number of the songs in this *Rolling Stone* 4/4 dataset could be put in that category.

and kick drums play every beat simultaneously. Usually, one metrical level within these songs is close to our "ideal" tactus rate and thus emerges as the preferred candidate. (The rate of the kick/snare beats in "Satisfaction," 136 BPM, is quite acceptable for the tactus.) In some songs, the kick/snare alternation is present but at a rate well outside the usual tactus range: do we really hear a tactus of 234 BPM in Chuck Berry's "Maybellene," or 47 BPM in Michael Jackson's "Human Nature"?[3] In still other songs, the drums play the conventional pattern but shift from one level to another within the song. An example is the Clash's "Should I Stay or Should I Go"; after the first two verses of the song (at around 1:00), the kick-snare alternation doubles in speed. Does our perception of the tactus shift from one level to another? (Ask yourself: If you were dancing to "Should I Stay or Should I Go," would you feel compelled to dance twice as fast when the drum pattern changes?) More generally, does there even have to be a single tactus level at each moment, or can multiple levels enjoy some degree of perceptual "tactusness" simultaneously? These are open questions.

The issue of the tactus can also arise in songs that have some kind of triple division. In a typical compound meter rock song like Example 4.4A, the tactus is pretty clearly the notated dotted-quarter level; this level is conveyed by the conventional drum pattern and is well within the usual tactus range (116 BPM). In Example 4.4B, the dotted-quarter level is again marked by the snare on beats 2 and 4, and again this is a reasonable tactus level (84 PM); in this case, the triply-divided level is the one *below* the tactus (the dotted eighth). (There is no standard time signature for this.) In Example 4.4C, the situation is more ambiguous. The drum pattern presents the usual alternating kick/snare pattern, marking the one-measure level (assuming the notation in the example), but this is much slower than the usual preferred tactus, only about 30 BPM; the dotted-quarter level, 90 BPM, would be much closer to the norm. Suppose the tactus was the dotted quarter, yielding a triple meter (with tactus beats grouped in threes); from the drummer's point of view, how should this be articulated? There is no very satisfactory option: patterns like "kick rest snare | kick rest snare" or "kick snare snare | kick snare snare" sound awkward and are rarely used. So perhaps the drummer, feeling that there had to be a kick-snare alternation *somewhere*, defaulted to the measure level for this pattern, even though it is actually not the tactus. I would say, then, that the tactus in "Take It to the Limit" is really the dotted quarter,

---

3. London (2004) has suggested that there are limits to the range of beat levels that can be perceived as a tactus; 234 BPM and 47 BPM are close to these upper and lower limits.

Example 4.4A. The Beach Boys, "California Girls"

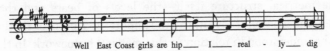

Well East Coast girls are hip___ I___ real - ly___ dig

Example 4.4B. Toto, "Rosanna"

All I want to do when I wake up in the morn-ing is see your eyes___ Ro-

Example 4.4C. The Eagles, "Take It to the Limit"

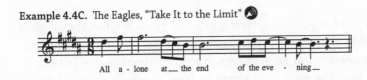

All a - lone at___ the end of the eve - ning___

Example 4.4D. Led Zeppelin, "Kashmir"

guitar

kick snare

notwithstanding the drum pattern. The meter of the song is then *compound* triple meter, since the tactus itself is divided in three. This situation is quite rare in rock, however. (Some songs are in a gray area between compound duple meter and triple meter: in Carole King's "(You Make Me Feel Like) A Natural Woman," for example, I can hear a slow duple tactus or a faster triple one.) Uptempo songs in triple meter are even less common; again, they present a dilemma for the drummer. In Phil Collins's "Dance into the Light," the drummer (Phil Collins himself) adopts the simple solution of a hitting the snare on every tactus beat. Led Zeppelin's "Kashmir" is an interesting and unique case (Example 4.4D). The drums play a conventional duple beat, but superimposed on this is a guitar pattern suggesting a dotted-quarter-note level (a slow 12/8), the two together forming a pattern that repeats every six quarter notes; perceptually, it seems to me, we infer a 3/4 meter from this (as shown in the example) as a kind of compromise between the two. (Also very rare is 3/2 meter, in which each measure contains six tactus beats grouped in twos; Soundgarden's "Fell on Black Days" is one example.)

While there is sometimes some subjectivity in identifying the tactus level, the metrical structure itself—the levels of beats and their relationships—is usually clear.[4] Nearly all the important aspects of rhythm in rock must be understood in relation to this metrical framework. In this chapter we explore four such aspects: syncopation, harmonic rhythm, hypermeter, and irregular meter. Also important is the issue of how we *experience* rhythm, with regard to emotion and complexity: we will address this topic in chapter 7.

4.2 SYNCOPATION AND CROSS-RHYTHM

If the meter of a song is to be correctly inferred by the listener, then it must be conveyed by the music in some fairly consistent way. As noted earlier, the meter is usually clear enough even in songs without drums; indeed, we can usually infer the meter of a song just from hearing someone sing the melody of it. Music theorists have explored the complex cues that indicate the meter of a piece, focusing mainly on common-practice music (Lerdahl & Jackendoff, 1983; Temperley, 2001). In particular, we tend to infer strong beats on notes rather than rests, on longer notes rather than shorter ones,[5] on louder notes rather than quieter ones, on stressed syllables rather than unstressed ones (in vocal music), and on changes of harmony. These last four cues—long notes, loud notes, stressed syllables, and harmonic change—could be viewed as kinds of accent, sometimes called "phenomenal accents"; roughly speaking, meter perception involves inferring the metrical structure that provides the best fit to the phenomenal accents of the piece. In the first phrase of "America the Beautiful" (Example 4.5), the meter is made clear to us by the long notes on the syllables "beau-" and "spa-", suggesting that these are strong beats; it is reinforced in all four measures by the fact that the stressed syllables fall on beats 1 and 3 of the measure. (In this example and the following ones, stressed syllables

4. Common-practice music distinguishes between measures containing four tactus beats (4/4, 12/8) and those containing two (2/4, 6/8). This is a subtle distinction. The 2/4 and 4/4 time signatures have identical metrical grids, except that 4/4 has one additional level—but this might be present as a hypermetrical level in a 2/4 context. However, de Clercq (2016) argues that the measure is an important perceptual unit, especially as it relates to conventional formal patterns like the blues pattern and AABA; this might argue for positing 2/4 in some cases and 4/4 in others.

5. The "length" of a note is often defined as the time interval between its onset and the following note-onset—its "inter-onset interval"—rather than as its actual duration. The former measure is generally more meaningful, in relation to our understanding of rhythm.

Example 4.5. Samuel Ward and Katharine Lee Bates, "America the Beautiful"

Oh *beau* - ti - **ful** for spa-cious *skies* for *am* - ber **waves** of *grain*

are shown in bold, and highly stressed syllables are in bold and italicized.) We also tend to favor a metrical structure that is aligned with repeated rhythmic and melodic patterns (so that strong beats occur at the same location in each instance of the pattern), a factor known as "parallelism"; in Example 4.5, the repeated rhythmic pattern in the first two measures confirms the 4/4 meter implied by other cues. In large part, these same perceptual cues apply in rock music as well. But there is one very important difference.

The top staff of Example 4.6A shows part of the first verse of Michael Jackson's "Billie Jean." It is immediately clear that the conventional rules of alignment between accents and meter do not apply. Arguably, "more" is the most stressed of the first five syllables, and this lands on a relatively strong beat. But "beau-" and "queen" are certainly more stressed than "-ty," yet fall on weaker beats. In the second phrase, of the stressed syllables "mind," "do," "mean," "I," and "one," only the first falls on a stronger beat than the neighboring unstressed syllables. In the following short three-syllable groups ("who will dance / on the floor / in the round"), the most stressed syllable of each group is the last, but in each case it falls on a weaker beat than the first syllable of the group.

Based on this, one might suppose that phenomenal accents in rock melodies do not align with the meter at all. But a further observation makes sense out of this seemingly chaotic situation. It can be seen that the highly stressed syllables on weak beats (bold and italicized) tend to fall just *before* a strong tactus beat (1 and 3): this is true of "beau-," "one," and "round." If we shift some of the notes one eighth note to the right, the stresses and the strong beats can be made to line up almost perfectly, with the stressed syllables metrically stronger than the unstressed ones and the highly stressed syllables strongest of all (see the second staff of the example). It appears, then, that rock does respect the usual correspondence between accents and meter, with the exception that phenomenal accents are allowed to fall just before strong beats.

This phenomenon—sometimes known as *anticipatory syncopation*—is a pervasive feature not just of rock, but of earlier popular styles such as jazz, blues, and Tin Pan Alley. In general, syncopation refers to some kind of conflict between the accents of a piece and its meter; frequently

Example 4.6. Michael Jackson, "Billie Jean." The top staff shows the original melodic lines; the second staff shows "de-syncopated" versions.

A. Part of the first verse

B. Part of the first prechorus

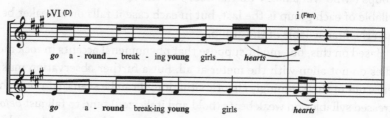

C. End of the first prechorus

D. Part of the guitar solo

it creates metrical instability or even ambiguity. By contrast, the anticipatory syncopations of rock and related styles are not usually heard as destabilizing the underlying meter (which is usually conveyed quite unambiguously by the instruments in any case). I would suggest that we hear the metrically weak stressed syllables in "Billie Jean" as "belonging" on the following strong beats—perhaps unconsciously inferring something like the "de-syncopated" rhythm shown on the second staff; in this way, the syncopated events are understood as being quite compatible with the underlying meter. One function of syncopation is that it provides a kind of rhythmic flexibility, allowing melodic rhythms that closely fit the natural pacing of the words; compare the actual melodic rhythm of Example 4.6A to the rather stilted de-syncopated version shown below. (There is some uncertainty as to exactly what this de-syncopated version should be. It seems clear that some of the unstressed syllables have to be shifted as well as stressed ones—if "beau-" was shifted but "-ty" was not, they would both land on the same beat!—but it is not always obvious how this should be done; in the fourth measure, should "am" and "the" be shifted or not?)

All the syncopations in Example 4.6A involve shifting a note by one eighth note, but this is not the only possibility. In the prechorus of "Billie Jean" (Example 4.6B), on the line "peo-ple always told me," "al-" is syncopated by one sixteenth and "told" is syncopated by one eighth (again, the de-syncopated version is shown beneath); the following measure contains a similar pattern. Consider also the syllable "hearts" at the end of Example 4.6B. I would argue (as indicated in the example) that this syllable is doubly shifted, first at the eighth-note level, then at the sixteenth-note level, so that it actually occurs three-sixteenths before the beat it belongs on. Such double syncopations are rare, but they do occur in some other songs; the last syllable in the title phrase of Fleetwood Mac's "Go Your Own Way" is another instance of this. In the vast majority of cases, syncopation occurs either at the sixteenth-note level or eighth-note level. Syncopations at the tactus level occur only occasionally; "way" in "Go Your Own Way" is an example. Syncopations can also occur in compound meters; in Example 4.4A, each of the last five syllables falls an eighth note before the beat it belongs on.

We see, then, that treating certain surface events as displaced from underlying positions brings stressed syllables and strong beats into close alignment. Similar reasoning can be applied to other metrical cues. In Example 4.4A, shifting the last five notes to the right aligns them with tactus beats rather than eighth-note beats, reflecting the general preference for note onsets to fall on strong beats. Note length is also a factor; in Example 4.6A, several long notes fall on weak beats ("queen," "mean," and "one"); shifting these notes aligns them with stronger beats.[6] Harmony is also a consideration. Consider the final phrase of the chorus of "Billie Jean," which ends on scale degree $\hat{5}$ (Example 4.6C). If this note were left in its surface position, it would create an odd clash with the underlying iv harmony (though such clashes do sometimes occur in rock, as we will discuss in the next chapter). If the syllable is shifted, then it coincides with i, which contains $\hat{5}$, making much more harmonic sense. (See Temperley, 1999b, for additional examples.)

Syncopations may also occur in instrumental lines. The guitar solo in "Billie Jean" consists largely of repetitions of the pattern in Example 4.6D. This pattern could be viewed as syncopated in the same way as the first measure of Example 4.6B; shifting the long note at the end of the pattern allows it to fall on a strong beat. A more complex case is seen in Example 4.7—the Jackson 5's "ABC." Notice the placement of each instrument's notes (including the voice) in relation to beats 1 and 3 of the measure. The kick drum consistently lands on beat 1 but anticipates beat 3. (Following convention, the snare marks beats 2 and 4 and the hi-hat marks every eighth-note beat; these are not shown.) The bass lands on beat 1 in the verse, but anticipates beat 1 in the chorus; it is silent on beat 3. The vocal lands on beat 1 and anticipates beat 3 in the verse (though elsewhere in the verse it anticipates beat 1); in the chorus, the vocals anticipate beat 1 and are silent on beat 3. The guitar line anticipates both beats 1 and 3; the piano in the chorus anticipates beat 3. In short, events on beat 3 are consistently syncopated, but beat 1 has complex combinations of syncopated and unsyncopated events at different times. The interplay between these components of the ensemble, sometimes landing right on the beat and sometimes just before it, creates a rich and satisfying texture.

Some have questioned the idea of treating syncopated events as "displacements" of unsyncopated ones (Moore, 2012); what is the justification for it? The argument so far has been that it allows the principles of accent-meter alignment found in common-practice music and other styles to apply to rock as well. There is also another source of evidence, coming from situations where the same melodic pattern is presented in both syncopated and unsyncopated forms. A subtle example is seen in Example 4.6A, where the three-note motive B–A–C♯ is presented first with syncopations ("beauty queen") and then without ("movie scene"). Much more obvious examples can also be found. In Bachman-Turner Overdrive's "Takin' Care

---

6. In the case of "do" and "hearts" in Example 4.6B, shifting the syllables places the long note at the end of the melisma on a *weaker* beat. In such cases, the preference seems to be to place the note that *begins* the melisma on a strong beat.

Example 4.7. The Jackson 5, "ABC"

A. First measure of first verse

B. First measure of chorus

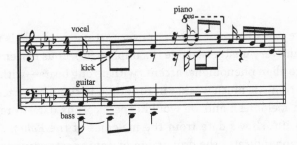

of Business," the first syllable of the title phrase ("*Tak*-in'") is unsyncopated at the beginning of each chorus, but syncopated after that.[7] In "ABC," the first syllable of the title phrase is almost always syncopated, but at the beginning of the third chorus—after an improvisational bridge—we get the unsyncopated version (Example 4.8A). Another example is seen at the end of Led Zeppelin's "Fool in the Rain"; in the line shown in Example 4.8B, heard five times at the very end of the song, the final syllable is syncopated in every presentation except the last. Such connections do not *prove* that the syncopated version of the pattern is understood as a displaced version of the unsyncopated one, but they are certainly consistent with that idea. In each of these cases, it is significant that the unsyncopated version of the event occurs at moment of great structural importance, making that moment especially stable and satisfying.

As can be seen from the previous examples, syncopation is a pervasive and essential element of the rock style. We sometimes even seen phrases that are *completely* syncopated—in which every note falls on a weak

---

7. This happens in an especially effective way near the end of the song. The title phrase is repeated a series of times, with the first syllable syncopated, over a "stop-time" accompaniment; this is followed by a full chorus, where the unsyncopated first syllable coincides with the climactic return of the full accompaniment texture (around 4:27).

Example 4.8A. The Jackson 5, "ABC"

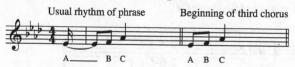

Example 4.8B. Led Zeppelin, "Fool in the Rain"

eighth-note beat (Example 4.9A), or every stressed syllable is metrically weaker than every unstressed one (Example 4.9B). Thus it seems that the tendency to align phenomenal accents with strong beats—with regard to *surface* rhythm—is much weaker in rock than in common-practice music (at least in melodies); and we would expect corpus data to reflect this. Example 4.10A shows data from the melodies of the *Rolling Stone* corpus; the graph indicates the proportion of note onsets occurring on each eighth-note beat of a 4/4 measure. It can be seen that, indeed, there is hardly any tendency to favor strong beats (positions 1, 3, 5, and 7) over weaker ones. By way of contrast, the graph also shows data for a corpus of European folk songs; here the alignment of note onsets with strong beats is clear and strong. But now consider Example 4.10B, showing the data for the same rock songs but distinguishing between stressed and unstressed syllables. Now there is a clear preference for stressed syllables on positions 1 and 5 (the half-note beats); the value for beat 8 (the last eighth-note beat of the measure) is also quite high, which surely represents anticipatory syncopation.[8] This suggests that there is *some* tendency in rock to align melodic phenomenal accents with strong beats, though much weaker than in common-practice melody. In instrumental parts, especially the bass and drums, the alignment between accents and meter is surely much stronger (though even here some syncopation may occur). The idea that syncopated events are less normative than unsyncopated ones will be important when we consider the issue of complexity in chapter 7.

8. This is preliminary data from a project by Ethan Lustig, Ivan Tan, and myself to add lyric and stress information to the *Rolling Stone* corpus; we hope to publish the full results soon. The rock data in Example 4.10A takes into account melismas (a syllable spanning multiple notes), counting only the first note of each melisma; the folk-song data counts all notes, so it is not a perfectly fair comparison.

Example 4.9A. The Police, "Message in a Bottle" (end of first verse)

Res - cue me___ be - fore I *fall*___ in - to___ de - *spair*___ oh___

Example 4.9B. The Jimi Hendrix Experience, "All Along the Watchtower" (part of first verse)

Said the *jo* - ker **to** the *thief*___

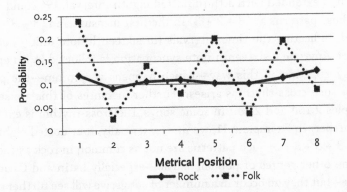

Example 4.10A. Distribution of note onsets on beats of the meter in melodies in 4/4, for a subset of the *Rolling Stone* corpus ("rock," 66 melodies) and the Essen corpus of European folk melodies (Schaffrath, 1995) ("folk," 1,585 melodies)

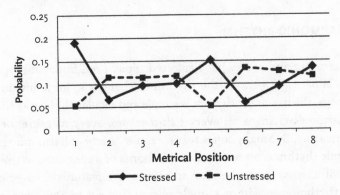

Example 4.10B. Distribution of note onsets on beats in the same subset of the *Rolling Stone* corpus, with syllables labeled as stressed or unstressed

A final topic for this section, related to syncopation, is cross-rhythm. Going back to Example 4.6B, I suggested that the pattern in the first two measures could be viewed as a sixteenth-note syncopation followed by an eighth-note one. However, there is another possible interpretation: the

Example 4.11. Jackson 5, "Dancing Machine"

She's a dance dance dance dance danc-ing ma-chine

two syncopations could also be viewed as subtly suggesting a dotted-eighth-note metrical level, going against the underlying meter. This possibility is shown in parentheses above the staff. In the first measure, the pattern is extended with a third dotted-eighth interval. We could represent these patterns as "3 + 3 + 3" in the first measure and "3 + 3" in the second, indicating the time intervals (in sixteenth-note units) between accents. Anytime a sixteenth-note syncopation is followed by an eighth-note syncopation in this way—which happens very often—the potential for such cross-rhythms arises. (Further instances of this are seen in Examples 2.16A and 2.18.) In some songs, the cross-rhythm is extended still further: In Example 4.11, we find, essentially, four dotted eighths in a row, 3 + 3 + 3 + 3. Such patterns are not as common in rock as they are in some other genres of popular music—especially Latin and Caribbean genres—but they do occur in a number of songs; we will see further examples later on. Traut (2005) presents an impressive list of songs from the 1980s with cross-rhythms.

4.3 HARMONIC RHYTHM

An interesting and somewhat neglected topic, even in common-practice theory, is *harmonic rhythm*: the rhythm of changes in harmony. In many rock songs, the harmonic rhythm is simple and regular all the way through, with harmonic changes on every half-measure, every measure, or every other measure. But many songs feature some variety of harmonic rhythm. Harmonic rhythm is often faster in the chorus of a song than in the verse, as we will discuss in chapter 8. And some songs features changes of harmonic rhythm even within a single phrase. The riff to Tom Petty's "Free Fallin'" is illustrative (Example 4.12). One could argue that there is anticipatory syncopation here, implying the underlying rhythm shown beneath the original rhythm; but even this rhythm is somewhat syncopated, with the IV chord held over the bar line and changing to I only on the second beat of the measure. (Here I use "syncopation" in the more general sense, referring to a conflict between phenomenal accents and meter, without

Example 4.12. Tom Petty, "Free Fallin'," showing harmonic rhythm of guitar riff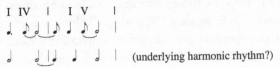

Example 4.13. Led Zeppelin, "Over the Hills and Far Away"

A. Introduction

B. "Many times I've loved . . ."

C. Transition into guitar solo

D. End of vocal ("really ought to know, oh, oh . . .")

implying displacement.) In this way, Petty manages to make the rather common chord progression I–IV–I–V sound fresh and appealing.[9]

Led Zeppelin's extraordinary song "Over the Hills and Far Away" is (among other things) a brilliant study in harmonic rhythm. Four passages from the song are shown in Example 4.13. In each one, the harmonic rhythm is complex and irregular; at a number of points we see chord changes on weak tactus

9. Details of the chord voicings give the progression extra charm: The IV chord lacks a third (though this is added in later) and has a ninth above the bass, while the V chord has a fourth above the bass. These added notes are $\hat{5}$ and $\hat{1}$, respectively, and could perhaps be regarded as upper-voice pedals, as they are prolonged throughout the whole progression—and subtly reinforced by a synthesizer in the background.

beats, eighth-note beats, or even sixteenth-note beats. As in "Free Fallin'," one could argue for anticipatory syncopations in some cases; for example, the IV and I chords in Example 4.13C perhaps "belong" one eighth note later. But most of the syncopations cannot be convincingly explained away in this manner. One could also think of some of the chords on sixteenth-note beats as non-harmonic "suspensions" from the previous chords, so that the underlying chord changes really happen *before* the surface ones (as shown by the alternative analysis below the staff in Example 4.13B). But this, too, is most unusual in a rock context. Notice, also, the imaginative ways that John Bonham's drum parts reinforce the harmonic changes. Other Led Zeppelin songs also feature interesting harmonic rhythms, such as "When the Levee Breaks" and "The Rain Song." They seem to be one of the few bands to have recognized the potential of this valuable musical resource.

4.4 HYPERMETER

It was noted earlier that metrical structures may extend above the level of the measure. This brings us to the topic of *hypermeter*, widely studied and discussed in common-practice theory. By general consensus, hyper-meter is nearly always duple, such that every other downbeat is strong in relation to the ones in between, as shown in Example 4.14. We call such downbeats *hyperdownbeats*; the metrical segments that they initiate are *hypermeasures*. (Passages in triple hypermeter are extremely rare in classical music, and even more so in rock; the outro to David Bowie's "Ashes to Ashes" is perhaps one example.) Most theorists agree, also, that phrases and sections (as well as whole pieces) typically begin with a strong measure (Lerdahl & Jackendoff, 1983; Rothstein, 1989). One could also posit levels higher than the two-measure level—perhaps a level in which every fourth measure is strong (as shown in Example 4.14), or even every eighth measure. This creates hypermeasures that mirror the structure of a 4/4 measure at a higher level. However, intuitions about hypermeter generally get weaker the higher up we go; it would seem questionable, for example, to say that the beginning of the verse of a song is metrically strong in relation to the beginning of the chorus.

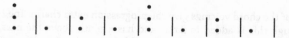

Example 4.14. A typical hypermetrical structure (showing only beats at the one-measure level and higher)

Example 4.15. Boston, "Peace of Mind" (second half of first verse)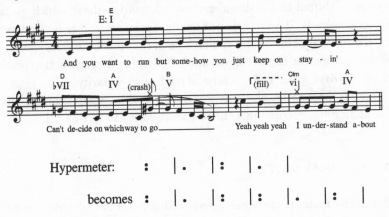

Hypermeter: : | . | : | . |

becomes : | . | : | : | . | : |

Many songs feature a completely regular hypermetrical structure, falling neatly into four-bar and eight-bar hypermeasures. This regularity is often reinforced by cues in the music—repeated harmonic and melodic patterns, and clear sectional boundaries; even if it is not, we may tend to infer it, given our perceptual preference for binary regularity at all levels. What is interesting, of course, is cases where the hypermeter is *not* completely regular. A simple, and common, use of irregular hypermeter is seen in Example 4.15. Following a four-bar hypermeasure at the beginning of the verse (not shown in the example), the second hypermeasure is five measures instead of the expected four; this is made clear by the continuation of the fourth measure's harmony (V) into the fifth measure, and by the new harmony and melodic phrase that starts in the measure after that, marking this as a hyperdownbeat. (The drums also play an important role here, as we will discuss in section 6.3.) Given the strong expectation for a four-measure unit here, we might well hear the five-measure unit as an "extension" (or "expansion") of an underlying four-measure one—a well-established concept in common-practice theory (Rothstein, 1989; Caplin, 1998).[10] Hypermetrical irregularities frequently create ambiguities as well. The fifth measure of Example 4.15 clearly seems weak, but is the fourth measure strong or weak? Perhaps we initially hear it as weak (understanding it to be the fourth measure in a four-measure unit), but once the fifth measure is heard, we reinterpret the fourth measure as the first measure in a two-bar hypermeasure (this is illustrated in the diagram below the example). This

10. Caplin (1998) uses "extension" when the final harmony of a phrase is lengthened, and "expansion" when an internal harmony is lengthened; I try to maintain that distinction here, though not all cases are clear-cut.

has the nice effect of placing the last syllable in the line (once it is "de-syn-copated"—shifted to the downbeat) on a hyperdownbeat, which gives it further emphasis. The extension of the four-measure unit to five measures also creates a bit of instability and tension at the end of the verse—increasing the anticipation for the chorus and heightening the satisfaction when it arrives, clarifying the hypermeter and restoring regularity.

There is more to say about hypermeter, but this requires consideration of melodic phrase structure, which we will address in section 5.1.

4.5 IRREGULAR METER

While duple meter is overwhelmingly predominant in rock (triple meter is extremely rare, as noted earlier), there are other possibilities. Occasionally we find songs with irregular meters, such as 5/8 or 7/8, or with shifts from one meter to another. Biamonte (2014) explores this topic and presents a number of examples. Regarding metrical shifts, one effective strategy is the use of anticipatory syncopation to prepare the transition from one meter to another. Soundgarden's "Spoon Man" employs this technique. The riff of this song, shown in Example 4.16A, is itself metrically irregular, spanning seven quarter-note beats; the syncopations within it have strong cross-rhythmic implications, hinting at a dotted-sixteenth-note level (similar to Example 4.11 above). At a certain point (Example 4.16B), the riff leads into a new section in which this dotted-sixteenth-note level is the tactus, shifting the song into compound meter. Because we have been hearing so many dotted-sixteenth-note intervals, the transition is quite smooth and indeed not immediately apparent. (The fact that the kick drum in the compound-meter section is syncopated obscures the shift still further; because of this

Example 4.16. Soundgarden, "Spoon Man"

A. Opening riff

B. Shift from quarter-note pulse to dotted-eighth pulse

syncopation, the compound meter section begins with the same 4 + 3 + 3 pattern that begins the riff.) The song later shifts back to a quarter-note pulse (not shown here) in a similarly ingenious way.

Irregular and shifting meters are particularly characteristic of progressive rock—a genre that flourished in the 1970s (but lived on in later decades) and that specialized in the exploration of complex rhythmic (and also harmonic and formal) techniques. Songs like Yes's "Heart of the Sunrise," Jethro Tull's "Living in the Past" (in 5/4 throughout), Rush's "Limelight," and Radiohead's "Paranoid Android" are illustrative. Here we consider one especially skillful use of irregular meter, Peter Gabriel's "Solsbury Hill" (Example 4.17). The song is almost entirely in 7/4. Maintaining such a meter through an entire song can be a challenge; each measure creates a kind of jolt (we never really get used to 7/4), which can eventually become tedious. The song avoids this pitfall by varying the subdivision of the measure and by departing from 7/4 at a crucial moment. The riff (the first measure of Example 4.17) features complex syncopations (again hinting at a dotted-sixteenth cross-rhythm); the rhythmic pattern of the first three beats is repeated starting on the fourth beat, suggesting a 3 + 4 division of the measure. In the first part of the verse, each vocal phrase begins on the fifth beat of the measure, making this beat seem strong and creating a 4 + 3 division of the measure. This 4 + 3 feel persists through the entire verse, though the vocal melody expands into the first half of the measure; the phrase "I did not be-*lieve*," though syncopated, creates an implied stress on the fifth beat. At the end of the section (one could call it a refrain), the meter shifts to 4/4 for just two measures. This prepares the cadential move to I (on "home"), which overlaps into the next verse (we will say more about

Example 4.17. Peter Gabriel, "Solsbury Hill"

RHYTHM AND METER [85]

cadential overlaps in section 9.1). Despite the fact that the song has been in 7/4 up to this point, we still expect duple meter more than anything else; moving into 4/4 at this point allows the cadence to be set up in a predictable, satisfying way. The two 4/4 measures lead back into the 3 + 4 pattern of the riff, creating an elegant symmetry: 4 + 3 + [4 + 4] + 3 + 4.

4.6 QUESTIONS

1. Each of these songs presents a metrical structure that is unusual in rock: the Jimi Hendrix Experience, "Manic Depression"; Pink Floyd, "Money"; the Police, "Synchronicity 1"; Soundgarden, "My Wave." Notate two measures of each song, showing the time signature and one melodic line (instrumental or vocal).

2. Some interesting uses of cross-rhythm: Bill Withers' "Ain't No Sunshine" contains a cross-rhythmic pattern taken to an extreme. In the opening of the Goo Goo Dolls' "Iris," cross-rhythm is used to make a smooth transition from one meter to another. Explain in more detail what is happening in these two cases.

3. Billy Joel's "She's Always a Woman" presents an interesting situation from the point of view of meter and hypermeter; how so? Transcribe the first verse-refrain (up to "always a woman to me").

4. Notate the first solo vocal line of the Beatles' "Good Morning Good Morning" ("Nothing to do..."). The time signature is not regular; you must decide on the best way to notate it. The melody is also (or may be) syncopated against the time signature; do anticipatory syncopations play a role here? What about cross-rhythms?

CHAPTER 5

Melody

In the 1990s, a board game called *Humm. . .ble* was popular for a brief time. In this game, players would hum or whistle the melodies to well-known songs and other players would try to guess them. Playing the game, I was often struck at how easy it was to identify the melody of a song, just from a few notes. (Even seemingly amorphous melodies like the Troggs' "Wild Thing" were instantly recognizable.) What this shows us is the crucial role of melody in defining a song's identity: The melody of a song is, in a way, its very essence. The importance of melody is also reflected in music plagiarism lawsuits, in which someone sues someone else for stealing their song or part of it; in such cases, melody is usually a large part, sometimes the main part, of the alleged "stolen" material.[1] To my knowledge, no one has ever been sued simply for stealing a chord progression.

Rock music, like most kinds of popular music, is generally constructed in such a way that the melody is very strongly highlighted, with all other parts of the ensemble relegated to a supporting role—what is sometimes called "melody-and-accompaniment texture." This is generally true even in instrumental sections, such as guitar solos. Even when backing vocals are present, one line usually stands out clearly as the main melody, though there are occasional cases of ambiguity. (Which line is the melody in the chorus of the Rolling Stones' "Honky Tonk Women"?)

In this chapter, we consider several topics relating to melody in rock, including both pitch and rhythmic aspects. One important rhythmic

---

1. At least, this was true before the age of digital sampling. See Conner-Simons (2007) for numerous examples of music plagiarism lawsuits.

aspect of melody, syncopation, was addressed in the previous chapter. We begin this chapter by addressing another facet of melodic rhythm, namely, grouping. We then consider the topics of motive, repetition, and rhyme, which relate to both pitch and rhythm (and also to text). Finally, we turn to some issues that pertain specifically to the pitch dimension of melody: the relationship between melody and harmony, and mediant mixture and "blue notes."

5.1 MELODIC GROUPING

As we hear the melody of "She Loves You" (Example 5.1), we do not perceive the notes as an unbroken stream; rather, we group them together in a complex, hierarchical way. Roughly speaking, every two measures form a unit (though each unit begins just before the bar line, with one or two "pickup" notes); these two-measure units group into larger four-measure units; and the two four-measure units themselves form an eight-measure unit. These units are shown with brackets above the staff. "Dancing in the Street" (Example 5.2) shows a similar pattern of segmentation, with

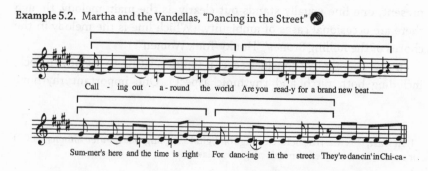

Example 5.1. The Beatles, "She Loves You," showing melodic grouping structure

You think you've lost your love___ Well I saw her yes-ter-day___ It's

you she's think-ing of___ And she told me what to say___

Example 5.2. Martha and the Vandellas, "Dancing in the Street"

Call-ing out · a-round the world Are you read-y for a brand new beat___

Sum-mer's here and the time is right For danc-ing in the street They're dancin' in Chi-ca-two-measure and four-measure segments grouping into an eight-measure segment. (In this and subsequent examples, the eight-measure bracket is not shown.)

At issue here is what is known in music theory as "grouping structure" (or sometimes "phrase structure"): the organization of the surface events of a piece into smaller and larger segments. The factors involved in the perception of grouping have been studied extensively, and are sometimes quite subtle (Lerdahl & Jackendoff, 1983). With regard to rock melody, grouping is usually a fairly simple matter. The most important factor is an obvious one: Notes that are close together in time tend to form groups, with rests indicating a boundary between one group and the next. These group boundaries are usually clearly reinforced by the lyrics, corresponding to natural phrases of the text. (Occasionally a long note or a syntactic break in the lyrics might signal a group boundary, even if there is no rest; the boundary between the first two groups of "Dancing in the Street" is an example.) As noted with regard to "She Loves You," grouping is assumed to be hierarchical, with smaller groups combining to form larger ones. Some people use the term "phrase" to refer to groups of any size; I prefer to use the term "sub-phrase" for very short groups, such as the two-measure groups in Examples 5.1 and 5.2, reserving "phrase" for larger (four-measure and eight-measure) groups.

So far we have only considered grouping with regard to the melody; what about the accompaniment? In a case like "She Loves You," we have a sense that the accompaniment texture divides into segments, corresponding roughly to those of the melody, but they are much less clearly defined—the accompaniment seems more like a seamless flow of sound. And the segment boundaries might not coincide exactly with those in the vocal; if forced, I would probably place them right at the bar lines, aligned with the meter and the harmony. It is not usually important to define exactly where accompaniment segments begin and end, so we will not dwell on this; but the general concept of phrases, including both the melody and accompaniment, *is* important, and we will make use of it in later chapters. Grouping can also be extended to still larger levels; phrases combine into sections (such as verses and choruses). A variety of factors can affect our perception of sectional boundaries, such as changes in harmonic pattern, vocal register, and instrumental texture. By convention, large-scale grouping is considered part of the topic of *form*, which we will address further in chapter 8. For now, our concern is with lower-level grouping, and only with the melody.

Example 5.3 shows two other melodies with their grouping structures. Example 5.3A begins with two two-bar sub-phrases, followed by a longer, unbroken unit; we can think of the latter unit as a four-measure phrase,

Example 5.3A. The Who, "Won't Get Fooled Again"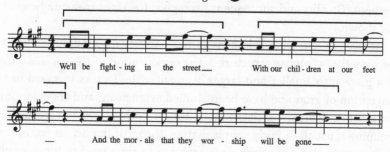

We'll be fight - ing in the street___   With our chil - dren at our feet

___   And the mor - als that they wor - ship will be gone___

Example 5.3B. Nirvana, "Smells Like Teen Spirit"

Load up on guns___ bring your friends It's fun to lose___and to___pre - tend___

though the fourth measure is empty.[2] This 2 + 2 + 4 pattern, common in rock, is known as a "sentence" (Caplin, 1987). In common-practice theory, this term carries specific harmonic implications; here, we will use it simply to indicate a grouping structure with 1:1:2 proportions. The grouping in Example 5.3B is superficially similar to that of Examples 5.1 and 5.2: two-measure units combine into four-measure units, which combine in turn to form an eight-measure unit (the second four-measure unit is not shown in the example).[3] There is a crucial difference, however, relating to the alignment of the units with the meter. In Examples 5.1 and 5.2, each unit begins on a strong beat (or just before it in some cases); the same is true in Example 5.3. Given a two-measure hypermetrical level in which odd-numbered measures are strong (which seems fairly clear in all four of these cases), the strongest beat within each group in Examples 5.1, 5.2,

2. Defining the lengths of groups is slightly tricky: Does a group include the rest between it and the next group? In examining the alignment of grouping and meter (which is our concern here), all that matters is the notes within the group; rests at the end have no effect, so it is clearer not to include them. But when assigning measure lengths to groups, it is customary to do it in such a way that the entire span under consideration (and any larger span) is exhaustively partitioned into groups, so that the sum of the group lengths equals the total length. If we labeled Example 5.3A (and the following repetition of the phrase) as "2+2+3," this would imply (incorrectly) that the total length of the section was 14 measures.

3. The first two-measure group could perhaps be further divided into two one-measure groups, though this is debatable. Uncertainties of this kind are common in grouping structure.

and 5.3A is right at (or near) its beginning; if we assume a higher four-measure hypermetrical level (with hyperdownbeats in the first and fifth measures), the same is true of the four-measure units as well. By contrast, in Example 5.3B, each two-measure segment begins just *after* a hyperdownbeat, and ends on the following hyperdownbeat. (Anticipatory syncopation is crucial here: literally the final note of each group in Example 5.3B falls on the last eighth of the measure, but these notes are heard as belonging on the following downbeats.) In Example 5.3B, then, the strongest beat within each group is right at the end, not at the beginning. We could refer to the groups in Example 5.3B as "end-accented" and those in the other three examples as "beginning-accented."

The distinction between beginning-accented and end-accented groups is well established in music theory (Lerdahl & Jackendoff, 1983; Temperley, 2003). There has been much discussion over the years about which pattern is more normative or stable; the consensus now is that both patterns are used, and both have virtues. If we think of hypermeasures as units, it seems natural for the melodic groups to align with these units; this implies that each group would start at the beginning of a hypermeasure (or perhaps just before). (The same principle also explains the fact, noted in the previous chapter, that we tend to hear the first measure in a piece or section as metrically strong—sometimes known as the "strong beat early" rule [Lerdahl & Jackendoff, 1983].) The beginning-accented pattern is undoubtedly the most common, in classical music and in rock as well. On the other hand, a strong beat is a natural point of *stability*, and it is satisfying for a melodic phrase to end at such a point: end-accented groups have a goal-oriented quality that beginning-accented groups do not. The fact that the groups in Example 5.3B do not align with the hypermeasures could be said to create a subtle kind of rhythmic conflict or complexity; but one could also say that it creates cohesion, like overlapping layers of bricks in a wall. In any case, the crucial point is that beginning-accented and end-accented phrases are very different in their effect. Because of their rarity, end-accented melodies are especially noteworthy; a few well-known examples are Led Zeppelin's "Houses of the Holy" (verse), Madonna's "Like a Prayer" (chorus), the Smashing Pumpkins' "1979" (verse), Bush's "Glycerine" (verse), and Natalie Imbruglia's "Torn" (chorus).

Example 5.4 shows three other possibilities for grouping-meter alignment. (In this case, hypermetrical symbols are shown in the score: two dots indicate a two-measure hyperdownbeat; three dots, a four-measure one.) In Example 5.4A, each two-measure group begins just after the hyperdownbeat, but still ends well before the following one; we might call these groups "unaccented," since they contain no hyperdownbeat (though

Example 5.4A. The Cars, "Just What I Needed"

I don't mind you com-ing here   And wast-ing all my time

Example 5.4B. Bob Seger, "Old Time Rock and Roll"

Just take those old re-cords off the shelf   I'll sit and lis-ten to them by my-self

Example 5.4C. Bruce Springsteen, "Dancing in the Dark"

I get up in the eve - ning   And I ain't__ got noth - in' to say__

they end on or near weak downbeats). Example 5.4B is superficially similar to Example 5.3B, in that the strongest beat in each two-measure group occurs near the end of it. At the four-measure level, though (grouping the two two-measure groups together), the strongest beat is much nearer the beginning of the group than the end; thus the four-measure group is better described as beginning-accented. (This analysis depends on hearing the first notated downbeat of Example 5.4B as the hyperdownbeat, but I think this is clear; this is the point at which the accompaniment enters.) In cases such as these, it can be confusing to label an entire melody as beginning- or end-accented; one must specify what level of grouping is at issue. Other ways of combining accentual types are also possible; in Example 5.4C, an unaccented two-measure group is followed by a second, end-accented one, forming an end-accented four-measure unit.

Many songs feature highly symmetrical, repetitive grouping structures, with the same structural type at multiple levels—beginning-accented (like Examples 5.1 and 5.2), end-accented (like Example 5.3B), or unaccented (like Example 5.4A); other songs combine these structural types in a regular, consistent pattern (like Examples 5.4B and 5.4C). But other songs mix different alignments of meter and grouping, and segments of different lengths, and this opens up an endless variety of possibilities. Example 5.5 shows one example, the Beatles' "Yesterday." The melody begins with a

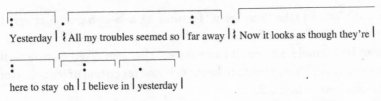

Example 5.5. The Beatles, "Yesterday," showing grouping and hypermeter

one-measure group—just a single word. The following group is end-accented, ending just after the third downbeat; the third group is parallel to the second, ending after the fifth downbeat. Two short beginning-accented groups complete the verse-refrain section. The entire section is seven measures, and is immediately repeated, so there must be an irregularity in the hypermeter somewhere, though it is not exactly clear where it happens. If it occurs at the sixth measure (as shown in the example), then measures 6–7 form a two-measure beginning-accented group. Michael Jackson's "Billie Jean" (shown earlier in Example 4.6) reflects a similar variety of grouping structures; in this case the underlying hypermeter is perfectly regular, but the groups align with the hypermeter in complex and varied way. This melody also features a complex network of motivic relationships, which is the topic of the next section.

5.2 MOTIVE, REPETITION, AND RHYME

Once the segments of a melody have been identified, the next step is to examine their relationship to one another. Two important aspects of this are pitch pattern and rhyme. Example 5.6 shows "She Loves You" and seven other melodies, indicating their patterns of pitch repetition and rhyme; I use **a/b/c** to indicate pitch patterns and **x/y** to indicate rhymes. "She Loves You" represents perhaps the most common pattern of all, in which the first and third sub-phrases share the same pitch pattern and rhyme, and the second and fourth do as well. "Dancing in the Street" is similar, though only the **b** phrases rhyme, not the **a** phrases. In this case, also, both the **a** phrases and the **b** phrases differ slightly in rhythm and pitch pattern; I use the prime symbol (′) to indicate cases where one segment is a close variant of another. In "Honky Tonk Women," an **a–b–a–c** pitch pattern is used, with the **b** and **c** (approximately) rhyming; in this case the units are four measures long instead of eight. (Since the first eight-measure phrase in this song ends on V and the second one on I, both phrases beginning the same way, the passage is what is known in classical theory as a "parallel period.") "Smells Like Teen Spirit" features an **a–b–a–b** pitch pattern, like "She Loves You," but with a different rhyme scheme, **x–x–y–y**. The patterns shown in Example 5.6 are all from verses; choruses often feature similar patterns, though there tends to be more literal repetition of text phrases in choruses (see section 8.3).

Sentence structures yield still more possibilities for pitch repetition and rhyme schemes. AC/DC's "You Shook Me All Night Long" reflects the most typical pattern for a sentence, **a–a–b** (the third segment is twice as long as the first two, as in all sentences); all three segments rhyme with one another. In "Saturday Night's Alright for Fighting," the first two sub-phrases are melodically contrasting but rhyme; the third sub-phrase is contrasting in both pitch pattern and rhyme (though it rhymes with the end of the *following* four-measure phrase). In "Won't Get Fooled Again," the first two sub-phrases share the same pitch pattern and rhyme; the third sub-phrase starts the same way but ends differently, hence the labeling **a–a–a′**.

These examples give a taste for the many ways that rhyme schemes and pitch repetition patterns can be combined in rock. There are other possibilities as well; I will not try to enumerate them all here. Suffice it to say that nearly all rock songs have some pattern of pitch repetition and rhyme, and identifying this pattern is an important part of analyzing the song. For the most part, rhyme schemes in rock are simple and repetitive, but occasionally one finds more complex ones. Pink Floyd's "Wish You Were Here" (at the end of Example 5.6) is a nice example; the verse falls into four two-measure groups, but the rhymes cut across them, so that the second measure of the first group rhymes with the first measure of the second.

The repeated pitch patterns indicated in Example 5.6 exemplify the more general concept of "motive." As the term is used in music theory, a motive is simply any repeated musical idea; it can involve either pitch or rhythm, or both. Common-practice composers played complex games with motives, elaborating and transforming them (e.g., through inversion—turning the pattern upside-down), fragmenting them (using just one part of a motive as a new motivic idea), stretching them out or compressing them in time, repeating them at different pitch levels, and so on. In my opinion, this kind of motivic development plays a fairly limited role in rock (though one can find almost any two segments to be motivically related if one tries hard enough!). We do find fairly simple kinds of variation and elaboration. For example, the second group of "Dancing in the Dark" (Example 5.4C) begins as a variant of the first, but ends differently; similarly, the third segment of "Won't Get Fooled Again" (Example 5.3A) begins like the first two but then deviates. Often, melodic variation in rock simply involves slight adjustments to the melody to incorporate a different stress pattern or number of

1. Beatles, "She Loves You"

   a   x b   y
   You think you've lost your love   Well I saw her yesterday
   a   x b   y
   It's you she's thinking of And she told me what to say

2. Martha and the Vandellas, "Dancing in the Street"

   a   —   b   y
   Calling out around the world Are you ready for a brand new beat
   a´   —   b´   y
   Summer's here and the time is right For dancing in the street

3. Rolling Stones, "Honky Tonk Women"

   a   —   b   y
   I met a gin-soaked bar-room queen in Memphis She tried to take me upstairs for a ride
   a   —   c   y
   She had to heave me right across her shoulder 'Cause I just can't seem to get you off my mind

4. Nirvana, "Smells Like Teen Spirit"

   a   x   b   x
   Load up on guns, bring your friends It's fun to lose and to pretend
   a   y   b   y
   She's overboard, self assured Oh no I know, a dirty word

5. AC/DC, "You Shook Me All Night Long"

   a   x   a   x
   She was a fast machine She kept her motor clean
   b   x
   She was the best damn woman I had ever seen

6. Elton John, "Saturday Night's Alright for Fighting"

   a   x   b   x
   It's getting late Have you seen my mates
   c   —
   Oh tell me when the boys get here

7. The Who, "Won't Get Fooled Again"

   a   x   a   x
   We'll be fighting in the streets With our children at our feet
   a´   —
   And the morals that they worship will be gone

8. Pink Floyd, "Wish You Were Here"

                            x
   So, so you think you can tell
                    x   —
   Heaven from Hell, blue skies from pain.
                   —   y
   Can you tell a green field from a cold steel rail?
              y   x
   A smile from a veil? Do you think you can tell?

Example 5.6. Patterns of pitch repetition (**a/b/c**) and rhyme (**x/y**) in eight melodies

syllables in the lyrics. In "Dancing in the Street" (Example 5.2), the first and third groups differ slightly in both pitch and rhythm, but are clearly closely related; the same could be said for the second and fourth groups. This kind of thing is of interest since it suggests that melodic phrases might be built on an underlying structure, varied or elaborated in different instances depending on the lyrics and other considerations—though it is often difficult to say exactly what that "underlying structure" is.

We do occasionally see quite complex patterns of motivic connection in rock. The opportunities for this are particularly rich in cases where the grouping structure of the melody is irregular. Consider "Billie Jean" (the transcription in Example 4.6A shows the grouping structure). The first two-measure group breaks (weakly) into a longer group followed by a shorter one; the second of these groups echoes the B-A-C♯ ending of the first (though without the syncopations). The rhyme between these segments ("queen," "scene") reinforces their motivic connection. The second two-measure group then mirrors the beginning of the first, but deviates from it at the end, pushing over to the next hyperdownbeat (assuming the underlying rhythm in the "de-syncopated" version) and forming an end-accented structure. (As usual, we assume that odd-numbered measures are metrically strong.) Three short half-measure groups then follow, all using the same motive (slightly varied in the third group); altogether they form a two-measure end-accented group, matching the previous phrase. The next four measures (not shown in the example) echo the second half of this eight-measure phrase. The following prechorus (Example 4.6B) features a one-measure motive; this is essentially a purely *rhythmic* motive (defined by the cross-rhythm discussed earlier), repeated with a variety of different pitch patterns. At a more global level, we find a motivic connection between the fourth measure of the chorus (not shown here—"I am the one") and the parallel point in the verse (with the same lyrics). All of these motivic connections help to hold the melody together. The melody also keeps things interesting by featuring repetition at a variety of different levels: half a measure, one measure, and two measures.

A curious feature of rock melodies is the relative rarity of *sequences*. A sequence is a pattern of melodic intervals that is shifted along the scale. In common-practice music, sequences are ubiquitous: consider the first eight notes of Beethoven's fifth symphony, or the "Gloria" section of "Ding Dong Merrily on High." Everett (2009) cites a number of rock songs that contain sequences. In most of these, the sequential passages follow standard classical conventions. In the bridge of Roy Orbison's "Pretty Woman" (Example 5.7A), the harmony descends by fifths (except for one descending third, I–vi) while the melodic pattern descends by step—a so-called "descending fifths" sequence. Sequences that go beyond classical conventions are fairly rare. Perhaps this is due to the murky nature of scales in rock: When the scale is unclear, it is not clear exactly how a pitch pattern should be shifted. One does occasionally see sequences that are

Example 5.7A. Roy Orbison, "Pretty Woman"

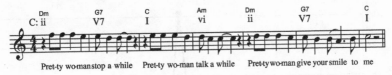

Pret-ty wo-man stop a while   Pret-ty wo-man talk a while   Pret-ty wo-man give your smile to me

Example 5.7B. TLC, "Waterfalls"

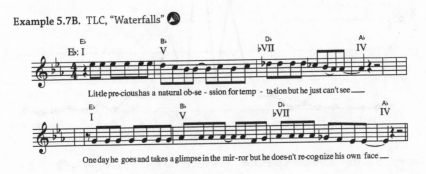

Lit-tle pre-cious has a natural ob-se - - ssion for temp - ta-tion but he just can't see ___

One day he goes and takes a glimpse in the mir-ror but he does-n't re-cog-nize his own face ___

quite unlike classical ones. Example 5.7B shows two phrases from TLC's "Waterfalls": the first and third four-measure phrases from the second verse. The second halves of the two phrases are identical in interval pattern (even in chromatic interval pattern), so this might be considered a type of sequence; in this case, though, both instances of the pattern are over the same harmonic progression, which is rarely the case in classical sequences.

5.3   "MELODIC-HARMONIC DIVORCE"

So far we have said rather little about the pitch organization of melody. In chapter 2 we addressed this in a "global" fashion—examining the overall scale-degree distributions in songs. And in the previous section we considered the role of repeated pitch patterns. But what other factors govern the moment-to-moment organization of rock melodies? As a starting point, we can examine the distribution of melodic intervals (intervals from one melody note to the next) in the *Rolling Stone* corpus, shown in Example 5.8. (Intervals are shown in semitones: for example, –1 indicates a descending half-step.) Notice the preponderance of small intervals: 70% of intervals are either repetitions (zero) or stepwise motions (major or minor second) from the previous pitch. Descending steps are more common than ascending ones, and ascending skips are slightly more common than descending ones (compare +7 to –7, for example). The local ups and downs in the distribution are no doubt due to the scalar character of rock: for example, major seconds are more common than minor seconds because there are

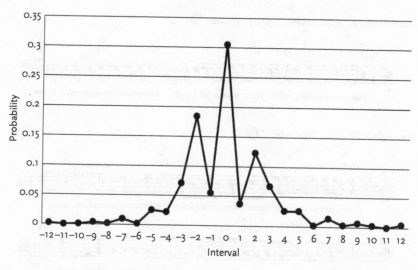

Example 5.8. The distribution of melodic intervals in the *Rolling Stone* corpus 🔊

more major than minor seconds in the scales that rock commonly uses, such as pentatonic and diatonic scales. In all of these respects, rock melody is similar to many other melodic idioms, both Western and non-Western (Huron, 2006).

An interesting—and more distinctive—aspect of rock lies in the relationship between melody and harmony. Consider first the melody of the Beatles' "I Want to Hold Your Hand," shown in Example 5.9. Most of the notes are chord tones—members of the underlying harmony: for example, $\hat{5}$ and $\hat{3}$ over I in the first measure, $\hat{4}$ and $\hat{2}$ over V in the second (the $\hat{4}$ is a chordal seventh), then $\hat{3}$ over vi and $\hat{7}$ over iii. The remaining notes—"non–chord tones"—are handled in highly constrained ways. The C in the first measure and the B in the second are approached by step and left by step in the opposite direction—"passing tones"; the first A in the final measure is a "neighbor tone," approached and left by step from the same side. The E's in the pickup could also be said to resolve by step, if treated as a single note; this could be considered an "incomplete neighbor." All this follows the normative use of non–chord tones in common-practice music (see, e.g., Laitz, 2012). In the great majority of cases, classical non–chord tones are approached and left by step; even when they are approached by leap (or not approached at all, like the first note of Example 5.9), they are most often resolved by step—sometimes known as the rule of "stepwise resolution." Non–chord tones resolving by leap are occasionally found—"escape tones"—but these tend to occur in highly stylized situations such as certain cadential gestures.

Example 5.9. The Beatles, "I Want to Hold Your Hand"

If Example 5.9 suggests that the treatment of non–chord tones in rock follows classical norms, the passages in Example 5.10 paint quite a different picture. In Example 5.10A, the first two-measure sub-phrase seems to follow the rule of stepwise resolution: the Fs and Cs move by step (or to a repetition, in the case of the second C). But the D and B♭ at the end of the second sub-phrase, not part of the underlying ♭VII chord, are left hanging with no resolution; similarly, the third sub-phrase ends with D, which is not part of IV (B♭ could be a chordal seventh). (Notes of interest are marked with asterisks.) Notably, these unresolved non–chord tones are all part of the tonic triad (B♭ is ♭$\hat{3}$ and D is $\hat{5}$). Thinking about harmony in a hierarchical way (see section 3.5), one could argue that tonic harmony is "prolonged" through the phrase—present at a higher structural level; in relation to this level, one might say, $\hat{1}$, ♭$\hat{3}$, and $\hat{5}$ are chord tones and do not require resolution. In other cases, though, this explanation does not help us. In Example 5.10B, the unresolved B at the end of the first measure is $\hat{4}$, not part of the local harmony (♭III), nor is it part of tonic harmony (which is surely the "structural" harmony, if there is one). Similarly, the D♯ ($\hat{6}$) at the beginning of Example 5.9C is not part of tonic harmony and not resolved.

When discussing stepwise resolution, we must be clear about what scale is being assumed. So far we have been assuming a diatonic scale, which is surely justified in the case of "I Want to Hold Your Hand"; in the melodies in Example 5.10, however, it could well be argued that the underlying scale is pentatonic rather than diatonic. This changes things significantly, because some diatonic leaps are pentatonic steps: for example, $\hat{1}$ to ♭$\hat{3}$ is a step on the pentatonic minor scale. This could potentially explain some of the unresolved non–chord tones in these examples. The F♯ ($\hat{1}$) marked with an asterisk in the second measure of Example 5.10B is unresolved in diatonic terms, but in pentatonic terms it moves by step to ♭$\hat{3}$; similarly, the A♯ in the second measure of Example 5.10C resolves by step on the major pentatonic. But this still cannot explain away the unresolved $\hat{4}$ in

Example 5.10. Examples of melodic-harmonic divorce. Asterisks mark unresolved non–chord tones.

A. Elton John, "Saturday Night's Alright for Fighting"

B. Oasis, "D'You Know What I Mean?"

C. Whitney Houston, "How Will I Know"

the first measure of Example 5.10B or the unresolved $\hat{6}$ at the beginning of Example 5.10C.

What we seem to find here is a kind of independence, or at least partial independence, between melody and harmony. Unresolved non–chord tones are perhaps the clearest indicator of this phenomenon, but not the only one. In general, we can ask: How strongly does the melody seem to outline or express the harmony? In "I Want to Hold Your Hand," the melody seems to outline the underlying triads quite clearly; the fact that the notes on strong beats are all chord tones (except for the first pickup note) adds to this effect. (We might not actually *guess* the harmony from the melody, but they seem fully compatible.) This is not the case for the melodies in Example 5.10. In Example 5.10B, we find essentially the same melody in the first half of the first measure and the first half of the second—an alternation between E and F♯; it seems far-fetched to claim that these notes express i in the first measure and ♭VII in the second. A similar point could be made about Example 5.10A (compare mm. 3–4 with mm. 7–8). The sense we get here, rather, is that the melodies are "doing their own thing," largely oblivious to the underlying chord changes.

The relative independence of melody and harmony in rock, compared to common-practice music and other genres, has been widely observed. It was perhaps first noted by Moore (1995), who referred to it as "melodic-harmonic divorce"; several other authors have also employed this term (Temperley, 2007a; Clement, 2013; Nobile, 2015). Historically, it most likely originates from the influence of the blues, where a similar independence between melody and harmony is found. Typically in blues songs, the same melody (or a close variant) is used over the first and second four-measure phrases, though the second phrase is harmonically different, moving to IV (Titon, 1994); this is analogous to the repeating of melodic phrases over different harmonies seen in Example 5.10A and 5.10B. The fact that melodic-harmonic divorce in rock occurs most often with minor-pentatonic melodies, the characteristic scale of the blues, is further evidence for this connection. This also relates to the frequent practice (discussed in chapter 2) of combining melodic ♭3̂ with harmonic 3̂—itself a kind of melodic-harmonic independence, and also a reflection of blues influence. Melodic-harmonic divorce does not always involve pentatonic melodies, however. In "Smells Like Teen Spirit" (Example 5.3B), the verse melody is diatonic, but note the clash between the final G (2̂) and the underlying i chord; in the Police's "Message in a Bottle", also diatonic, the D♯ at the end of the phrase in Example 4.9A clashes with the underlying F♯ minor chord.

Note, finally, that all the examples shown in this section are from *verses*. Melodic-harmonic independence seems to be most common in verses of rock songs, with choruses tending to feature a closer coordination between the two; we will return to this point in chapter 8.

5.4 MEDIANT MIXTURE AND "BLUE NOTES"

We now turn to one rather specific but very characteristic aspect of rock melody: the combination or "mixture" of the two forms of the mediant scale degree, 3̂ and ♭3̂. No conventional scale, diatonic or pentatonic, contains both of these degrees. Yet we saw in chapter 2 that the "minor" melodic profile of the *Rolling Stone* corpus reflected a fairly high frequency of 3̂ as well as ♭3̂; closer examination shows that, indeed, many songs contain both. Mediant mixture is also an important factor in the relationship between melody and harmony; I noted in section 2.2 that many songs feature $\flat\hat{3}$ in the melody and $\hat{3}$ in the harmony. Here, however, our focus is on the purely melodic aspect of mediant mixture. For songs that use both forms of the mediant in the melody, what are the factors influencing the choice between these two degrees at specific moments?

Sometimes choices between $\hat{3}$ and $\flat\hat{3}$ are guided by the harmony. The verse of the Who's "I Can See for Miles" (Example 5.11) starts with $\hat{3}$ over a bare fifth on I in the guitar and bass; when the accompaniment moves to $\flat$III, the melody shifts to $\flat\hat{3}$ along with it. (In this and subsequent examples, scale degrees $\hat{3}$ and $\flat\hat{3}$ are marked on the score.) One often sees a move to $\flat\hat{3}$ over subdominant harmony; "Satisfaction" (shown in earlier in Example 2.16B) illustrates this, shifting to $\flat\hat{3}$ in the fourth measure over IV. This, too, could be explained harmonically, if we assume that that $\flat\hat{3}$ forms a dominant-seventh chord ($\hat{4}$–$\hat{6}$–$\hat{1}$–$\flat\hat{3}$)— though in this case only the triad is present in the accompaniment. A more subtle case is seen in the second phrase of Example 5.7B: $\hat{3}$ is used in the first measure ("One day . . . ") and $\flat\hat{3}$ in the third ("re-cog-nize"). The $\flat\hat{3}$ degree is not part of $\flat$VII, but somehow it seems more compatible with it, as it is scale-degree $\hat{4}$ of $\flat$VII (whereas $\hat{3}$ would be $\sharp\hat{4}$). In general, $\flat\hat{3}$ seems to be preferred over $\flat$VII; the G$\natural$ in the third measure of Example 4.15 is another instance of this. Perhaps the $\flat$VII chord in such cases creates a very subtle "tonicization"—not so much establishing itself as a tonal center, but steering the melody momentarily toward its own major scale.

Other choices between $\hat{3}$ and $\flat\hat{3}$ cannot be explained by harmony. Consider the first phrase of the Jackson 5's "ABC," shown in Example 5.12A. The melody features $\hat{3}$ at "went" but $\flat\hat{3}$ at "never never." The accompaniment is the same under both the $\hat{3}$ and the $\flat\hat{3}$ (really just $\hat{1}$, but I take it as implying a major triad), so this cannot be the explanation. The determining factor here seems to be the fact that the first half of the line gravitates around $\hat{5}$, and the second half around $\hat{1}$. In general, $\hat{3}$ tends to be favored in proximity to $\hat{5}$, and $\flat\hat{3}$ in proximity to $\hat{1}$. A similar pattern is seen in a number of other songs; the other excerpts in Example 5.12 are

Example 5.11. The Who, "I Can See For Miles"

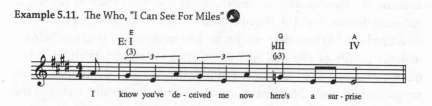

Example 5.12A. The Jackson 5, "ABC"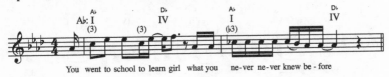

You went to school to learn girl what you ne-ver ne-ver knew be-fore

Example 5.12B. Tina Turner, "River Deep, Mountain High" (bridge)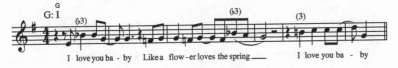

I love you ba - by Like a flow - er loves the spring ⸺ I love you ba - by

Example 5.12C. Guns N' Roses, "Sweet Child O' Mine"

She's got a smile that it seems to me ⸺ Re-minds

Example 5.12D. The Beatles, "Birthday"

You say it's your birth - day It's my birth-day too ⸺ yeah

illustrative.[4] In "Satisfaction" (Example 2.16B), this explains the use of $\hat{3}$ (with $\hat{5}$) at the beginning of the first section, and $\flat\hat{3}$ (with $\hat{1}$) in the second section. The Beatles' "Birthday" (Example 5.12D) offers an especially clear example; in this case the $\hat{3}$ and $\flat\hat{3}$ are heard almost simultaneously in different voices. This pattern may be due to the fact that, in pentatonic terms, $\hat{5}$–$\hat{3}$ and $\flat\hat{3}$–$\hat{1}$ are neighbor motions (in the major and minor pentatonic scales, respectively); this makes these intervals seem especially natural and comfortable to sing (though $\flat\hat{3}$–$\hat{1}$ is often filled in with $\hat{2}$, as in Examples 5.12A, B, and C). By this view, each of these melodies features a mixture of the two pentatonic scales—a common occurrence in rock melodies, also reflected in the idea of the "pentatonic union" scale.

4. The F♭ in Example 5.12C is a bit high—possibly a "blue note" (a concept discussed later in this section).

Example 5.13A. Crosby, Stills, Nash & Young, "Woodstock" (end of chorus)

Example 5.13B. Alice in Chains, "No Excuses" (end of first verse)

There is also a tendency to use $\hat{3}$ rather than $\flat\hat{3}$ at the end of a section—what we might loosely call "cadential" points (though elsewhere I have defined "cadence" rather more specifically). The inherent stability of the major triad (due to its physical basis in the overtone series) makes it especially well-suited for the end of a section.[5] In the chorus of Crosby, Stills, Nash & Young's "Woodstock" (Example 5.13A), $\flat\hat{3}$ is used throughout the chorus but shifts to $\hat{3}$ on the final word, coinciding with the cadential move to tonic: "And we've got to get ourselves back to the *gar*-den." In Alice in Chains' "No Excuses" (Example 5.13B), $\flat\hat{3}$ is used consistently through the verse (over prolonged tonic harmony); only in the final two measures do the vocals shift to $\hat{3}$. Here again, the move to $\hat{3}$ coincides with the end of the section. (The melisma from $\hat{3}$ down to $\flat\hat{3}$ in the upper voice is curious; I suspect this is to smooth the transition into the $\flat$VI chord that begins the chorus.) Choices between $\hat{3}$ and $\flat\hat{3}$ may also be influenced by expressive considerations; in "Woodstock," the shift to $\hat{3}$ at the end of the chorus perhaps represents the triumphant return to the "garden" (we will see further examples of the expressive aspect of mediant mixture in chapter 10). Finally, there seems to be some tendency to favor $\hat{3}$ more in choruses rather than verses—reflecting a more general difference between the pitch content of verses and choruses, as we will discuss in section 8.3.[6]

5. A similar phenomenon is seen in classical music: one often finds a major tonic harmony at the end of a minor-key section, known as a "Picardy third."

6. Occasionally we find $\hat{3}$ and $\flat\hat{3}$ in close alternation, as in the guitar riff to the Doors' "Love Me Two Times" and the first vocal phrase of Bachman-Turner Overdrive's "Takin' Care Of Business." In a common-practice context, these $\flat\hat{3}$s would probably be notated as $\sharp\hat{2}$s; whether this is justified in the case of rock is an interesting question. The same issue arises with the "sharp-ninth" chord, in which $\flat\hat{3}/\sharp\hat{2}$ is used above $\hat{3}$, as in the Jimi Hendrix Experience's "Purple Haze"; see van der Bliek (2007) for discussion.

The use of $\hat{3}$ and $\flat\hat{3}$ in rock melodies provides further evidence—if any were needed—that pitch organization in rock cannot be neatly explained in terms of conventional diatonic and pentatonic scales. There is an even deeper issue, however, which is the reality of the chromatic scale itself. All of our discussion so far has assumed that melodic notes are selected from one of the twelve chromatic categories; but it has been suggested that notes in rock melodies may sometimes "fall between the cracks" of these categories—so-called microtonal notes, or (in this more specific context) "blue notes."[7] As the term suggests, such notes are most characteristic of the blues (Titon, 1994; Moore, 2002b), but a number of authors have pointed to them in rock (broadly defined) as well (Tallmadge, 1984; Brackett, 1994; Weisethaunet, 2001). Blue notes have most often been observed between $\flat\hat{3}$ and $\hat{3}$, though they may occur in other parts of the scale as well. They are most often found in vocal melodies; they can also be produced on some instruments such as the guitar (by "bending" and other techniques).

Observations about blue notes by previous authors have been based on aural ("by-ear") analysis. In an exploratory study, Iris Ren, Zhiyao Duan, and I sought to examine the issue of blue notes in a more objective way.[8] We chose to focus on the Jackson 5's song "ABC," for two reasons. First, the melody includes numerous examples of both $\hat{3}$ and $\flat\hat{3}$, and therefore seemed like a situation where blue notes in between $\hat{3}$ and $\flat\hat{3}$ might also occur. Second, a recording of the song is available on the internet including just the vocal; this makes it easy to identify the pitch of the vocal using automatic pitch-tracking software. (For further technical details of our procedure, see Temperley, Ren, & Duan, 2017.) After automatically identifying the complete pitch contour of Michael Jackson's lead vocal, we divided it up into individual notes (assuming one note per syllable), and identified the mean pitch of each note. (The song contains only a few melismas—where one syllable spans several notes—but it does contain a number of gliding notes; steeply gliding segments of pitch, and notes containing no stable segment at all, were excluded from our analysis.) We wondered if, perhaps,

7. Some authors have used "blue note" in a different way, to refer to minor-mode chromatic scale categories used in a major-mode context (Wagner, 2003). Here I use the term only in the microtonal sense.

8. I do not wish to question aural transcription in general; of course, the current book heavily relies on it. Aural analysis may be less accurate, however, when microtonal judgments are concerned; there may be some tendency toward "categorical perception" (assigning a note to a chromatic category when its true pitch is quite far from the mean of the category) and other biases (Burns, 1999).

the distribution of these mean pitches would show a distinct blue-note category halfway between $\hat{3}$ and $\flat\hat{3}$.

The results are shown in Example 5.14; here notes are sorted into pitch categories of one-tenth of a semitone. We can observe a strong peak close to $\hat{3}$, and a (smaller) peak close to $\flat\hat{3}$. There is also a peak halfway between the two, which might suggest the presence of blue notes. Inspecting these possible blue notes, we found that several of them were very brief or gliding segments that did not convincingly suggest an intended blue note. There were only a few cases where the pitch did seem to linger on or near the halfway point. Interestingly, these tended to be cases where the abovementioned criteria for $\hat{3}/\flat\hat{3}$ choices were in conflict. One is shown in Example 5.15. The pitch of the note on the syllable "love" is exactly halfway between $\flat\hat{3}$ and $\hat{3}$. This note is heading down towards $\hat{1}$, and is also over a IV harmony, both of which favor $\flat\hat{3}$; but it is at a cadential point, which favors $\hat{3}$. Perhaps in this case, the conflict between the factors caused Jackson to "compromise" by hitting a pitch in between the two mediant degrees.

On the whole, the evidence from this study does not suggest that blue notes are a common phenomenon in rock music. We did find a few possible blue notes in "ABC." But recall that we chose this song specifically because we thought it was a likely situation for blue notes to occur. We also

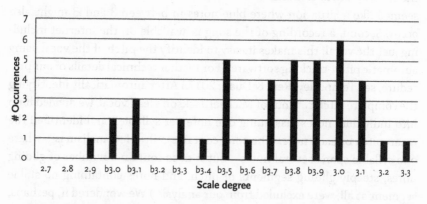

Example 5.14. The distribution of mediant notes in the melody of the Jackson 5's "ABC." Pitches are indicated by a tenth of a semitone; for example, $\flat3.5$ is exactly halfway between $\flat\hat{3}$ and $\hat{3}$.

Example 5.15. A possible blue note in the Jackson 5's "ABC" (at 2:26), marked with $\flat$?).

examined several passages from other songs, and here, too, found very little evidence of blue notes. If blue notes do exist in rock, they appear to be fairly rare. However, this is a very preliminary and exploratory study; certainly the topic of blue notes deserves further exploration.

5.5 QUESTIONS

1. The verses to these four songs have a melodic grouping structure that is quite common but has not yet been mentioned: Eddie Cochran, "Summertime Blues"; the Doors, "L. A. Woman"; the Romantics, "Talking in Your Sleep"; Janet Jackson, "Runaway." Diagram the grouping structure (it is approximately the same in all four songs), showing how the groups align with the bar lines. The instruments play a more important role here than in other grouping structures; why?

2. The phrase structure in "Yesterday" (Example 5.5) reflects a rather common strategy: a very short (one-measure) group on the first downbeat, followed by an end-accented group ending on (or just after) the third downbeat. (Stephenson [2002] discusses this strategy.) Since this pattern spans two hyperdownbeats, it cannot simply repeat (unless it repeated two measures later, which would leave a large gap between phrases; this occurs in some early blues-based songs but rarely in later decades). So it generally continues in a somewhat irregular fashion, though this happens differently in different songs; in some cases the hypermeter becomes irregular as well. Consider the verses of these songs: Freda Payne, "Band of Gold"; the Spinners, "Could It Be I'm Falling in Love"; Deep Blue Something, "Breakfast at Tiffany's"; Sugar Ray, "Someday." In each case, diagram the phrase structure and hypermeter, as shown in Example 5.5.

3. The music of the Smiths reflects a highly unusual approach to rock melody. Consider the song "This Charming Man," and how it follows or rejects the norms of melodic organization discussed in this chapter, with regard to rhyme, motive, and phrasal regularity. The song also reflects an extreme degree of melodic-harmonic independence; discuss and give specific examples.

4. As we have seen, the mediant scale-degree can be handled in various ways in rock: it can be major ($\hat{3}$) in both melody and accompaniment, or minor ($\flat\hat{3}$) in both; it can be minor in the melody and major in the accompaniment; it can also be mixed in the melody (and/or the accompaniment), using both $\hat{3}$ and $\flat\hat{3}$. In some cases, the mediant may be totally absent in the accompaniment. Consider these songs and discuss mediant usage in each one (in each case, consider just the first eight measures

of the vocal): The Who, "I Can't Explain"; the Kinks, "You Really Got Me"; Creedence Clearwater Revival, "Bad Moon Rising"; Eric Clapton, "Cocaine"; John Cougar Mellencamp, "Rain on The Scarecrow."

5. *Counterpoint* refers to the use of simultaneous melodic lines, independent but carefully coordinated. (Sometimes the lines are equal in melodic importance—as in a Baroque fugue—but not always.) Counterpoint is hugely important in common-practice music, and in the theory and study of it. Could we speak of counterpoint in rock? Why or why not? Is this a possibility that rock musicians and songwriters could explore more fully?

The Musical Language of Rock

CHAPTER 6

Timbre and Instrumentation

Examples 6.1A and B show the opening melody of the song "Handy Man," in two different versions: the original, by Jimmy Jones (1959), and a later version by James Taylor (1977). Represented as notation, the two passages are quite similar. They are in different meters (compound versus simple) and the melodic elaborations diverge slightly; but they seem like close variants of the same tune. Yet how different the two songs sound! It is partly the instrumentation: while Taylor's ensemble of acoustic guitar, electric piano, and gentle Latin and rock percussion creates a mellow effect, the more forceful drums, bright acoustic piano, and background vocals (not to mention the unusual whistling part) in Jones's version conveys a much higher energy level. Crucially, the vocal *timbres* (sound qualities) of the two singers are utterly different as well: Jones's vocal is higher—in absolute terms, but more importantly, in relation to the singer's natural range, which gives it an intense, somewhat strained character, while Taylor's voice is relaxed and open. Related to this is the sense of space conveyed by the two recordings: Jones's suggests a large, resonant space, while Taylor's suggests a small and intimate one. These differences between the two versions— coupled with the significant tempo difference—greatly influence their expressive effects. Jones's handyman is brash and cocky, trying to win over the "girls gather[ed] 'round" with his braggadocio (perhaps trying a bit too hard); Taylor's persona, by contrast, is cool and confident—here I am, take it or leave it (but I bet you'll take it).

Cover song comparisons like this one bring out the enormous importance of timbre and instrumentation in rock music. (By instrumentation, I mean the set of instruments used in a song, as well as the specific notes

Example 6.1. The opening phrase of "Handy Man," in two versions (both transposed to C)

A. Jimmy Jones's version

B. James Taylor's version

they play.) In this chapter we explore these two closely related topics. We will also consider aspects of the recording process that impact the sound and effect of a song. Some words of caution are in order, however. While previous chapters have attempted to treat the topics at hand with some depth and thoroughness, this is simply not possible in the current case, for a couple of reasons. With regard to timbre, our current understanding of the subject is quite limited—not just with regard to rock music, but in general. This is reflected in the vague way that timbre is usually defined: according to one source, "the attribute distinguishing sounds that are equivalent in pitch, duration, and loudness" (Thompson, 2014; most other definitions are similar). Basic questions—the components and dimensions by which timbre is mentally represented, the factors determining similarity between timbres, and their expressive and extramusical effects—remain largely mysterious, despite some valiant attempts to answer them (see McAdams, 2013, for a recent survey). In my fairly brief treatment of timbre, I review some of what we do know about the topic as well as some open questions, and broadly survey the timbral world of rock music.

With instrumentation, we have, in a sense, the opposite problem: there is a vast literature on the instruments of rock—guitar, bass, drums, keyboards, and secondary instruments like saxophone—and how to play them. I have neither the space nor the expertise to treat these topics in depth. In any case, much of this literature concerns matters such as fingering techniques and equipment choices, which are somewhat tangential to the listener-based focus of the current study. My focus here will be on aspects of instrumentation that relate to the structural musical dimensions discussed in previous chapters, such as meter, harmony, and form. Instrumental parts relate to musical structure in certain rather obvious ways: the guitar and bass often determine the harmony of a song, for example, and the drums establish its meter (as explained in section 4.1). But there are more subtle questions to consider as well. For example, how can a drum part help to convey the hypermeter, phrase structure, and form of a song? How do improvised guitar solos reflect the melodic conventions of rock that we have discussed previously—scale structures, patterns of syncopation, motive, alignment with the harmony, and so on?

Timbre and instrumentation would seem to be vital concerns with any kind of music—certainly with common-practice music. While I would not go so far as to say that timbre is more important in rock than in common-practice music, there are some stark differences between the two that deserve mention. One difference is the sheer range of timbres that are available. The variety of sounds that can be produced by an electric guitar—equipped with the full range of special effects (distortion, flanging, echo, etc.)—far exceeds what any classical instrument allows (though one might say that the greater variety of actual instruments in a classical orchestra, compared to a rock band, partly makes up for this). The mind-boggling array of possibilities allowed by modern synthesizers is an even more extreme case. Here again, the issue of the composer/performer distinction arises. In classical music, the composer decides on the instrumentation; the performers have some control over the timbre of their instruments, but within a relatively narrow range. In rock, the fact that individual instruments allow so much timbral variety gives the individual musicians great power to shape the overall sonic effect. (Production effects—such as reverb and equalization—also play an important role here.) And as we have noted, the members of a band may be largely responsible for choosing the *notes* of their parts as well. All this bears on the question of who deserves credit for the various instrumental parts that I will be discussing, both their timbres and their notes; this is a very complex question that I largely evade here. For simplicity, I will generally attribute each instrumental part to its nominal player, as listed on the recording; but it should be borne in mind that others (songwriters, producers, other band members) may have contributed to these components of the song in important ways.

6.1 APPROACHES TO TIMBRE

A discussion of timbre must begin with some acoustics (with apologies to those with some knowledge of this topic). A musical pitch, in its most basic form, is caused by something vibrating in a regular sine wave pattern. The higher the speed or *frequency* of the vibrations (usually measured in hertz, or cycles per second), the higher the pitch; each time the frequency doubles, the pitch goes up an octave. In practice, a musical note usually involves many vibrations, one that corresponds to the pitch of the note (the "fundamental") and a number of faster vibrations at multiples of the fundamental (known as "harmonics" or "overtones"). If the basic vibration is middle C (262 hertz), there might be overtones at 524 hertz, 786 hertz, and so on. The fundamental and the overtones of a note combine together to produce a complex, repeating pattern of vibration. Example 6.2A shows part of the wave form (about a thirtieth of a second) of the opening guitar note of the Rolling Stones' "Satisfaction"; the large pattern repeating four times in the figure represents the fundamental pitch, while the smaller ups and downs represent the overtones. A useful way of representing a sound is with a *spectrogram*, a two-dimensional representation with time on the horizontal axis and frequency on the vertical, showing the frequencies that are present at each point in time (see Example 6.2B); darkness or color is usually used to show the strength of each frequency at each time point.

It has long been known that the timbre of a note is largely determined by two things: (a) the overtones in the sound—which ones are present, and

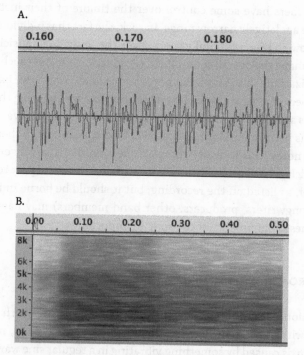

Example 6.2. The first guitar note of the Rolling Stones' "Satisfaction." (Numbers on the horizontal axis represent seconds; numbers on the vertical axis represent Hertz, e.g. 2k = 2,000.) (A) A small segment of the waveform of the note. (B) A spectrogram of the entire note.

with how much energy (i.e., loudness)—and (b) the way these overtones change over time. Roughly speaking, a note with more and higher overtones will sound "brighter" in timbre. On some instruments (such as an organ), the overtone content of a note is relatively constant over its duration, as is the loudness of the note as a whole; in other sounds, the loudness may change, with overtones rising or falling at different rates. In the "Satisfaction" spectrogram, the dark vertical band indicates the part of the note where the energy is highest. On a piano, a note dies down or "decays" rapidly after it begins, with higher overtones decaying faster. Some sounds may also be composed of random, non-repeating vibrations; these sound like unpitched "noise." Most percussion sounds are of this nature. (Noise can be of higher or lower frequency: a kick drum's noise is low in frequency, a snare drum is higher, and a cymbal is higher still.) And still other sounds may combine pitched ("periodic") components and unpitched ones; for example, a bowed violin note generally has a small burst of noise at the beginning.

While this explanation of timbre is accurate as far as it goes, it does little justice to the tremendous richness and complexity of timbre as we *experience* it. A fundamental with just the first overtone added sounds quite different in quality from one with just the second overtone; different combinations of overtones produce an almost endless variety of tone qualities, to which a single dimension such as "brightness" hardly does justice. And this is just for steady-state tones; adding changes in overtone content over time expands the possibilities enormously. To further complicate things, we could add vibrato (fluctuations in pitch), tremolo (fluctuations in loudness), and production effects such as reverb (which can make the sound seem like it was recorded in a small room or a cavernous church).

In exploring timbre from a perceptual viewpoint, it is useful to focus on non-pitched sounds: this allows us to devote our full attention to timbre. A natural object of study is the snare drum, which is present in the vast majority of rock songs and offers huge timbral variety. Table 6.1 lists eight well-known songs containing isolated (or almost isolated) snare drum sounds (the sounds can be heard at the book's website). I think you will agree that the sounds are all quite different, and that this impacts our experience of the songs in which they occur. But how do we describe these differences? Some of the differences can be described concretely: some sounds are more reverberant than others (compare Densmore's snare with Wonder's); some of them sound slightly pitched (Kinney's has a rather distinct pitch around D3). We might also want to use more impressionistic terms like tight versus loose, or thin versus fat. Efforts have been made to model such intuitions—for example, by reducing timbre to a small number of dimensions representing different perceptual qualities (Grey, 1977;

Table 6.1 SONGS CONTAINING ISOLATED SNARE DRUM SOUNDS[a] 🎧

Song Title	Artist	Drummer
Light My Fire	The Doors	John Densmore
Honky Tonk Women	Rolling Stones	Charlie Watts
Rock and Roll	Led Zeppelin	John Bonham
Superstition	Stevie Wonder	Stevie Wonder
No Time This Time	The Police	Stewart Copeland
Billie Jean	Michael Jackson	Leon "Ndugu" Chancler
Black Hole Sun	Soundgarden	Matt Cameron
No Excuses	Alice In Chains	Sean Kinney

[a]The sounds are all heard in the introductions, except in "Rock and Roll," "No Time This Time" and "Black Hole Sun," where they occur in drum breaks in the middle of the song.

McAdams, 2013). This approach is useful up to a point, but it tells us relatively little about the *expressive* effects of the sounds and how they function in their larger musical contexts.

An alternative approach to timbre builds on the *ecological* theory of perception (Gibson, 1966; Clarke, 2005). A fundamental idea of this approach is that the perception of an event depends largely on our inferences about the physical situation in which it was produced, and how that situation might impact us. In relation to timbre, this could involve inferences about the size and material of the resonating object, the way it was struck or set in vibration, and the space in which the event occurred—though these inferred properties may have little resemblance to the way the sound was actually produced. Several recent studies have examined timbre in rock from this perspective. Moore (2012) suggests, for example, that the staccato, high register piano octaves in Annie Lennox's "Walking on Broken Glass" convey the image of the song's title (and also the careful, delicate way that one might walk through such objects). Zagorski-Thomas (2014) explores how a dry, non-reverberant recording environment can suggest intimacy and, along with that, honesty and sincerity. Heidemann (2016) applies ecological theory to vocal timbre, and Osborn (2016) to the music of Radiohead. The ecological approach seems highly suggestive with regard to the snare sounds presented in Table 6.1. To my ears, Watts's snare suggests a large object being hit, while Chancler's suggests a small one; Cameron's has a more metallic sound, Wonder's a more wooden sound; Copeland's suggests a more forceful "hit," Bonham's a gentler one. (A drum expert who knows how the sounds were actually produced might draw quite different inferences!) And it is easy to see how some of these inferences might have further expressive implications—in particular, a sound being hit harder suggests more energy, a concept that we will return to in chapter 7.

If the timbral possibilities for the snare drum are great, those of the electric guitar are even greater. Different brands of guitars have different sound qualities (the same is true of drums and other instruments); guitarists debate the relative merits of the Fender Stratocaster and the Gibson Les Paul. But guitar technology also allows much more striking and easily recognizable differences in timbre. One important dimension of variation is the amount of sustain, overdrive, or distortion in the sound. These three effects are closely related (fundamentally the same thing): they all involve amplifying the original sound, perhaps to the point where the amplifier cannot handle it and it becomes distorted. (At least, that was the original cause of distortion; in later years, it was achieved by other means.) Acoustically, distortion involves clipping the waveform (imagine literally chopping off the peaks of the sound wave in Example 6.2A), which introduces other frequencies into the sound and sometimes noise as well. Boston's "Peace of Mind" offers us a clear demonstration of the effect: we hear the same chords played on an acoustic guitar in the introduction and, later in the song (around 3:55), on a highly sustained electric guitar. Another important guitar effect is the wah-wah pedal; this effect "filters" the sound, boosting a narrow range of frequencies as the pedal is depressed, which can create an almost speech-like sound. Jimi Hendrix is especially associated with this effect. At the beginning of "Voodoo Child (Slight Return)," Hendrix damps the strings high on the fretboard and strums them, creating an unpitched sound that then passes through the wah-wah pedal; the absence of pitch draws our attention to the effect itself.

Another set of guitar effects includes phasers, flangers, chorus, and echo. These four effects all involve the more general principle of *delay*: making a copy of the sound and shifting it in time in relation to the original sound. Phasers, flangers, and chorus effects shift the copied sound by a tiny time interval (a few milliseconds); this can create a thicker sound, but it also boosts or suppresses certain frequencies in the sound. The time interval is varied smoothly, creating a swooshing sound that rises and falls. The differences between these three effects are subtle, both technically and aurally; experts sometimes disagree as to which one was used on particular songs. The phaser is heard in Pink Floyd's "Have a Cigar," a flanger in the Police's "Walking on the Moon," and the chorus effect in Nirvana's "Come As You Are" (in each case, the effect is heard in the guitar part at the very beginning of the song). An echo effect is the same principle, except that the time interval between the original sound and the copy is much longer (as much as half a second or more), so that each delayed sound is heard as a distinct

Example 6.3. U2, "Where the Streets Have No Name" (excerpt from introduction). Combining a guitar pattern (upward stems) with a delayed version of itself (downward stems) creates a composite pattern.

event. U2's guitarist, the Edge, uses echo in imaginative ways, sometimes interweaving a melodic pattern and its echo to create new patterns (see Example 6.3).

Keyboard instruments have been widely used throughout rock's history, greatly enriching its timbral range. The use of the piano goes back to the 1950s (heard in songs such as Elvis's "Jailhouse Rock" and Jerry Lee Lewis's "Whole Lotta Shakin' Goin' On") and comes to the fore again with 1970s soft rock artists such as Carole King, Elton John, and Billy Joel. An important keyboard type in the 1960s was the Hammond organ. This instrument contains a rotating speaker which creates slow fluctuations in timbre; the introduction to the Spencer Davis Group's "Gimme Some Lovin'" is a nice illustration. In the late 1960s, the electric piano became popular; in this instrument, the keys strike metal rods, creating a mellow, bell-like sound, heard in songs such as Billy Joel's "Just the Way You Are."

Synthesizers offer the most timbral variety of any instrument, at least in theory: it should be possible to synthesize any sound that can be imagined, aurally or physically. But in practice, commercially available synthesizers (at least those widely used in rock music) have offered a relatively limited range of possibilities, and the range of sounds commonly used in rock is more limited still. Most synthesizers offer some control over the range of overtones in the sound, thus controlling its "brightness," as well as the way that volume and brightness change over time; other effects such as vibrato, chorus, and portamento (sliding between notes) are also available. Portamento was a source of fascination in early rock (perhaps because it is not easily achieved on most other instruments), as seen in the Who's "Bargain" and the Beatles' "Here Comes the Sun." Progressive rock of the 1970s offers many creative uses of synthesizers, such as Kansas's "The Spider" and Genesis's "Follow You Follow Me" (the keyboard solo in the latter is an especially beautiful use of portamento). In the 1980s, a novel technique known as frequency modulation became fashionable (epitomized by the Yamaha DX7 synthesizer); this tended to produce abrasive, metallic sounds, such as those in the introduction to Depeche Mode's "People Are People." Also fashionable in the 1980s were sampling keyboards, in which each key plays a short digital recording or "sample" of sound, with different keys shifting the sound up or down in pitch. The sampled sound could be anything; the samples in Yes's "Owner of a Lonely Heart" (at around 2:20) seem to combine a human voice with a chord played by an orchestra. The 1990s saw a return to the warmer, purer sounds of early synthesizers, and renewed interest in effects such as portamento; Madonna's "Music" is illustrative.

Some might say that the most expressive instrument of all, from a timbral perspective, is the human voice—yet the voice presents special challenges in the analysis of timbre. The production of a vocal sound is uniquely complex (and not easily observed), depending on several parameters: the movement of the vocal folds that produce the sound, the shape of the vocal tract (the mouth and throat), the amount of breath that is released, and sympathetic vibrations throughout the body (Heidemann, 2016). An additional complication is that the variation in the sound of a sung pitch depends partly on the linguistic sounds being sung; this variation is very difficult to separate from timbral variation. (From an acoustic point of view, vowel sounds are essentially timbres, defined by different combinations of overtones over the fundamental.) Here again, the ecological perspective is useful, and in particular the idea that our experience of a vocal sound depends partly on the imagined experience of producing it ourselves. Heidemann (2016) applies this approach to an analysis of Aretha Franklin's vocals, sometimes taking pleasure in sounds that she knows she could *not* produce herself, but also noting sounds that suggest long-term strain and fatigue. We will say a bit more about vocal timbre in chapter 10.

Having briefly surveyed the timbral world of rock, we now turn to the issue of instrumentation. How are rock instruments actually played, and, in particular, how does this relate to the structural dimensions of rock discussed in earlier chapters? I will explore the guitar and drums in some depth and then comment more briefly on other instruments.

6.2 GUITAR

The central role of the guitar in rock is due not only to its great variety of timbres, but also to the many ways that it can be played. It is one of the few instruments that can play both chords and melodies. (Keyboard instruments can play both chords and melodies, and of course they are widely used in rock as well; but it's hard to jump around the stage with a keyboard instrument!) And that leads us to the primary distinction in rock guitar playing: between *rhythm guitar* and *lead guitar*. The lead guitar part in a song involves melodic lines of some kind: improvised solos, melodic riffs that occur in the introduction and at sectional boundaries, and interpolated "fills" (sometimes improvised, sometimes not) between vocal phrases. The rhythm guitar part is accompanimental—usually outlining the harmony in some way. Many bands have a dedicated rhythm guitarist and lead guitarist, the Beatles most famously (John and George, respectively).

Most broadly, rhythm guitar techniques can be grouped into two categories. One is strumming, where the entire right hand hits multiple strings. Often (though not always) this is done in a rapid up-and-down motion; I find this technique especially appealing because of its visceral rhythmic effect, which no other instrument can approximate (except closely related instruments like the ukulele). An up-and-down strumming pattern naturally conveys two metrical levels, the faster level of the individual chords and the slower level of the "down" chords, which are generally louder than the "up" ones (one naturally performs the "down" motion with greater force). This can clearly be heard in a simple strumming pattern like the introduction to the Smiths' "Bigmouth Strikes Again." Certain up or down chords may be left out (though the motion of the hand normally continues to maintain the rhythmic feel), creating complex rhythmic patterns, a common practice in funk and disco; an example is seen in Chic's "Le Freak" (Example 6.4A). Generally, the "down" chords (the ones on eighth-note beats) are emphasized, but several "up" chords are heard with no following "down," creating nice syncopations.

The other broad class of rhythm guitar techniques involves striking individual strings, either with the fingers ("fingerstyle") or with a pick. Like strumming, these techniques often convey subtle rhythmic patterns. The

Example 6.4. Rhythm guitar patterns (guitarists shown in parentheses)

A. Chic (Nile Rodgers), "Le Freak"

B. Fleetwood Mac (Lindsey Buckingham), "Landslide"

C. The Police (Andy Summers), "Message in a Bottle"

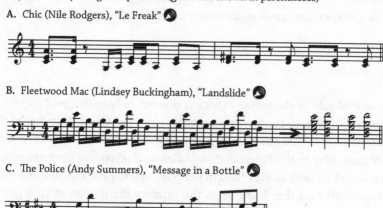

introduction to Fleetwood Mac's "Landslide" (Example 6.4B) could be viewed as a simple arpeggiation of the harmony, but it can also be seen as presenting four contrapuntal lines; the lowest one lands on the beats and thus conveys the meter, while the highest one suggests a syncopated melody. Rhythm guitar patterns normally emphasize triadic chord tones (or perhaps sevenths), but not always; in the Police's "Message in a Bottle" (Example 6.4C), Andy Summers adds a ninth above the root to each chord (D♯ over C♯, and so on).

With regard to lead guitar, our focus will be on the guitarist's moment in the spotlight: the guitar solo. Conventional wisdom has it that guitar solos are usually improvised—that is, generated spontaneously on the spur of the moment. In fact, interviews suggest that many guitar solos are quite carefully planned.[1] Still, it is clear that guitar solos are often quite different in character from the composed parts of a song (the vocal melody and other instrumental sections): in particular, they tend to be less structured, less repetitive, more "through-composed." A particularly interesting issue with guitar solos is their approach to the underlying harmony. (Most solos take place over harmonic patterns used elsewhere in the song, usually the verse or chorus; we will say more about this in chapter 8.) As we have seen, rock melody in general varies greatly in its adherence to the harmony, and this is true of guitar solos as well: some solos follow the harmony quite closely, others not at all. Two short solos will illustrate contrasting approaches to this issue.

Example 6.5A shows Eric Clapton's guitar solo for the Beatles' "While My Guitar Gently Weeps." Like many solos, this one exclusively uses notes of the minor pentatonic scale. I would say that this solo is almost completely oblivious to the complex harmonic progression beneath. Yes, it begins by emphasizing chord tones of A minor, and also ends on A as the harmony returns to that chord; but in between, I see little influence of the harmony. Let us not think that Clapton was incapable of following a chord progression; his exquisite fills elsewhere in the song prove otherwise (see Example 6.5B, emphasizing the G♯ of the underlying V chord). Breaking free from the harmony here was a deliberate choice. But if there is no harmonic structure in the solo, what gives it its logic, its coherence? There are certain motivic ideas, notably the repeated four-note figure at the beginning and the sequential two-note idea (G–A, A–C, C–D, D–E) near the end. But much of the rest of the solo has an unstructured, through-composed

1. *Guitar World* magazine's article "50 Greatest Guitar Solos" (2009) has informative interviews with guitarists about their creative processes.

Example 6.5A. Eric Clapton's guitar solo in the Beatles' "While My Guitar Gently Weeps." (The first two notes, in small noteheads, are part of the previous fill.)

Example 6.5B. A guitar fill from the second verse

quality—more like musical prose than poetry. It does, however, have a satisfying overall shape, both in terms of register (peaking in the middle, sweeping down to a low point and then rather quickly back up to the peak again) and also in terms of note density: Practically every measure has more notes than the previous one (4, 4, 8, 6, 9, 12, 12, 16). Also important to the effect of the solo (but not shown in the notation) are the many bends and glides between notes—a technique used in many of Clapton's solos but especially in this one, perhaps to convey the "weeping" suggested by the song's title.

In contrast to Clapton's solo, Elliot Easton's solo on the Cars' "Just What I Needed" is strongly built around the harmonic progression (Example 6.6). This particular progression is more challenging than most: It is quite fast, with two changes each measure (it is the same progression as in the verse but at twice the speed, for some reason), and the second harmony of each measure is syncopated, starting on the fourth eighth of the bar. The progression also does not stay within any conventional scale; the III chord introduces the #$\hat{5}$ degree (B♯). For the most part the solo outlines the harmony in the conventional manner, with chord tones or stepwise-resolving non–chord tones. At a few points, though, it rubs against the progression in unusual ways. Consider the E at the end of the third measure, the first A in the fourth measure, and the low B♯ in the sixth measure (these notes are marked with asterisks); these notes are not chord tones or stepwise

Example 6.6. Elliot Easton's guitar solo on the Cars' "Just What I Needed" 🔊

resolving. Notice, though, that each note belongs to the *following* chord; in common-practice terms, they could be described as "anticipations."[2] This gives the solo a rushing, impatient feeling, as if the guitar is getting ahead of the other instruments. The second C♯ in the fifth measure is also an unresolved non–chord tone, but this—6̂ leaping down to 3̂—is a common idiom of "melodic-harmonic divorce," often seen in vocal melodies as well (see Example 5.10C). These slightly misbehaved notes give the solo a quirky, playful quality. Here Easton shows that he is not only capable of following a tricky progression, but comfortable enough to goof around with it a bit as well.

The rise of multitrack recording in the 1960s and 1970s created vast new possibilities for the use of guitars in rock: a band with one or two guitarists could now create complex arrangements. An extreme case is the Eagles' "Hotel California"; the use of guitars in this song can only be described as orchestral. The introduction features a 12-string acoustic guitar pattern, with occasional bass notes, joined by organ and a second guitar in the second half. When the vocal enters (along with the bass and drums), an electric guitar is added, simply playing a rhythmic pattern with muted strings (sometimes known as the "waka waka" technique—similar to Jimi Hendrix's pattern on "Voodoo Child," discussed earlier). The second half of the first verse adds two guitars playing sustained chord tones in a fairly low register—similar to what would normally be done by an organ or string section. In the first chorus, a strumming guitar joins the fingerstyle one,

---

2. I have trouble hearing these as anticipatory *syncopations*. In the case of the E in the third measure, the following beat that it would "belong" on if it were shifted already has a note, and that note does *not* seem syncopated.

and a lead guitar plays fills between vocal phrases. The second verse continues the texture of the first, joined in the second half by two more guitars playing a sequential pattern (Example 6.7 shows just two measures of this section). And then there is the famous guitar solo at the end of the song, eventually joined by a second guitar in close harmony with it. Other bands of the late 1970s, such as Queen and Boston, also experimented with complex guitar arrangements.

Virtuosity—the display of great technical ability, valued as an end in itself—has long been a part of rock, particularly with regard to the guitar. In the late 1960s, Eric Clapton and Jimi Hendrix were idolized for their technical prowess; in the 1970s, progressive rock bands such as Yes and Emerson, Lake & Palmer included virtuosic passages for all the band members. Guitar virtuosity took a leap forward in the late 1970s with Van Halen's guitarist, Eddie Van Halen, who developed a technique called "tapping." In this technique, both hands are used on the fretboard, allowing

Example 6.7. The Eagles, "Hotel California," first two measures of second half of second verse. (Some parts are barely audible in this particular segment. See Example 6.8 regarding the drum notation.)

extremely complex and rapid note sequences; guitar solos in Van Halen's "Jump" and Michael Jackson's "Beat It" offer nice illustrations.

6.3 DRUMS

Example 6.8B shows an unremarkable drumbeat from an unremarkable song: John Cougar Mellencamp's "Hurts So Good." (The conventions I will use for notating drum sounds are shown in Example 6.8A.) The drums begin the song more or less alone (apart from a few tentative guitar chords), so they can be heard quite clearly. The kick drum marks beats 1 and 3 of each measure, the snare drum marks beats 2 and 4, and the hi-hat (a pair of cymbals pressed together, making a sound best represented as "tst") marks every eighth-note beat. The final downbeat of the example is marked with a cymbal "crash" (the cymbal is struck hard and allowed to ring freely). This is the point where the guitar enters with the song's riff, along with the bass, and it is definitely a hyperdownbeat; cymbal crashes typically mark hyper-downbeats. Just preceding the cymbal crash is a "fill." Fills are moments of freedom and prominence for the drummer; a huge variety of patterns may be used, often employing the toms, the other main components of the rock drum set. (Lacking the "snare," the metal net that creates the buzzy noise of a snare drum, toms have a purer and sometimes almost pitched sound.) Drum fills typically occur just before hyperdownbeats; like the guitar fills described in the previous section, they are often found in breaks between vocal phrases (though not in this case), but they also serve a particular structural function that will be discussed below.

The drumbeat just described—kick drum on 1 and 3, snare on 2 and 4, hi-hat on every eighth note—might be regarded as the most basic rock drumbeat, but it is not especially common; more often, this basic pattern is varied or elaborated in some way. (Even Example 6.8B elaborates it slightly, with an extra kick drum hit on the last eighth of each measure.) A number of other drumbeats from well-known songs are shown in Example 6.8C through J. All of these occur unaccompanied, either at the beginning of the song or in the middle (as explained in the caption). They really only have one thing in common: in every case, beats 2 and 4—the "backbeats"—are accented, usually by the snare (though the snare may mark other beats as well, as in 6.8C and D). This is an extremely consistent principle of rock drumming. In some cases the "backbeat" function is filled by other sounds, such as a "rimshot"—a drum-stick hit on the metal rim of the snare drum (as in beat 2 of 6.8I)—or hand claps; in 6.8H, the entire part is synthesized, but even here, beat 2 of each measure is marked by a snare-like sound, and beat 4 is marked for emphasis

Example 6.8. Drumbeats in some famous songs (drummers shown in parentheses). All drum parts are heard unaccompanied (or nearly so); all are at the beginning of the song, except "Funky Drummer," which occurs near the end (5:20). Drum sounds are represented by staff positions as indicated in (A). In cases where the drum part is synthesized (H and I), the description of the sounds is only approximate.

A. Key to drum notation conventions used in this and other examples

kick   snare   hi-hat   open hi-hat   crash   toms

B. John Cougar Mellencamp (Kenny Aronoff), "Hurts So Good"

C. The Rolling Stones (Charlie Watts), "Get Off of My Cloud"

D. James Brown (Clyde Stubblefield), "Funky Drummer"

E. Led Zeppelin (John Bonham), "When the Levee Breaks"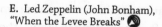

F. Aerosmith (Joey Kramer), "Walk This Way"

G. Donna Summer (Keith Forsey), "Hot Stuff"

H. Prince (drum part synthesized), "When Doves Cry"

I. TLC (drum part synthesized), "Waterfalls"

J. Alice in Chains (Sean Kinney), "No Excuses"

by the rest on the following eighth-note beat. The marking of beats 1 and 3 by the kick drum is somewhat less consistent; quite often it hits beat 1 but not beat 3, as in 6.8D and E. An important variant is 6.8G, in which the kick drum marks *every* tactus beat, including 2 and 4; this pattern, known as "four on the floor," became popular in the disco era and has remained common in dance music since then (often with the snare omitted).

In relation to rock's musical language as a whole, a drum part such as that in Example 6.8B functions in several ways. The basic kick/snare/hi-hat pattern conveys three levels of the metrical structure: the eighth-note, quarter-note, and half-note levels. It is natural that the kick pattern marks the stronger beats; in general, lower-frequency sounds in music tend to adhere to the meter more strongly. (In the "oom-pah-pah" accompaniment pattern of a waltz, for example, the lower-frequency "oom" is on the downbeat.) However, the fact that the conventional snare pattern (on beats 2 and 4) appears more consistently than the kick pattern (on 1 and 3) may also serve a communicative function: because the kick drum relies on very low frequencies, it might not be clearly heard in some situations (a small portable radio on the beach, for example), whereas the snare covers a wide frequency spectrum and is almost always audible. Cymbal crashes mark hyperdownbeats, and fills (which typically occur just before hyperdownbeats) serve this function as well; this can be especially informative when the hypermeter is irregular. In Example 4.15, discussed earlier, the five-measure phrase could potentially be confusing for the listener; the cymbal crash on the downbeat of the sixth measure (marked on the score), along with the preceding fill, helps to convey the beginning of the new hypermeasure. (The crash marking the fourth downbeat of the phrase—normally a weak measure—is of interest too; perhaps this helps us anticipate that an extended phrase is coming, and prepares us for the hyperdownbeat two measures later.) In addition, recall that melodic phrases in rock are most often beginning-accented; typically, they leave a gap near the end of the hypermeasure. This is therefore a natural place for a fill—keeping the musical activity and interest going for the listener; the same point could be made about many guitar fills, like Example 6.5B.

Changes in instrumental patterns can also help to articulate form. The shift from the verse to the chorus is often marked by a change in guitar timbre, usually to a more sustained, power-chord sound, as in Boston's "More Than a Feeling" and Semisonic's "Closing Time." The drums can play an especially important role in articulating section boundaries. In the Beatles' "I Want to Hold Your Hand," Ringo Starr uses the open hi-hat in the verse-refrain sections, producing a rather noisy, sustained sound, but switches to a closed hi-hat in the bridges for a more muted effect.

Having considered some of basic conventions of rock drumming, we now consider several drummers who transcend the ordinary. Neil Peart, the drummer of Rush, is known for his virtuosity, but he also stands out for his thoughtful treatment of very simple materials. Example 6.9A shows a passage near the beginning of "Tom Sawyer." The riff repeats the same rhythmic motive four times, occupying just the first half of the measure and leaving the second half to the drums. The snare marks beat 4 of the measure each time, but the kick drum pattern is different in each measure: we hear it once, then twice, then three times, then four, building up the density with methodical care. A few measures later we hear the passage in Example 6.9B, suggesting a dotted-eighth cross-rhythm. Peart establishes a repeated pattern in the first part of the cross-rhythm but then breaks it; why did he not continue the pattern (as shown by "why not"), especially since this would have aligned with the guitar-bass melody? I suspect Peart's intent here was to set up the following hyperdownbeat as strongly as possible (which is, after all, the primary function of a fill), and he felt—quite rightly—that this could be done more effectively by hitting the final two sixteenths of the measure. (He gives extra emphasis to these two sixteenths with "flams"—hitting the snare with both sticks at once.) In addition, leaving a bit of space after the fourth beat adds strength to it; this helps to ease us back into the underlying 4/4 meter, preparing us for the hyperdownbeat in another way.

Example 6.9. Two passages from Rush's "Tom Sawyer"

Example 6.10. Led Zeppelin, "Living Loving Maid" (second part of first verse) 🔊

I have already mentioned Led Zeppelin's drummer, John Bonham, but he deserves recognition again here. What sets Bonham apart is not just his thick, reverberant sound, but also his great sensitivity to what the other band members are doing. Example 6.10 shows a short segment from "Living Loving Maid." In the third and fourth measures, Bonham follows the guitar/bass rhythm, catching the syncopated downbeat. He then fills in the short gaps after "living" and "loving" with snare hits combined with cymbal crashes; in the following measure, the snare accentuates the syllables "*she's* just a *wom-an*." Note the unusual, accelerating pattern of snare hits that results from this (shown beneath the score). This creates a subtle dotted-eighth cross-rhythm; it also places one hit on beat 3 of the sixth measure, which nicely prepares his transition to a "half-time" feel (kick on beat 1, snare on beat 3) in the following chorus. This change in beat serves a structural function: it helps to convey the sectional boundary to the listener, which might not be obvious given the unusual structure of the verse (two six-measure phrases, the second of which is shown in the example).

Another unique drummer is the Police's Stewart Copeland. Copeland's playing incorporates elements of reggae; in the first verse of "Message in a Bottle" (Example 6.11), he hits the kick drum on beat 3 only, a standard reggae beat. However, he went far beyond this to develop a highly original style.[3] In "Message in a Bottle," he plays a different pattern on each of the

---

3. This characterization applies to the Police as a whole; they take the reggae style as a starting point but expand it with original touches and borrowings from other styles. See Spicer (2010) for discussion.

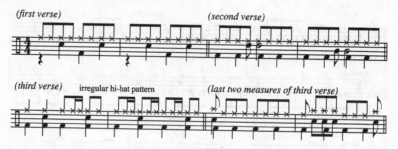

Example 6.11. The Police, "Message in a Bottle," showing Stewart Copeland's drumbeats for sections of the song 🎵

three verses, as shown in the example. The "snare-plus-cymbal-crash" (also used by Bonham, as mentioned above) is something of a trademark for Copeland, often occurring just before a hyperdownbeat; toward the end of the third verse of "Message in a Bottle," these gestures become increasingly dense, almost hysterical, mirroring the desperate tone of the song's lyrics.

Soul and funk music have their own tradition of great drummers; recent popular music (especially hip-hop) has paid these musicians the ultimate compliment of sampling their solo passages ("drum breaks") in numerous songs. Here we consider Clyde Stubblefield, one of James Brown's drummers in the 1960s, whose drumbeat from "Funky Drummer" has been especially widely used in sampling (the beat was shown earlier in Example 6.8D). We can probably all agree that this pattern is especially infectious and appealing; what makes it so? It has some notable commonalities with Peart and Bonham's drum parts discussed above. A beat is clearly established in a conventional way and then subverted just at the end of the measure, by withholding the conventional kick and snare placements and also by suggesting alternative meters: in particular, there is a strong implication of cross-rhythm (just as in Examples 6.9B and 6.10). In all of these cases, the subversion of the meter at the end of the measure (or hypermeasure) creates a moment of instability and complexity that is resolved in a satisfying way on the following hyperdownbeat. (We could speak of a small-scale trajectory of tension here, a concept that I will return to in later chapters.)

Some additional factors set Stubblefield's pattern apart from Peart's and Bonham's. One is dynamics: whereas there is little variation in loudness in Peart's and Bonham's snare hits, Stubblefield hits the snare noticeably more strongly on beats 2 and 4 than on other locations. Some transcriptions identify additional snare hits on the 12th and 15th sixteenth-note beats (Greenwald, 2002; Butler, 2006), which may indeed be quietly present. (We should note, also, that the pattern varies subtly from one measure to another.) Also of interest here is "microtiming": subtle departures from strict metrical timing. Drummers often speak of the importance of placing a hit a little bit ahead of the beat or a little bit behind, or of dividing the beat slightly unevenly ("swing"); this is thought to be of particular importance in funk and soul (Iyer, 2002; Bowman, 1997, 61–62).[4] Interestingly, in this repertoire, swing applies to the division of the eighth-note beat, not the quarter-note (tactus) beat as in jazz. In a study of funk drum passages including "Funky Drummer," Frane (2017) found that they had an average "swing ratio" (the ratio between the first and second halves of the beat) of 1.2, which is about the minimum that could be perceived; in "Funky Drummer" the swing ratio was just 1.1. Regarding the tactus, Frane found a slight delay of beat 2 (about 2%) in funk drum patterns, but little other evidence of microtiming deviations. On the whole, then, microtiming in funk drumming appears to be a very subtle phenomenon. This is not to say that it is illusory or unimportant; certainly, though, it is quite a different phenomenon from swing in jazz, which typically involves swing ratios of 1.5 or more (Friberg & Sundström, 2002).[5]

6.4 OTHER INSTRUMENTS

Virtually every rock song has a bass line, and this is normally provided by an electric bass guitar (though in the later decades of rock it is sometimes synthesized). We have already said that the vast majority of harmonies in rock are in root position, and this makes the bassist's normal function clear: to play the roots of chords, most often on strong beats of the meter. But even with this constraint, there is great room for variety: other tones can be added (usually *above* the root—most often the fifth, sometimes the third, and sometimes even passing and neighbor tones), and all manner of rhythmic patterns can be used, either supporting or complementing other rhythmic patterns in the texture. Randy Meisner's bass pattern in the verses of "Hotel California" (Example 6.7) is illustrative; using just the root and fifth, he fashions a distinctive motive which is a crucial part of the song's sonic identity. As another example, Flea's leaping, sliding bassline in the Red Hot Chili Peppers' "Give It Away" contributes greatly to the song's powerful groove (Example 6.12A).

4. *Rolling Stone*'s article "The 100 Greatest Drummers of All Time" (2016) contains numerous comments by drummers about other drummers, sometimes indicating the importance of microtiming; see for example Nirvana drummer Dave Grohl's remarks on John Bonham's "swing" and "behind-the-beat swagger."

5. Occasionally in funk one finds much more uneven divisions of the eighth-note beat; for example, listen to the drums in the opening of Stevie Wonder's "Superstition." One might consider this *too* uneven to be swing—more like an actual 2:1 ratio, implying a triple division of the beat (like that shown in Example 4.4B). There is a frequently a gray area between these two interpretations.

Example 6.12. Rock bass lines (bass players are shown in parentheses). Each bass line is from the opening vocal phrase of the song.

A. Red Hot Chili Peppers (Flea), "Give It Away"

B. The Beatles (Paul McCartney), "With a Little Help from My Friends"

Allowing inversions opens up a huge range of additional options for the bass player. Each inversion of a triad—root position, first inversion (with the third in the bass) and second inversion (with the fifth in the bass)—has a distinctive sound; inversions also expand the possibilities for motions between chords, and in particular, *linear* motions. Example 6.12B shows Paul McCartney's bass line at the beginning of "With a Little Help from My Friends": using a root position I, first-inversion V, and second-inversion ii (followed by root-position ii), he creates an expressive linear pattern. (The more active pattern in the final measure fills in a gap in the melody—serving a function similar to a drum or guitar fill.) In other contexts, the natural instability of inversions can create an unsettling effect. In the Supremes' "You Keep Me Hangin' On" (shown earlier in Example 3.15), notice how the great Motown bassist James Jamerson plays the fifth of the ♭VII chord, D♭, on the third downbeat of the chorus.[6] While this avoids the dull effect of simply repeating the root from the previous measure, the resulting second-inversion chord also injects an element of tension, well-suited to the anxious mood of the lyrics.

Early uses of the piano in rock were greatly influenced by the subgenre of blues known as "boogie," with triadic right-hand patterns often mixing the major and minor third; the piano solo in Jerry Lee Lewis's "Whole Lotta Shakin' Goin' On" is illustrative. In later years, a very different style of rock piano emerged, and I can think of no better example than Elton John's performance on "Tiny Dancer" (Example 6.13). In the introduction to the

---

6. The A♭ on the third beat of the third measure is curious. One might wonder if Jamerson was thinking of D♭ as the root here, but the G♭ at the end of the measure suggests otherwise. We could perhaps think of this A♭ as hinting at a pedal point—keeping the underlying tonic present in the listener's mind. The upper-voice $\hat{5}$ pedal in the guitar, mentioned earlier, might serve the same purpose.

Example 6.13. Elton John, "Tiny Dancer," first two measures of piano part

song, a one-measure pattern is heard four times, slightly different on each occurrence (only the first two measures are shown in the example). Rock piano parts generally arpeggiate the harmonies, in ways that sometimes resemble a guitar fingerstyle pattern; but the piano allows a more complex and contrapuntal texture, and Elton takes full advantage of this. The top line of the pattern, E5–D5–C5, anticipates the vocal melody that enters in the fifth measure (the syncopations are identical); Elton brings out the first two notes by harmonizing them in sixths below (this explains the rather odd F after the second beat). Accented non–chord tones are a trademark of Elton's style, especially from the second above the root to the third, as seen on the third beat of each measure. Another trademark is the accenting of certain notes, sometimes in irregular and unpredictable ways (e.g., the middle-voice C near the end of the second measure) but sometimes quite systematically. In the introduction to "Goodbye Yellow Brick Road," notice how he accents the second and fourth chords—approximating the effect of the backbeat snare.

Two other instruments are quite often used in rock solos: the saxophone and the harmonica. The sax is seen in a range of genres, from Aretha Franklin's "Respect" to Bruce Springsteen "Born to Run" to Billy Joel's "Just the Way You Are"; the harmonica was made famous by Bob Dylan in songs such as "Like a Rolling Stone," and appears later in songs like the Doobie Brothers' "Long Train Runnin'." Both the sax and harmonica permit the bending of notes, thus allowing the kinds of expressive, blues-influenced gestures seen in guitar solos. Other instruments are more often seen in an accompanying role, providing harmonic support and occasional fills, such as the string section in Simon & Garfunkel's "Bridge over Troubled Water" and the horn section in Wilson Pickett's "In the Midnight Hour." Strings can be used melodically as well; the instrumental section of a 1960s Motown or soul song is more likely to have a composed violin melody than a guitar solo. The high point for string writing in rock was probably late-1970s disco; a number of disco songs feature quite complex violin parts, such as Gloria Gaynor's "I Will Survive" and Chic's "Dance, Dance, Dance." Horn sections in rock typically feature some combination of sax, trumpet, and/or trombone; the music of Chicago offers a particularly fine example, in songs such as "Make Me Smile" and "Does Anybody Really Know What Time It Is?"

Finally, we consider an instrument of a very different character: the sequencer. A sequencer is a device (or, more recently, a software program) that allows the creation and editing of note patterns using graphic interfaces, music notation, or other means, thus bypassing the process of real-time performance. The note pattern can then be fed into a synthesizer to produce the desired timbre. (Related to this is the drum machine, essentially a sequencer that produces drum patterns.) Sequencers first became prominent in the synth-pop of the 1980s, represented by songs like the Human League's "Don't You Want Me" and New Order's "Bizarre Love Triangle." Sequencers allow all kinds of note sequences that no human performer could produce (I would challenge any keyboardist to replicate the chords in the introduction to "Bizarre Love Triangle"!). On the other hand, their output can seem mechanical and lifeless, lacking the nuances of dynamics and timing that characterize human performance. They also allow full control of the creative process by a single individual; again, this could be seen as an advantage, but it also sacrifices the collaborative approach that has worked so well in rock in the past. For now (through the 1990s and even today), there still seems to be plenty of enthusiasm for the traditional rock model: a joint effort of musicians producing sounds on traditional instruments in real time. But I expect the tension between humanly and electronically produced music will be a persistent issue in rock (and whatever takes its place) in the coming decades.

6.5 THE RECORDING PROCESS

As noted in chapter 1, a rock song is normally defined, first and foremost, by a recording; as such, all aspects of that recording must be considered essential aspects of the work. This includes structural elements treated in earlier chapters (harmony, rhythm, and so on), as well as timbral aspects discussed in this chapter; it also includes aspects introduced by the recording process itself. This process shapes the sound and effect of a song in fundamental though often subtle ways (Cunningham, 1998; Zak, 2001; Moorefield, 2005). What follows is only the briefest survey of this huge field, focusing on a few important topics. This also allows us to acknowledge—at least in a general way—an important part of the team that creates a rock song: the producer and sound engineers. (Producers are often involved in other matters besides recording, such as choosing material and managing personnel.)

A crucial aspect of recording is "ambience"—the aural impression of the space in which the music was recorded. This largely depends on the amount and character of "reverb"—the reflection of sound off of walls and other surfaces and its blending with the original sound. This can be affected by the actual recording space, as well as by the placement of microphones and artificial reverb simulators. The boomy sound of John Bonham's drumming in Led Zeppelin's "When the Levee Breaks" is due in part to the large stone hall in which it was recorded. The effect of reverb is clearest when it shifts within a song: At the end of Earth, Wind & Fire's "Shining Star," the reverb is suddenly reduced to almost nothing, making it seem as if the singers are just inches away from us. Rock of the 1950s and early 1960s generally has high levels of reverb; the producer Phil Spector, who produced many girl-group songs (e.g., the Ronettes' "Be My Baby"), was especially famous for this. Sometimes recordings would be played back in reverberant spaces and re-recorded to add additional reverb; Spector used a converted bathroom (Zak, 2001, 77–78). In later years, much lower levels of reverb became fashionable. I suspect the very obvious difference in *sound* between early and later rock songs—often apparent within a fraction of a second—is partly due to the much lower levels of reverb in the latter. (Compare the two versions of "Handy Man" discussed earlier.) Related to reverb is echo, which refers to a reflection of the sound that is distinct from (not blending in with) the original. This was discussed earlier as a guitar effect, and is frequently used elsewhere as well; the echo in the opening vocal of Led Zeppelin's "Black Dog" can be heard clearly at the end of each phrase.

An important issue in any rock recording is the way the instruments and voices are "mixed" or balanced against one another. The aesthetics of mixing have changed significantly over the decades: in the early years, the vocals tended to be highlighted, but since the 1970s—especially in dance music, but in other genres as well—more emphasis has been given to the drums and bass.[7] An important trend in this regard has been the growth of multitrack recording, from two tracks in the late 1950s to 24 or more in the 1970s. This permits a very precise and controlled approach to mixing (each instrument can be recorded and edited individually); it also allows the creation of complex textures through overdubbing ("Hotel California" was cited earlier as an example) and virtuosic "one-person band" feats, such as Stevie Wonder playing all the instruments on "Living for the City." With the rise of stereo in the 1960s, mixing also required the placement

7. The producer Brian Eno offers a fascinating commentary on this trend, quoted at length in Moorefield (2005, 58).

of each track between the right and left channels. Most often the aim of this is simply to allow the parts of the texture to be heard more clearly, but stereo can also be used in more striking ways; at the beginning of Pink Floyd's "Money," note how the looped "cash register" sounds switch from one side to the other.

Two other important tools in the recording process are equalization and compression. Equalization (or filtering) refers to the boosting or suppression of certain frequencies within the sound. Naturally, this affects timbre, since (as discussed earlier) the timbre of a sound depends largely on the relative strength of the frequencies within it. A dramatic use of equalization is in the introduction of Pink Floyd's "Wish You Were Here." The song begins with a solo guitar passage in which the low frequencies have been completely removed, making it sound like it was coming through a small radio or a telephone. At around 0:40, a second guitar enters, unfiltered; the incomplete sound of the first guitar makes the second one seem especially rich and satisfying. Compression refers to the automatic adjustment of volume to obtain a more consistent level; this can be used to balance loudness across sections of a song, but can also affect timbre—for example, by softening the attack of a note in relation to the later portion. Compression was used on the last chord of the Beatles' "A Day in the Life" (produced by three simultaneous grand pianos) to give it an abnormally long decay (Moorefield, 2005, 34).

Rock recording has also made use of many special effects. A famous example is the backwards-tape effect, seen for instance in the slurping sounds at the end of the Beatles' "Strawberry Fields Forever." Another is gated reverb, in which the strong reverb on each recorded sound is abruptly cut off, epitomized by Phil Collins' drum break in "In the Air Tonight" (at around 3:40). (From an ecological point of view, the appeal of this timbre may be that it evokes a space that is actually physically impossible.) More recently we have seen the rise of Auto-Tune, which adjusts the smoothly varying intonation of the voice to discrete pitch categories. This can be used unobtrusively to correct imprecise singing, but is also sometimes applied more conspicuously; in Cher's "Believe," it gives a somewhat robotic quality to the vocal line.

6.6 QUESTIONS

1. Each of these song sections has a drumbeat that is unusual, lacking (consistent) snare hits on beats 2 and 4: the Ronettes, "Be My Baby" (intro and verse); the Foo Fighters, "Learn to Fly" (verse); Fleetwood

Mac, "Go Your Own Way" (verse); Led Zeppelin, "Whole Lotta Love" (second verse, around 0:50). Transcribe each pattern—at least the snare and kick drum, and possibly other elements as well.

2. Transcribe part of Don Felder's guitar solo in "Hotel California." (You could do as little as four measures, or as much as the whole solo. You could also use an existing transcription, but be careful: transcriptions of guitar solos often indicate only the finger positions, which may not correspond to the pitches heard, due to string bending.) The solo has a complex relationship with the underlying harmonic progression (which was shown earlier in Example 3.8A), sometimes following the harmony closely and sometimes going against it; find specific examples of each.

3. Choose a song (or perhaps just a section of it) and do a timbral analysis of it. This means identifying the instruments that are used, and also describing their specific timbres. What kinds of sounds do you hear from the guitar, drums, keyboards, and/or other instruments? What is the timbral quality of the voice? You may use technical language if you can (e.g., specific guitar effects), but it is also fine to describe the sounds in more subjective terms, using whatever adjectives or metaphors come to mind.

4. Each of these songs features a solo by an instrument that is unusual in a rock context: The Beatles, "Fool on the Hill"; the Mamas & the Papas, "California Dreamin'"; Simon & Garfunkel, "The Boxer"; Crosby, Stills & Nash, "Wasted on the Way." Which instrument is used, and why do you suppose it was chosen? What is its expressive effect? Does the instrument bring to mind specific situations, or other musical styles?

CHAPTER 7
Emotion and Tension

Recently I taught a large music psychology class, and I asked the students at the beginning of the semester what topics most interested them. Many topics were mentioned, but there was a clear favorite: about one-third of the students mentioned *emotion* or something related. This did not surprise me; in my experience, the emotional impact of music is, more than anything else, what makes it valuable and important to people. Emotion is a highly subjective aspect of musical experience; two different people may respond to the same piece quite differently. But there are also strong commonalities, and research in music psychology has revealed much about the ways that specific emotions are musically communicated. Now that we have surveyed the basic building blocks of the rock style, we can begin to consider how these elements are used to achieve emotional effects. And in exploring this, we may gain insight into how specific rock songs—and indeed the rock style as a whole—have such a powerful impact and appeal.

Research on music and emotion typically distinguishes between *felt emotion*, the emotion that a piece makes us feel, and *perceived emotion*, the emotion that we perceive it to express (Evans & Schubert, 2008). (These are also called *emotional induction* and *emotional recognition*, respectively.) The two are related, but they are not the same thing: A melody that seems sad does not necessarily make us feel sad (though it may). Felt emotion is particularly subjective—for example, a piece may make us feel happy or sad simply because we associate it with the situation in which we first heard it; thus it is difficult to study in a general way. (Felt emotion also relates closely to the issue of musical *preference*—the kind of music that we like or enjoy listening to; this, too, obviously varies hugely among listeners.)

Perceived emotion is more consistent across listeners and thus more amenable to scientific study. My main concern in this chapter is with perceived emotion: the musical means that rock uses to convey or express particular emotions. We will also consider musical complexity and the associated idea of *tension*—another important aspect of musical experience.

7.1 THE VALENCE DIMENSION

Much psychological research on emotion has employed a two-dimensional representation known as the *circumplex model* (Russell, 1980; see Example 7.1). One dimension, commonly called *valence*, represents positive versus negative emotions, and the other dimension is something like activity, energy, or arousal (I will refer to it as the *energy* dimension here). Roughly speaking, we can think of this two-dimensional space as having four quadrants (representative emotions of each quadrant are shown in parentheses): +valence +energy (joy, excitement), +valence −energy (calmness), −valence +energy (fear, anger), −valence −energy (sadness). While the

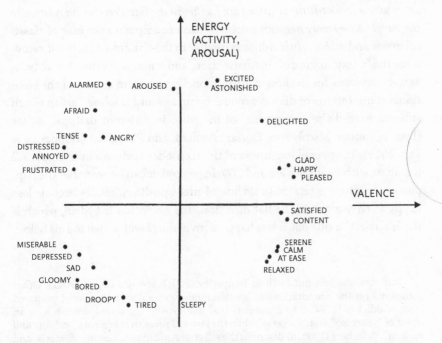

Example 7.1. A two-dimensional representation of emotions (axis labels added by the current author). From J. Russell (1980), "A circumplex model of affect," *Journal of Personality and Social Psychology*, 39, 1168. Published by the American Psychological Association; reprinted with permission.

circumplex model is not universally accepted, I find it to be an extremely powerful tool for the exploration of emotion in music. In this section we will focus on the valence dimension; we turn to the energy dimension in the following section.

In common-practice music, it has been found that the primary determinant of the valence dimension is mode, in the common-practice sense of the term: major or minor (Gabrielsson & Lindström, 2001). Even young children are sensitive to these connotations—for example, pointing to a happy face when they hear a major melody and a sad face when they hear a minor one (Kastner & Crowder, 1990). I would submit that the valence dimension is expressed in a similar way in rock, though with an important difference. As we saw in chapters 2 and 3, there is something analogous to the major/minor distinction in rock, but a great deal of rock music blurs the distinction between the two—for example, combining ♭$\hat{3}$ in the melody with $\hat{3}$ in the accompaniment, or combining the major tonic triad with "flat-side" harmonies. I suggested earlier (sections 2.2 and 3.3) that we think of pitch organization in rock songs in terms of the more general "line-of-fifths" axis, representing each song by its mean position on the line, so that songs may be flat-side or sharp-side to varying degrees. Given this model, I submit that *songs whose line-of-fifths positions are further in the flat direction (in relation to the tonic) convey more negative emotion.*[1] This encompasses the case of classical major and minor, since minor is further in the flat direction, but it recognizes the "fuzzy" nature of this distinction, and it makes further distinctions as well. Evidence for the line-of-fifths model comes from a study of the emotional connotations of diatonic modes by myself and Daphne Tan, in which subjects judged the "happiness" of melodies in different diatonic modes (Lydian, Ionian, Mixolydian, Dorian, Aeolian, and Phrygian) (Temperley & Tan, 2013). The overall happiness of the six modes is shown in Example 7.2 (compare with Examples 2.3 and 2.7). In general, it can be seen that the happiness of a mode is related to its line-of-fifths position: modes become less happy as they move in the flat direction. The exception is Lydian, which is the "sharpest" mode but is less happy than major; I will return to this below.

---

1. This idea was first put forth in Temperley (2001); see also Moore (2012). Other comments on the connotations of specific modes generally fit the model proposed here. Middleton (1972, 166) comments that modes with the raised seventh have an effect of "yearning" and "progress" while the lowered seventh represents "stability and realism"; Björnberg (1985, 4) describes the effect of Aeolian mode as one of "stasis" and "coldness"; Moore (1995, 188) writes that Aeolian implies "resignation," while Dorian "at least carries the illusory possibility of escape"; Covach (1997, 18) suggests that the effect of Dorian mode in Yes's "Close to the Edge" is "primitive" and "chaotic," in contrast to the "refined" and "life-affirming" effect of major mode.

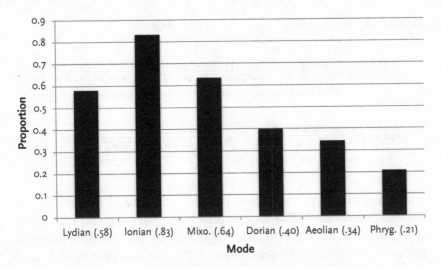

Example 7.2. The "happiness" of diatonic modes (from Temperley & Tan, 2013). Numbers represent the proportion of trials in which one mode of a pair was judged as happier.

The line-of-fifths position of a song is a crucial part of its expressive meaning. Consider two songs discussed in chapter 2, "Satisfaction" and "She Loves You," represented with their line-of-fifths positions in Example 2.13.[2] The emotional contrast between the two songs is clear, even without considering their lyrics: the mood of "She Loves You" is thoroughly positive, while "Satisfaction" projects a darker feeling. The effect of line-of-fifths position is especially apparent in cases where the lyrics are emotionally neutral or ambiguous. Consider the opening of Michael Jackson's "Billie Jean" (Example 4.6). The first line of the song—"She was more like a beauty queen from a movie scene"—could go either way expressively; based on this lyric alone, the song might well turn out to be a happy love story. But the flat-side orientation of the verse—reflected not only in the melody but also in the Dorian accompaniment pattern that begins the song—tells us that something more ominous is in the works. The line of fifths is also useful in describing shifts of mood within a song, as I will discuss at several points later in the book.

In this context, it is interesting to consider heavy metal. Unlike other genres of rock, heavy metal (especially since the 1980s) makes frequent use of the ♭2̂ and ♭5̂ degrees. Example 7.3, Metallica's "King Nothing," shows

2. In chapter 2, we defined the line-of-fifths position of a song as the mean position of its melodic pitches on the line. One could also use the pitches extracted from a song's harmonic progression for this; alternatively, one could devise a measure that combined melodic and harmonic pitches. I will not explore these possibilities further here.

Example 7.3. Metallica, "King Nothing" (end of chorus)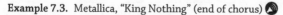

a case in point: ♭2̂ is emphasized both melodically and harmonically in the fourth measure, and ♭5̂ appears prominently in the guitar riff. Walser (1993) and Biamonte (2010) have suggested that this practice represents use of the Phrygian and Locrian modes. This would imply that ♭2̂ is used instead of 2̂, and ♭5̂ instead of 5̂; while this may sometimes occur, many metal songs use both versions of these degrees. In either case, the use of ♭2̂ and ♭5̂ pulls these songs strongly in the flat direction; we would expect the line-of-fifths position of such songs to be further to the flat side than a Dorian or Aeolian song, for example. The line-of-fifths model predicts that such songs will tend to convey very negative emotions, and I would say this is generally true. Certainly the lyrics of heavy metal tend to be very negatively charged, often dealing with topics such as violence, alienation, and death. In the lyrics of "King Nothing," the negative connotations are readily apparent—both in the subject of the song, a delusional narcissist whose life is a pathetic sham, and in the mocking, pitiless tone of the narrator. Thus, the line-of-fifths theory predicts the extremely negative emotional connotations of heavy metal in a way that a simple major/minor dichotomy does not.

Some may raise objections to the line-of-fifths model of musical emotion. What about all the sad songs in major mode—the Beatles' "Yesterday," for example? And what about disco, much of which is in Dorian mode: does this music really convey the "moderately negative" emotional tone that the line-of-fifths model would predict? It is possible that, in certain stylistic contexts, the usual line-of-fifths connotations of scales simply are not operative. But even here, perhaps we should not give up on the line-of-fifths model so easily. In a song like "Yesterday," I feel that the major mode of the song *does* have a positive emotional connotation: it suggests a stoic, reflective attitude in the singer—"smiling through the tears," one might say—that makes the song even more touching. (If the song were in minor, it might seem that the singer was feeling *too* sorry for himself.) As for disco: It is true that much of this music is about nothing more than persuading you to get up and dance, a message that would seem to have few negative undertones. But even in this situation there is an element of risk, of mild danger—perhaps just the danger of being embarrassed, or of doing something that one will regret. If there was no risk, no persuasion would be necessary! In a flat-side disco song like Chic's "Le Freak," the music brings out on the risky side of the situation (which is perhaps appealing in itself), while a major-mode disco song like Van McCoy's "The Hustle" or DeBarge's "Rhythm of the Night" focuses on the innocent upside.

7.2 THE ENERGY DIMENSION

The valence dimension of emotion—the distinction between positive and negative—is certainly crucial to musical expression. But this is only part of the story of musical emotion. This becomes clear when we consider the huge contrast between emotions that are similar in valence: joy versus serenity, or anger versus gloom. To capture these distinctions, we turn to the second component of Russell's theory: the energy dimension.

Clearly, music is able to portray contrasts in energy in very powerful ways: within a few seconds, we can identify a song as joyful or serene, angry or gloomy. How is this achieved? Many factors come into play here. (The following discussion relies heavily on the survey in Gabrielsson & Lindström, 2001.) Higher melodic register connotes higher energy, as do higher loudness levels and brighter timbres (though brighter timbres can have connotations of negative valence as well). Tempo plays a large role: music with a faster beat conveys higher energy. Also important is rhythmic activity or note density; a higher density of notes can increase the energy level even if the tempo is constant. In the context of rock, this might depend largely on the degree to which the sixteenth-note level is active. Texture has an effect as well; adding instruments into the mix can boost the energy level, both by increasing rhythmic density and by increasing loudness.

These fairly simple factors—tempo, rhythmic density, register, loudness, timbral brightness—go a long way to explaining contrasts in energy level that we perceive in rock. For one thing, they relate to distinctions in style. When we speak of "hard rock" versus "soft rock," I suggest that this distinction largely relates to the energy dimension: hard rock tends to be louder, higher in melodic register (at least in relation to the singer's natural register—hard rock singers often sing near the top of their range), faster in tempo, and brighter in timbre; it also uses noisier and more sustained timbres, which conveys more energy as well. Consider a pair of songs by the same artist, Elton John's "Your Song" and his "Saturday Night's Alright for Fighting"; it is largely the differences in tempo, melodic register, loudness, and timbre that makes the former seem "soft" and the latter "hard." There are other components to this distinction as well (e.g., different harmonic practices, as discussed in chapter 3), but differences in energy level certainly play a major role.

The energy dimension also helps us to capture expressive shifts *within* songs. Consider Led Zeppelin's "Stairway to Heaven." The song falls into three contrasting sections, creating a trajectory of energy from low to medium to high. The first section, featuring mainly acoustic guitar and a single vocal, has a slow tempo, a relatively low-register melody, and almost no sixteenth-note motion. In the second section (starting around 4:15), the drums enter, the tempo increases slightly, and the rate of rhythmic activity also increases, with significant sixteenth-note activity in both the guitar and the bass. In the third section (around 5:50), the tempo increases substantially, the vocal moves to a higher register (and is doubled), and sixteenth-note patterns become pervasive in both the melody and the instruments (we even hear triplet sixteenths in the guitar solo). One also detects a significant increase in loudness across the song—partly in the literal loudness of the recording, but more importantly in what might be called its *implied* loudness. We can tell that Robert Plant is singing much louder in the third section, and John Bonham is hitting the drums harder, even if the actual loudness has not changed much. "Stairway to Heaven" is a rather unique case; there are also more conventional ways that rock songs express trajectories of energy, as we will discuss in chapter 8.

7.3 COMPLEXITY AND TENSION

Another important factor in the experience of music is complexity. You have probably noticed this: some music seems so complex as to be almost overwhelming, requiring great mental effort and attention, while other music might seem so simple as to be boring. Musical complexity can involve a variety of factors (Heyduk, 1975; Conley, 1981), but to a large extent, these can be reduced to two. First, a piece will seem more complex if it has more rhythmic activity—more events per unit time (notes or any other kind of events, e.g., percussion sounds). Second, a piece will seem more complex if the events are unpredictable in some way. It has been found, for example, that larger melodic intervals seem more complex than smaller ones (Maher & Berlyne, 1982); this can be attributed to predictability, since large intervals are relatively rare. It follows from this that a piece with a lot of repetition will seem simpler, since the repetition in itself makes things more predictable. Conley (1981) found that both harmonic and rhythmic variety contributed to complexity. Both predictability and event density connect with the mathematical concept of *information*. If a message (of any kind—linguistic, musical, or other) contains a lot of events, it conveys a lot of information, and the information it conveys is higher if the events are surprising or unexpected.[3]

How does complexity relate to rock? Most obviously, a piece will seem more complex if it has a higher level of rhythmic activity—a higher density of events. With regard to predictability, complexity is caused by events or patterns that go outside the norms of the style. Since much of this book so far has been concerned with identifying the norms of the rock style, we are now in a good position to consider what kinds of things would violate these norms. In terms of harmony, notes that go outside the supermode— $\flat\hat{2}$ and $\sharp\hat{4}$—could be considered to increase complexity. Given the very high frequency of tonic harmony, any phrase not containing any tonic harmony (or avoiding it on hyperdownbeats, where it is especially common) could also be mildly complex. With regard to meter and grouping, any deviation from the strong norm of duple (two-measure and four-measure) hypermeter, and the regular grouping structures that are usually aligned with it, is likely to increase complexity. Norms can also be established within a single song—what are sometimes called "intra-opus" norms—and violation of these norms, too, will cause complexity. A scale collection established within a song could be considered a kind of intra-opus norm, and notes and chords that go outside that collection might increase complexity: for example, a flat-side chord in a major-mode context. And songs with little repetition—with a constant flow of new rhythmic, harmonic, and melodic material—will tend to seem complex as well.

With regard to rhythmic complexity, another important factor is syncopation. It was noted earlier that syncopated events, while common in rock, are somewhat less common than unsyncopated ones, so syncopations in themselves contribute a mild degree of complexity; and some kinds of syncopations, especially simple anticipatory ones, are more normative than others. Studies by Heyduk (1975) and Povel and Essens (1985) found that more syncopated patterns were judged as more complex (though the stylistic context and listeners' expectations matter greatly here; syncopations are

---

3. Information, in turn, relates to probability: events that are low in probability are high in information. Information and probability provide a rigorous mathematical framework for modeling the phenomena of complexity and tension that I discuss here (see Temperley, 2007b), but this level of rigor is not necessary for present purposes.

much less common in classical music than in rock). Returning to "Stairway to Heaven," there is a feeling of increasing rhythmic complexity from one section to the next, and this is due not only to the increased rhythmic density (already mentioned) but also to the use of syncopation. The first section has conventional syncopations in the vocal, but very little in the accompaniment; in the second section, the accompaniment too becomes syncopated; and the third section introduces complex cross-rhythms in the drums and other instruments.

A difficult issue is the relationship of complexity to emotion. Consider the factor of rhythmic density: while this contributes to complexity, I noted earlier that it is a factor in emotional connotations as well, contributing to the "energy" dimension. Rhythmic variety, which affects complexity, can also be a factor in energy level: varied rhythms can seem "angry" or "joyful"—emotions that are high in energy (Gabrielsson & Lindström, 2001). I would argue, however, that complexity is not merely a matter of emotion. Some aspects of the energy dimension, such as pitch register and loudness, seem quite unrelated to complexity. And there is an experiential aspect of complexity that does not seem adequately described simply as an increase in energy level. Complexity may have some effect on energy level—the increase in syncopation in "Stairway to Heaven" probably contributes to the increase in energy—but its primary effect, I believe, is not an emotional one. This will be important in later chapters, since we will see that complexity in rock is sometimes manipulated independently of energy level.

A concept that I find useful here is *tension*—something that has been studied extensively in music psychology. Perceived tension has been found to be affected by complexity; for example, chromatic notes or chords, which presumably add to complexity, also create tension (Bigand & Parncutt, 1999; Lerdahl & Krumhansl, 2007). Some have explained tension in terms of the two-dimensional circumplex model, as a high-energy, somewhat negatively valenced emotion (it is shown that way on Russell's diagram); other studies have treated it as a separate dimension (Ilie & Thompson, 2006; Keller & Schubert, 2011). I prefer to think of tension as the experiential aspect of complexity, and therefore as distinct from emotion.[4] It seems intuitive to me, and I hope to the reader also, that unexpected events such as chromatic chords and irregular phrases cause an increase in tension. This may be related to the fact that unexpected things are generally more difficult to

4. Tension in music is a complex and controversial topic; other scholars have approached it in quite different ways. See Margulis (2005), Huron (2006), and Farbood (2012).

process, thus requiring more cognitive effort—a well-known phenomenon in language processing (Levy, 2008).

Also of interest here is a line of research begun by Berlyne (1971). Berlyne posited that aesthetic pleasure—not just in music but in the other arts is well—is maximized when complexity is at a moderate level. When music is very simple, it becomes overly predictable and boring; when it is very complex, it becomes overwhelming and incomprehensible. A number of studies have tested Berlyne's theory, with generally (but not entirely) positive results (Vitz, 1964; Heyduk, 1975; North & Hargreaves, 1995; Witek et al., 2014). Berlyne's theory complicates the relationship between complexity and emotion still further, since it suggests that a moderate degree of complexity results in the most positive emotional response—though here, perhaps, we are talking about *felt* emotion more than *perceived* emotion. I think there is a lot of truth to Berlyne's theory, though the subjectivity of musical preference should be borne in mind. Certainly, I have often heard listeners complain about a piece of music being too complex to be enjoyable—or too simple and repetitive. For most listeners, I think, a song needs to have *some* degree of complexity, though that complexity may sometimes reside in very subtle aspects of the song. In Tom Petty's "Free Fallin'," as noted earlier (section 4.3), the rather commonplace harmonic progression contains an unusual syncopation that keeps it interesting; without this, I suspect, the song would have fallen flat. In other apparently very simple songs (e.g., with highly repetitive harmonic patterns), it may be elements of the rhythmic texture that provide complexity, or subtle nuances of timing and dynamics; think of the guitar pattern in "Le Freak" (Example 6.4A) and the drum pattern in "Funky Drummer" (Example 6.8D). As another application of Berlyne's theory, I suspect that the relatively low happiness of the Lydian mode (compared to major mode) in Temperley and Tan's experiment, discussed in section 7.1 above, is due to the fact that it employs $\hat{\sharp4}$, making it unexpected (and therefore complex) to an undesirable degree.

7.4 GROOVE

These ideas about emotion and complexity shed light on a topic that was mentioned at the beginning of chapter 4: the concept of "beat" (in the colloquial sense) or "groove." In examining this concept, we should first note the very general and deep connection between music and motion. "The most proper response to musical rhythm is to move" (Zbikowski, 2004, 296). It has been found that listening to rhythms activates motor areas of the brain—areas normally involved in the control of movement—even when the listener is not moving at all (Grahn & Brett, 2007). As noted by Margulis (2014), this can give us a sense of being inside the music, even creating the music. And of course much of the music discussed in this book was intended partly—if not primarily—as *dance* music. It seems clear that this music-movement connection is at the heart of "groove," and experimental studies have confirmed this: people feel a stronger sense of groove with music that they can tap to more easily (Janata et al., 2012). Indeed, Madison (2006, 201) defines the experience of groove as "wanting to move some part of the body in relation to some aspect of the sound pattern."

What are the musical factors that give rise to a sense of groove? It seems obvious that a strong and regular metrical structure is required, and rock nearly always offers that; but some rock songs "groove" much more than others. A study by Madison et al. (2011) found that the density of events and salience of the beat were both correlated with groove. The strength of "fast metrical levels" (e.g., sixteenth notes) was weakly correlated as well; as the authors note, this is closely related to event density. Not surprisingly, then, a fairly high energy level is required for music to "groove": if the music conveys energy, this encourages us to expend our own energy by dancing. Notably, in Madison et al.'s study, "microtiming"—small deviations from the metrical grid—was not correlated with groove; this is of interest, since microtiming has been found to be an important factor in groove in other genres, especially jazz (Iyer, 2002).

Of particular interest is a further study by Witek et al. (2014), which examined the effect of syncopation on groove. This study found that an intermediate amount of syncopation—not too much, not too little—was found to be optimal for the experience of groove, and also for pleasure.[5] This fits with Berlyne's theory of "optimal complexity": if we think of syncopation as contributing to complexity, as suggested earlier, Berlyne's theory would predict that a moderate degree of syncopation would be optimal. To my mind, this rings true; the songs that groove most strongly are the ones that lay down the beat clearly, but with enough rhythmic complexity and subtlety to keep us cognitively (and also physically) on our toes. Consider "ABC," a song that I think most would agree has a fairly infectious groove (see Example 4.7). Imagine how much less danceable it would be if the complex syncopations were removed—that is, if everyone were landing on the beat all the

5. Also of interest is a study by Keller and Schubert (2011), which examined the effect of syncopation (displacements of notes in a melody by one eighth note) on perceived tension. They found only a mild effect, but (as they observe) this might be expected, given the frequent occurrence of such patterns in modern popular music; they suggest that more extreme syncopations might have greater effects.

time. On the other hand, if the rhythm were made much more syncopated, then it would become overly complex and confusing; there is also a danger that the beat would simply be lost. It is the delicate balance between clarity and complexity that truly makes the music "move," and makes us want to do so as well.

A connection here could be drawn with our discussion of drumming in section 6.3. I noted there that it is common for drum parts to establish the meter clearly at the beginning of a measure or hypermeasure, but then to subvert it toward the end with kick and snare hits at unexpected places, creating syncopations or cross-rhythms; drum patterns by Neil Peart, John Bonham, and Clyde Stubblefield were used as illustrations. From the current perspective, the subversion of meter at the end of the metrical unit creates a brief tensional increase, which is then resolved by the clear marking of the (hyper)downbeat. This is a small-scale example of a tensional curve, something that will be seen at larger time scales in chapter 9.

Perhaps it will be useful to summarize the ideas in this chapter about musical emotion and complexity (see Example 7.4). I first noted the distinction between felt emotion (the emotion that a piece makes us feel) and perceived emotion (the emotion we perceive in it); my focus here, and in the following chapters, is on perceived emotion. I presented Russell's two-dimensional model of musical emotion, with one dimension representing valence (positive or negative) and the other dimension representing energy. I suggested that valence in rock is conveyed largely by

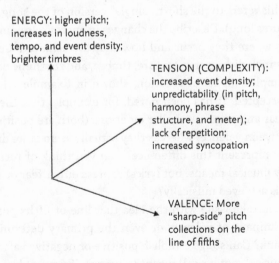

ENERGY: higher pitch; increases in loudness, tempo, and event density; brighter timbres

TENSION (COMPLEXITY): increased event density; unpredictability (in pitch, harmony, phrase structure, and meter); lack of repetition; increased syncopation

VALENCE: More "sharp-side" pitch collections on the line of fifths

Example 7.4. Three dimensions of musical experience, showing the main factors giving rise to "positive" values in each dimension

line-of-fifths position: songs whose scale-degrees are (on balance) further in the flat direction convey more negative emotions. Energy is conveyed by a variety of musical factors including register, dynamics, tempo, and rhythmic density. I then introduced the idea of complexity, which depends on the density of events and also on the level of predictability. Complexity is increased by things that violate our expectations—either general stylistic expectations (this would include notes and chords outside the supermode, and irregular meter and phrases) or expectations established by the piece (notes and chords outside the established scale of the piece, or a lack of repetition). The relationship of complexity to emotion is not simple; complexity may affect both the energy and valence dimensions of emotion (more complex things may seem higher in energy, and a moderate level of complexity may be most enjoyable). But to simplify things, I will say little about the emotional aspect of complexity in what follows, treating complexity as distinct from emotion. I will use *tension* to represent the experiential aspect of complexity: an increase in complexity results in an increase in tension. Of particular interest, in the following chapters, will be the ways that rock songs create trajectories in these three dimensions: valence, energy, and tension.

7.5 QUESTIONS

1. Bonnie Tyler's "Total Eclipse of the Heart" reflects a strong and clear trajectory of energy. Consider the first large section of the song: from 0:00 to 2:18 (this refers to the short, "single" version of the song, a little over four minutes long). Describe the changes in energy, pinpointing specific moments where they occur and how they are achieved. Consider such factors as melodic register, texture, timbre, and rhythmic density.

2. The circumplex model of emotion, shown in Example 7.1, is not universally accepted. It has been noted, for example, that the model represents fear and anger as similar emotions (both are positive in energy and negative in valence) whereas they actually seem quite different. But can music represent this difference? Can you think of rock songs that (by purely musical means, not lyrics) express either fear or anger? If so, how is this achieved musically?

3. Some would take issue with the idea that line-of-fifths position is the sole determinant of valence, or even the primary determinant. What do you think? Can songs establish positive or negative valence by other (purely musical, not lyrical) means? Give specific examples.

4. Analyze a song that you think has a particularly satisfying groove, and discuss the means by which this is achieved. This may require careful and detailed transcription of the drums (or electronic percussion) and other instruments. Are particular parts of the texture especially crucial for the effect? Is the idea of an optimal level of complexity relevant here?

CHAPTER 8
Form

At first thought, the topic of form in rock music may seem fairly simple. There are verses (with different lyrics on each occurrence) and choruses (with the same lyrics); there are bridges, instrumentals, intros, and outros. As a one-sentence summary of the topic, this is in fact fairly accurate. But closer study shows that form in rock is more complex and subtle than it first appears. While many rock songs divide cleanly and unambiguously into the section types described above, many others do not. Consider two iconic songs that we have already considered several times, the Beatles' "She Loves You" and the Rolling Stones' "Satisfaction." In "Satisfaction," the first section of the song ("I can't get no / satisfaction") features repeated lyrics on each occasion, while in the second section ("When I'm driving in my car") the lyrics change; but the second section is in some respects more "chorus-like" than the first. In "She Loves You," there are two possible candidates for the chorus, though one ultimately proves more convincing than the other. (We will return to both of these songs later in the chapter.) This kind of play with the conventions of form—as with other dimensions discussed in earlier chapters—is partly what makes a song interesting and memorable.

To understand how songs play with formal conventions, we must first understand the conventions themselves. In this chapter, we explore the types of sections that occur in rock songs and the ways they are typically arranged. In so doing, we will consider a large number of examples. It should be noted that formal analysis—the identification of the form of a piece—is one of the more subjective aspects of rock analysis. It involves both dividing a song into sections and labeling each section with regard to its formal category. My overall perspective on this topic is largely in accord with those of other authors, such as Covach (2005), Everett (2009), and de Clercq (2012); indeed, I build heavily on these authors' ideas. But I also depart from them in certain ways, introducing some novel concepts and approaches to certain aspects of rock form.

8.1 BASIC FORMAL TYPES

The formal conventions of rock have evolved somewhat over the decades, especially in the early years of the style. A brief survey of these changes will be useful and will allow us to introduce some important distinctions between formal types in rock.

The songs in Example 8.1 represent three different formal patterns, each one characteristic of a different period in rock history. Example 8.1A consists of repetitions of a fairly short section, just eight measures, or about 20 seconds long. While the first part of the section has different lyrics on each occurrence, the final part has the same lyrics each time; this final part is sometimes called a "refrain."[1] The entire repeating section is often called a verse; as shown in the example, I apply the term "verse" only to the part of the section before the refrain, for reasons that I explain below. The section is repeated six times; the fifth occurrence is a guitar solo, over the same chord changes as the other sections. This general formal pattern is highly characteristic of the late 1950s: many of the famous early rock & roll songs use it, such as Bill Haley & His Comets' "Rock Around the Clock," Little Richard's "Long Tall Sally," and Carl Perkins's "Blue Suede Shoes" (which was also a hit for Elvis Presley). The number of occurrences of the repeating section may vary, as well as the number of instrumental sections (the three songs just mentioned each have two instrumental sections).[2] Many of the songs in this category are blues-based, using the 12-bar blues progression or a variant of it (more on this in section 8.2). Some songs in the "folk rock" genre of

---

1. The term "refrain" is sometimes used more broadly, to refer to any line of text that is repeated in multiple sections. This can occur in a variety of ways in rock; for example, in John Lennon's "Imagine" and AC/DC's "Back in Black," the title phrase occurs at the beginning of each verse. To avoid confusion, I will use "refrain" only to refer to a short passage with unchanging text at the end of the main repeating section of a song.

2. In some songs of this type, a single set of lyrics may occur in multiple instances of the repeating section; in "Heartbreak Hotel," the second and final sections have the same lyrics. In Elvis Presley's "Hound Dog," one set of lyrics ("You ain't nothing but a hound dog") repeats three times, and could be regarded as a chorus; and there is just one other set of lyrics which also repeats three times. Cases such as this create a gray area between this formal type and verse-chorus form, discussed below.

Example 8.1A. Elvis Presley, "Heartbreak Hotel"

Verse	Refrain	V	R	V	R	V	R	V$_{inst}$	R	V	R
Since my baby left me ... I I I I	You make me so lonely ... IV I I V I I I	And although it's always crowded ...		Now the bellhop's tears keep flowin' ...		Well now if your baby leaves you ...		(Guitar solo)		And although it's always crowded ...	

Example 8.1B. The Beatles, "I Want to Hold Your Hand"

Verse	Refrain	V	R	Bridge	V	R	Br	V	R
Oh yeah I'll tell you something ... I I V I vi I iii I I I V I vi I iii I	I want to hold your hand ... IV V II vi I IV V III I	So please say to me ...		And when I touch you ... C: ii I V II I vi I ii I V II I	Yeah you've got that something ... G: V I I I I			Yeah you've got that something ...	

Example 8.1C. The Rolling Stones, "Honky Tonk Women"

Verse	Chorus	V	C	V$_{inst}$	C	C
I met a gin-soaked barroom queen in Memphis ... I I I IV I I I I V/V I V I I I I I IV I I I I V I I I I	It's the honky tonk women ... I I V II I I	I laid a divorcee in New York City ...		(same harmonies as verse)		

the mid-1960s also have this form, such as Simon & Garfunkel's "The Sounds of Silence."

Example 8.1B is somewhat similar to Example 8.1A. We have a short repeating section that comprises most of the song (in this case it is 12 measures long rather than eight); the section concludes with a four-measure refrain. The difference is that there is also a contrasting section, a *bridge*; the bridge occurs twice, after the second occurrence of the main section and after the third. The main section is strongly grounded in the tonic key, beginning and ending on tonic harmony; by contrast, the bridge emphasizes other harmonies, and the first part of it even tonicizes another key (the subdominant). This form emerged in the late 1950s and became common in the early 1960s. We see it in songs such as the Everly Brothers' "All I Have to Do Is Dream," the Miracles' "Shop Around," and the Dave Clark Five's "Glad All Over." This formal structure, too, has variants; there may be two iterations of the main section after the first bridge, and one of them may be an instrumental (as in the Beatles' "I Saw Her Standing There"). This form is rarely seen after the mid-1960s. When it does occur in later years, it is often in a nostalgic context that seems to deliberately evoke the early years of rock—either explicitly in the lyrics (e.g., Billy Joel's "It's Still Rock and Roll to Me") or implicitly, by employing other features of early rock such as the blues progression (e.g., the Electric Light Orchestra's "Don't Bring Me Down").

In Example 8.1C, we see something new: an alternation between a verse, with different lyrics on each occurrence, and a chorus, which always has the same lyrics. Unlike the refrains seen above, the chorus is a sizable section in its own right, and is also strongly differentiated from the verse by a number of musical parameters—melodic, harmonic, rhythmic, and textural. (The differences between verses and choruses will be discussed further in section 8.3.) Nearly all songs following this verse-chorus pattern begin with two iterations of the verse-chorus pair. After that, there is usually (though not always) an instrumental (as in Example 8.1C), a contrasting bridge section, or both; this is then followed by either a third verse-chorus pair, or just a chorus. (The song may then end with an additional chorus, as in Example 8.1C, or in other ways to be discussed below.) Since the mid-sixties, this general formal plan has been the norm for rock; indeed, it is reflected in most of the songs discussed in this book.

Covach (2005) offers a useful taxonomy for labeling these forms (many of the examples mentioned above are taken from his discussion). Those like Example 8.1A are "simple verse" forms. (Covach regards the refrain as part of the verse.) Songs like Example 8.1B are labeled as "AABA" form, with the As representing the verse-refrain sections and B representing the bridge. Here Covach draws a connection with early-twentieth century American popular music—Tin Pan Alley and jazz—in which a structure of AABA was normative, usually with each section occupying eight measures. (The earlier AABA form also resembles the rock form in that the bridge usually serves as some kind of tonal departure.) Finally, songs with a verse-chorus alternation are labeled as verse-chorus forms. A song with an instrumental that follows the chord changes of the verse or chorus (like Example 8.1C) is still considered verse-chorus form; however, if a song has a bridge as well as a verse-chorus alternation, it is a "compound" form.

There is much to recommend Covach's system. Especially useful is the basic distinction between simple-verse, AABA, and verse-chorus forms; I will adopt this framework in the remainder of the book. However, more needs to be said about the connections between the three formal types. Consider the following:

1. All three formal types—simple-verse, AABA, and verse-chorus—feature a repeating section that comprises most (or all) of the song. In all three forms, the repeating section normally consists of a first part with different text on each occurrence and a second part with unchanging lyrics (the refrain or the chorus). It is for this reason that I define the "verse"

in simple-verse and AABA forms as the part of the A *before* the refrain, analogous to the verse in a verse-chorus pair. This is somewhat unconventional, but I believe it is justified. Given the strong parallel between refrains and choruses, it is confusing to define the verse as including the former but not the latter.

2. All three formal types normally begin (after the introduction) with two iterations of the main repeating section. The consistency of this rule in rock is quite remarkable; very few songs violate it. One variant that is sometimes seen in verse-chorus forms is that the first verse-chorus pair may have two verses instead of one; John Lennon's "Imagine" and Lynyrd Skynyrd's "Sweet Home Alabama" are examples. Occasionally a song will begin with the chorus, but even then the initial chorus is usually followed by two verse-chorus pairs (this will be discussed further below).

3. In both AABA and verse-chorus forms, the opening two iterations of the repeating section are, in the great majority of cases, followed by something that breaks the pattern. In AABA songs, this is of course reflected in the AABA label itself. Occasionally, one finds verse-chorus forms consisting of nothing but three iterations of the verse and chorus: Elton John's "Candle in the Wind" is one. A few songs consist of just two iterations of the verse-chorus pair (Bonnie Raitt's "I Can't Make You Love Me") or more than three (Bob Dylan's "Like a Rolling Stone"). But much more often, the second chorus is followed by something contrasting: an instrumental, a bridge, or both. After this contrast, the song will almost invariably return to the repeating section—either in its complete form (this occurs in AABA songs and some verse-chorus songs) or perhaps just the chorus, as in Example 8.1C. To put it another way, verse-chorus forms typically reflect some kind of "AABA" as well.[3]

3. A slightly tricky issue here is the handling of instrumental sections that use the harmonic progression of the main repeating section (as they most often do). In verse-chorus forms, I am treating these as contrasting; in AABA songs, on the other hand (which often contain instrumentals), I am treating the bridge as the main contrasting section. We could perhaps think of instrumentals as *weakly* contrasting with the main vocal section, and bridges as *strongly* contrasting. (My notation reflects this: I label instrumentals as *variants* of the main repeating section, e.g., V_{inst}). In a song containing both instrumentals and bridges, the bridges are heard as the *primary* contrast within the song; if there is no bridge, the instrumental serves this function. The fact that instrumentals in verse-chorus forms occur very consistently after the second instance of the main repeating section, which is where bridges occur in AABA forms, suggests to me that they are serving a similar contrastive function. This raises an issue for simple-verse forms: by the current logic, we should think of instrumentals in simple-verse form as serving a kind of contrastive function as well—and thus not so different from AABAs. In simple-verse forms, though, the tendency for the instrumental to occur after *two* instances of the repeating section is much less consistent.

These considerations suggest that AABA and verse-chorus forms (lumping together Covach's "verse-chorus" and "compound" forms in the latter category) could well be viewed as variants of the same form. There are two primary differences. First, in AABA, what I have called the "repeating section" tends to be shorter than in verse-chorus forms, and the two parts of it tend to be less differentiated. Secondly, in AABA forms, the initial AABA is almost always followed by further material, most often another B and A, creating an AABABA structure (or sometimes AABAABA). (Ironically, "AABA" forms are almost never literally AABA, whereas verse-chorus forms usually are!) To summarize: An AABA song is one that has a fairly short repeating section (usually 12 measures or less), usually occurring at least four times, and also includes a bridge; a verse-chorus song has a longer repeating section (usually 16 measures or more) that occurs just three times (or occasionally only two). Simple-verse form, like AABA form, has a short repeating section, usually occurring four times or more; but unlike AABA form, it contains no bridge. This system does not cover all possibilities: some songs are on the borderline between two categories, and others do not fit any of them. But I believe it accounts for the common conventions of rock form reasonably well.

All three of our formal types have what I have called a "repeating section." This concept will prove to be very valuable in later sections and chapters; I will refer it as a "VCU" (verse-chorus unit) in verse-chorus forms and a "VRU" (verse-refrain unit) in AABA and simple-verse forms. It will be noted that the forms with a shorter repeating section (AABA form and simple-verse form) also tend to have more iterations of the repeating section. This is no accident, and it relates to the typical length of a rock song. In the early years, the AM radio format strongly favored songs of about three minutes in length. This became somewhat more flexible after the mid-1960s, but even then the great majority of songs stayed close to that length, usually between two and a half and five minutes.[4] If an AABA song (with, say, a 12-measure repeating section) was nothing but AABA, its duration might be well under two minutes; further material would be needed to bring it up to an acceptable length.

While the criteria I have proposed for distinguishing formal types usually lead to clear-cut decisions, there are occasional borderline cases. Consider the Beatles' "Please Please Me" (Example 8.2). The repeating section is 16 measures—on the cutoff point between a VRU and VCU, slightly favoring the latter—but the two short vocal phrases in the first half of the repeating

---

4. For all songs in the *Rolling Stone* corpus, the average length is 223 seconds (3:43); for songs from 1966 onward, it is 266 seconds (4:26).

Example 8.2. The Beatles, "Please Please Me" 🔊

Verse		Chorus (?)		V	C	Bridge	V	C
(S) Last night I said these words to my girl	*(R)* I know you never even try girl	*(D)* Come on (4x)	*(C)* Please please me oh yeah like I please you					
I I IV I bIII IV V I	I I IV I I	IV I ii I vi I IV I	I I IV V I I IV V I					

section hardly seem adequate for the verse of a VCU. This makes the first 16 measures seem more like a VRU, suggesting AABA form. We do indeed get an AABA; we then expect another B and a final A, as is typical with songs following this model. But the song simply ends, which makes it much more characteristic of verse-chorus form. Rather than quibbling about whether the song is "really" AABA or verse-chorus form, the important thing is to recognize that it shares features with both, and perhaps reflects the transition from the AABA-dominated era to the later period in which verse-chorus form was prevalent.

"Please Please Me" also connects with another formal structure in rock, this one proposed by Everett (2009): the SRDC structure, which stands for "Statement/Restatement/Departure/Conclusion." Typically each of the four segments is four measures (as indicated in Example 8.2). The S and R usually have the same melody and harmony with different lyrics; the D moves away from tonic harmony, and the C has a cadential function. This could be seen as a kind of large sentence structure (grouping the D and the C together as one unit): 4 + 4 + 8. A number of the Beatles' early songs followed this structure, as Everett points out: as well as "Please Please Me," "Ticket to Ride" and "The Night Before" are other examples. The SRDC has connections with both verse-refrain and verse-chorus forms, with the D and C mapping onto the refrain or chorus; as noted by Summach (2011), the D could also be viewed as a prechorus, a category we will return to in section 8.4.

8.2 THE BLUES PROGRESSION

We first encountered the blues progression in chapter 3, where I proposed it as a kind of harmonic schema. Given its length—12 measures—we might expect the blues progression to form a section in and of itself, and indeed it usually does. However, the way this progression maps onto the formal types described in the previous section and the associated section types—verse, chorus, refrain—is rather complex.

Example 8.3A. Big Joe Turner, "Shake, Rattle and Roll"

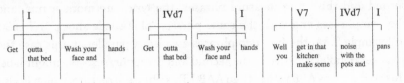

Example 8.3B. Elvis Presley, "Blue Suede Shoes"

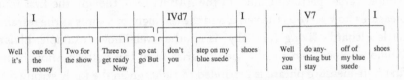

Let us first consider the melodic grouping structure of the blues progression. As observed by de Clercq (2012), two phrase patterns are commonly encountered, shown in Example 8.3. Both of these structures are found in actual blues songs—de Clercq gives examples—and were then carried over into early rock. In Example 8.3A, we find a structure of three four-measure groups. The second group is parallel to the first: it typically repeats the lyric of the first and is often melodically similar or even identical (though the underlying harmony changes). The third is contrasting melodically and lyrically, though it usually rhymes with the first two. We could describe this pattern as AAB. Each four-measure group may break down into smaller groups. The most typical segmentation is shown in Example 8.3A; note that the segmentation is uneven, with a beginning-accented group followed by an end-accented one. In other songs, the four-measure phrases divide evenly into two beginning-accented groups.

This AAB treatment of the blues pattern is used formally in several ways. In Elvis Presley's "Hound Dog," a simple-verse song, the AAB pattern comprises the entire VRU, with the third phrase constituting the refrain. In Big Joe Turner's "Shake, Rattle and Roll," by contrast—a verse-chorus form—one iteration of the entire pattern forms the verse, and another iteration forms the chorus. (Example 8.3A shows the verse. The phrase structures of the verse and chorus are somewhat different, but both of them adhere to the AAB model.) Chuck Berry's "Johnny B. Goode" is similar in this regard. In Berry's "Maybellene," the chorus uses the AAB pattern, while the verse is harmonically contrasting, simply featuring a prolonged tonic harmony.

Example 8.3B is similar to Example 8.3A in that the blues progression is segmented into three four-measure units. Beyond that, however, the two phrase structures are quite different. In this case, the first four measures of the progression support four short, rapid-fire melodic groups. In the second and third four-measure phrases, the lyrics are more sparse, and the two phrases end with the same phrase, "blue suede shoes." Whereas in Example 8.3A, the first two phrases are clearly parallel, in this case the stronger parallel is between the second and third phrases. (We might label this structure as ABB rather than AAB.) This phrase structure, which is also common in late 1950s rock, leads to quite a different formal treatment. Generally, the entire progression forms a VRU, most often repeating in a "simple-verse" pattern. Unlike in the AAB pattern, though, the first four measures now serve as the verse, and the last eight measures as the refrain. Little Richard's "Long Tall Sally" is another well-known example. Elvis's "Jailhouse Rock" can also be seen to arise from this pattern, though the first four-measure phrase is expanded to eight; given the fairly strong differentiation between the first half and the second, this starts to look more like a verse-chorus structure.

As mentioned in chapter 3, many later songs use variants of the blues pattern, most often retaining the first eight measures of the pattern but deviating from it in the last four. In most cases, the first eight measures constitute the verse (sometimes stretched out to sixteen measures), while the harmonically deviating section becomes the chorus (or perhaps the refrain). The Beatles' "Day Tripper," the Rolling Stones' "19th Nervous Breakdown," the Temptations' "The Way You Do the Things You Do," and Cream's "Sunshine of Your Love" all follow this model.[5] One interesting characteristic of both the AAB and ABB versions of the blues progression—when treated as an entire VRU—is that the verse begins on tonic harmony while the refrain begins on non-tonic harmony (either V in the AAB case or IV in the ABB case); this pattern is typical of rock in general, as we will see.

8.3 VERSE AND CHORUS

Try turning the radio dial to a station playing a rock song that is unfamiliar to you. Most likely, it will be playing either a verse or a chorus. I suspect that, after listening for a few seconds, you will be able to guess fairly

5. Michael Jackson's "Billie Jean," discussed earlier, is an interesting case in this regard (see Example 4.6). The verse is 12 measures: the first eight follow the blues pattern in minor form (i–i–i–i–iv–iv–i–i), but mm. 9–12 then repeat mm. 5–8. The phrase structure is reminiscent of the "ABB" blues pattern, with a densely-packed four-measure phrase followed by sparser phrases in the remaining eight measures.

Table 8.1 TYPICAL DIFFERENCES BETWEEN VERSES AND CHORUSES IN ROCK,
AS REFLECTED IN THE THREE SONGS SHOWN IN EXAMPLE 8.4

Features of chorus (compared to verse)	Tracks of My Tears	Hot Stuff	Livin' on a Prayer
Occurs second	X	X	X
Same lyrics on each occurrence	X	X	X
Includes song title	X	X	X
More internal lyric repetition		X	X
Lower syllabic density	X	X	
Thicker instrumental texture	X		X
More backing vocals	X	X	X
Higher melodic pitch	X	X	X
Closer melodic-harmonic coordination	X	X	
Faster harmonic rhythm		X	X
Cadential harmonic gestures	X	X	
More sharp-side pitch collections (in relation to tonic)			X

easily which one it is—verse or chorus. What cues do we use to make such guesses? Earlier I stated that a verse features changing lyrics on each occurrence, while a chorus has unchanging lyrics; while this is generally true, it is not useful in the current guessing game, since we are hearing the section out of context. One might also say that the verse usually occurs first; also true, but again, not useful here. There must be other attributes that signal to us what part of the song we are hearing.

It turns out that there are a large number of musical features that differentiate verses and choruses.[6] Here I build on de Clercq's (2012) exhaustive treatment of this topic, which brings together features stated by previous theorists, other features gleaned from their examples, and still other features not previously suggested. I will focus on 12 differences that seem to me to be especially important, shown in Table 8.1 (de Clercq cites several others). Three songs will help to illustrate these differences (see Example 8.4); in each case I show just the first four measures of the verse and the first four measures of the chorus.

---

6. Obviously our focus here is on verse-chorus form. There is less to say in this regard about verse-refrain forms; as noted earlier, verses and refrains tend not to be strongly differentiated. Refrains do have some of the same characteristics as choruses, though, as I will indicate below.

Example 8.4. Each of these examples shows the first four measures of the verse and first four measures of the chorus.

A. Smokey Robinson and the Miracles, "Tracks of My Tears"

B. Donna Summer, "Hot Stuff"

C. Bon Jovi, "Livin' on a Prayer"

We first consider some features relating to melody and text. In all three of our examples, the chorus contains the title phrase of the song (in "Tracks of My Tears" this occurs later in the chorus); this is certainly typical (though not helpful in our guessing game if we do not know the title). In "Hot Stuff," the title phrase is also repeated *within* each chorus; the same is true in "Livin' on a Prayer," where the title is repeated in the second four-measure phrase (not shown). There are also subtle rhythmic differences between the verse and chorus melodies. De Clercq asserts that choruses tend to have slower rhythms and also "less lyrical content"—essentially, fewer words. The second of these features seems to me to be crucial; more precisely, choruses tend to have fewer *syllables* (per unit time) and thus fewer notes—a lower syllabic density, one might say. This can be caused both by longer notes within groups, and by longer gaps between groups; both of these differences are apparent in "Tracks of My Tears." (In the verse, there is *no* gap between the first two vocal groups, after the word "party.") "Hot Stuff" also shows lower syllabic density in the chorus.[7] All of these features of the chorus—the use of the title phrase, the greater repetition of text within the section, the lower syllabic density—contribute to a general feature of choruses: they tend to be more memorable, the focus of the listener's attention.

Other differences between verses and choruses pertain to texture and instrumentation. In general, choruses have a thicker, more complex texture. In all three of the songs in Example 8.4, the verse features just a solo voice; the chorus adds backing vocals. Thickening of the instrumental texture is also characteristic of choruses: in "Tracks of My Tears," the chorus adds a brass section; in "Livin' on a Prayer," it adds a guitar playing sustained power chords. Related to this, the lead vocal in the chorus tends to be higher in register than in the verse; this is apparent in all three examples. Thinking back to our discussion of musical emotion in chapter 7, all of these changes relate to the energy dimension of emotion.[8] Higher pitch connotes higher energy; adding voices or instruments to the texture increases loudness (or at least *implied* loudness, even if the actual loudness is unchanged), and this also conveys an increase in energy. This also relates to the tendency (though not absolute) for the chorus to come second: a trajectory from low energy to high seems more natural, somehow, than the reverse. Syllabic density is interesting to consider here: presumably the lower syllabic density of choruses—as an aspect of rhythmic activity—tends to *lower* their energy slightly, though this is usually outweighed by other factors. (This is a significant point, and we will return to it.) In this respect, one could say that the "focal" function of choruses is in conflict with their "energetic" function.

7. I calculate syllabic density in an approximate way by counting the number of syllables in each section and dividing by the number of measures (rounding to the nearest whole number of measures). Syllabic density values for "Tracks of My Tears," verse = 4.125, chorus = 3.5; for "Hot Stuff," verse = 4.5, chorus = 3.5. The differences are fairly small but, I think, perceptible. In "Livin' on a Prayer," syllabic density is slightly higher in the chorus: verse = 2.625, chorus = 3.25.

8. Stephan-Robinson (2009) notes the rise in energy level in many choruses. Similarly, Doll (2011) points to a rise in "intensity," referring to this pattern as the "breakout chorus."

A final set of differences, perhaps the most interesting ones, relate to harmony. Many songs feature the same harmonic progressions in the verse and chorus ("Tracks of My Tears" is an example), but many others do not; and even in those that do, the sections may differ in the way melody and harmony interact. Recall from chapter 5 that rock generally features a looser coordination between melody and harmony than common-practice music; we often find unresolved non–chord tones. This seems to be more characteristic of verses than choruses. In "Hot Stuff," the A in the first measure of the verse and the Ds in the third are unresolved non–chord tones; in the chorus excerpt, all notes are either chord tones or resolve by step or to the same pitch (if we allow the Fs in the second and fourth measures as chordal sevenths). In "Tracks of My Tears," too, the melody seems to be outlining the harmony much more clearly in the chorus than in the verse. Another difference between verses and choruses is that the rate of harmonic change is faster in the choruses; this is apparent in "Hot Stuff" and "Livin' on a Prayer." These two differences may be related. When the chords are changing rapidly, the melody must support the harmonies in order for them to be clearly conveyed. But when a harmony is prolonged for a longer span of time in the accompaniment, there is plenty of time for the listener to absorb it; there is thus less pressure on the singer to constantly reinforce it.

Elsewhere (Temperley, 2007a) I have suggested that the thicker instrumental texture, addition of backing vocals, and tighter melodic-harmonic coordination that are typical of choruses all contribute to a sense of *unity* in the ensemble. This contrasts with the greater *individuality* of the verse, which draws more attention to the independent parts (or, one might say, just to the lead singer). I have called this the "loose-verse/tight-chorus" model. The greater unity of the chorus is sometimes reflected lyrically too. We see it for example, in the Beatles' "Come Together," where the title phrase at the beginning of the chorus coincides with the addition of backing vocals and guitar. We see it also in Crosby, Stills, Nash & Young's "Woodstock," which tells the story of a lone traveler who eventually joins a crowd that is "half a million strong"; here too the chorus features backing vocals and closer melodic-harmonic coordination than the verse (see Example 5.13A).[9]

9. It is also notable that pedal points (see section 3.6) tend to occur more often in verses than choruses. Consider the progression of "Jumpin' Jack Flash," shown earlier in Example 3.14A. One could simply ignore the tonic pedal, and treat the guitar chords as defining the harmony, alternating between I and ♭VII. In that case it is clearly an example of "melodic-harmonic divorce," since the melody (which hovers around $\hat{1}$ and $\hat{3}/\flat\hat{3}$) clashes frequently with the ♭VII chords. Alternatively, one could treat the tonic pedal as the underlying harmony; in that case the melody follows the

We can observe two further harmonic differences between verses and choruses. First, the harmonic progressions of choruses often have a cadential quality. As noted earlier (section 3.6), I simply define a cadence as a move to tonic harmony at the end of the chorus. However, we might consider any harmonic progression to be "cadential" in character—even if not actually a cadence—if it moves from non-tonic harmony to tonic under a vocal phrase (especially if the pre-tonic harmony is V or IV, the most characteristic pre-tonic cadential chords). The chorus of "Hot Stuff" features such progressions (in minor form, iv–v–i). Even if the harmonic progression is the same in the verse and chorus, the phrase structure of the chorus may give it a more cadential character. In "Tracks of My Tears," at the end of the chorus (not shown), the grouping structure of the melody places the final word "tears" over tonic harmony, creating a strongly cadential IV–V–I gesture. The harmonic progressions of verses rarely have this cadential quality. Often, verses consist largely of prolonged tonic harmony ("Hot Stuff" and "Livin' on a Prayer" are illustrative); in other cases, they consist of gestures that start on tonic and move to other harmonies. An especially characteristic pattern is where the verse features "tonic-to-non-tonic" gestures and the chorus features the reverse "non-tonic-to-tonic" pattern; this creates a satisfying trajectory of "departure and return."[10] The Beatles' "I Want to Hold Your Hand" is an example of this (though I consider this a "verse-refrain" rather than "verse-chorus" structure):

Verse		Refrain	
(tonic-to-non-tonic gestures)		(non-tonic-to-tonic gestures)	
Oh yeah I . . .	When I . . .	I want to . . .	I want to . . .
I	V	vi	iii	I	V	vi	iii	IV V	I vi	IV V	I	

One might say the "departure-and-return" trajectory is signified rather than actual here, since in reality each section features multiple trajectories. A number of other famous songs feature this pattern: The Beatles' "Ticket to Ride" and "Come Together," the Who's "Won't Get Fooled Again," John Denver's "Rocky Mountain High," R.E.M.'s "Losing My Religion,"

harmony, but the rate of harmonic change is very slow. So either way, this pattern seems characteristic of verses. De Clercq has also suggested (personal communication) that we could speak of "harmonic-bass divorce" in cases like this; perhaps this is another reflection of the greater feeling of "individuality" in verses.

10. This relates to the "open / closed" distinction, discussed by Moore (2001): a "tonic-to-non-tonic" gesture is what he calls an "open" progression. In Moore's usage, however, a closed progression is "tonic-to-tonic" rather than "non-tonic-to-tonic," which is what I posit here; there is no existing name for the latter, as far as I know.

Aerosmith's "Janie's Got a Gun," and Bette Midler's "Wind Beneath My Wings" are examples. In yet other songs, the verse de-emphasizes tonic harmony or avoids it altogether; this occurs, for example, in Prince's "Little Red Corvette" (Example 2.11A) and Michael Jackson's "Human Nature" (Example 2.18). In all of these cases, the chorus gives us the clear motions to tonic that were denied to us in the verse, providing a sense of arrival and resolution.

Finally, with regard to the global pitch organization of the two sections, de Clercq notes a tendency for the chorus to be in Ionian mode; verses, while often Ionian, have a stronger tendency to explore more flat-side scale collections. This usually occurs in one of two ways (illustrated in Example 8.5). In the first scenario, the verse and chorus maintain the same tonic but employ different scales. In the second scenario, the verse and the chorus employ different tonal centers but use the same scale. An especially common situation is when the verse is in Aeolian and the chorus is in the relative-major Ionian (this is the case illustrated in Example 8.5B); this parallels the "minor-to-relative-major" pattern commonly found in classical music. "Livin' on a Prayer" is an example of this (Example 8.4C). We will say more about shifts of scale and tonal center in section 9.5.

It appears, then, that verse and chorus are highly complex cognitive categories, each one characterized by a large number of features. These features seem to correlate strongly with one another—that is, the part of the song that has the title phrase tends to be relatively high in vocal register, relatively thick in texture, and so on—so that, in most cases, the labeling of verse and chorus is relatively clear-cut. However, it is rare to find a verse-chorus pair that reflects all of these features, and in some cases there is enough conflict between them to create real

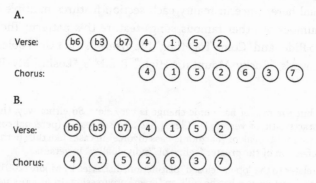

Example 8.5. Two forms of the "Ionian chorus" pattern, shown with scale-degrees on the line of fifths. (A) The verse is Aeolian and the chorus is Ionian with the same tonic. (B) The verse is Aeolian and the chorus is Ionian with a different tonic but the same scale.

ambiguity. Consider "Satisfaction." Certainly there is a large repeating section (heard three times in the song), which breaks roughly into two parts (we'll call it a VCU for now). The second part of the VCU ("I can't get no, I can't get no") is chorus-like in many ways: It has a higher register, thicker instrumental texture, and multiple vocals (at the beginning and end at least)—and of course, the mere fact that it is second makes it chorus-like. The beginning and end of the section also feature the title phrase, or part of it ("I can't get no" is part of the song's title, though in parentheses). On the other hand, the middle part of this section has different lyrics on each occurrence (it also has the highest syllabic density of any part of the song); by contrast, the lyrics in the first half of the VCU are always the same (except for "girl reaction" in the second half of the third occurrence of the section), and also contain the *complete* title phrase. So, which is actually the verse and which is the chorus? To my mind (and this is certainly subjective territory), musical features tend to outweigh lyrical ones, so that the second section feels much more like a chorus than the first.

The tendency for the chorus to come after the verse is certainly strong, but it is not inviolable; in some cases, other features make it fairly clear that the first section is the chorus. Well-known examples include Everly Brothers' "Cathy's Clown," the Byrds' "Mr. Tambourine Man," Chic's "Le Freak," and Guns N' Roses' "Paradise City." After the first chorus, songs of this type typically reflect an alternation of verses and choruses—perhaps with an instrumental or bridge somewhere— just as we would expect in a typical verse-chorus form. One interesting trait appears in a number of these songs, however; the Beach Boys "I Get Around" is illustrative (Example 8.6). The chorus is quite typical in most respects, featuring low syllabic density (in the lead vocal, anyway), backing vocals, and inclusion of the title phrase. But the verse is unusual: in particular, it avoids tonic harmony almost entirely. This is occasionally seen in verse-initial songs as well, as noted earlier, but it is much more characteristic of bridges. Because of this, and because the verse does not begin the song, one might be tempted to call it a bridge (treating the chorus as the main repeating unit of the song). But this analysis

Example 8.6. The Beach Boys, "I Get Around" 🔊

Intro	Chorus	V	C	Instrumental	V	C	Repeat of intro	C
Round round get around...	I get around, town to town...	I'm gettin' bugged...		A: V I I I I I IV I	We always take my car ...			
G: I I V/ii I ii I ♭VII V I	I I I V/ii I ii I I ii I I ♭VII I V I	ii V I (x4) I I I ii V I (x4)		I I I I V I A♭: V/ii				

seems doubtful for several reasons: (a) the lyrics of the second section (the verse or bridge) are different on each occurrence, (b) the first section is unlike a typical repeating unit (VCU or VRU) because its lyrics are the same on every occurrence (it is also chorus-like in other respects, as noted above), and (c) the second section occurs after only one occurrence of the first section, not two, which is most unusual for a bridge. So I would say it is definitely a verse, though it has characteristics of a bridge; following de Clercq (2012), we might say that it has a high degree of "bridge quality." This "blending" of bridge and verse features is also seen in a number of other chorus-initial songs: Buddy Holly and the Crickets' "That'll Be the Day," the Supremes' "You Keep Me Hangin' On," Sly and the Family Stone's "Family Affair," the Bee Gees' "Too Much Heaven," and Mötley Crüe's "Shout at the Devil" are examples. I will return to the significance of this pattern in chapter 9.

We have said little about the *internal* form of verses and choruses. Many verses and choruses simply repeat a simple two- or four-measure chord progression several times. In terms of phrase structure, too, many sections consist entirely of repetitions of a simple grouping pattern, such as those described in section 5.1. But verses and choruses can also be constructed in more complex and irregular ways. In the 16-measure verse of Green Day's "Longview," we find a 4 + 4 + 2 + 2 + 4 pattern in the phrase structure; this could be regarded as a kind of AABA within the verse. In Dobie Gray's "Drift Away" and Matchbox 20's "3AM," the verse consists of three similar phrases followed by a contrasting fourth one—an AAAB structure; in Poison's "Every Rose Has Its Thorn," we find AABC. (In cases where the latter part of the verse seems to constitute a distinct section—more than just a single phrase—we might want to posit a "prechorus," as discussed further below.) Another very common phenomenon is some kind of extension at the end of the verse or chorus. In addition, both verses and choruses often end with a distinctive harmonic gesture—setting up the transition to the chorus at the end of the verse (sometimes with a kind of "half-cadential" effect), or landing strongly on tonic at the end of the chorus. I will say more about these end-of-section strategies in chapter 9.

8.4 OTHER SECTION TYPES

In this section we examine the other basic components of rock form. We focus on the conventions that developed in the mid-sixties—with the rise of verse-chorus form—and remained fairly stable from then on.

Bridge

As we have already noted, songs in either AABA or verse-chorus form typically begin with two iterations of the VRU or VCU, respectively; after that, something else happens. If that "something else" involves vocal material, it is called a bridge. As we would expect, bridge sections usually seem designed to provide contrast with the earlier verse-refrain or verse-chorus material. In particular, bridges often feature a move away from tonic harmony—emphasizing non-tonic harmonies (especially at hypermetrically strong positions), or even tonicizing another key. In earlier (AABA) rock songs, certain harmonic patterns were especially characteristic of bridges, such as IV–I–IV–V (often elaborated with other harmonies): the Five Satins' "In the Still of the Nite" and the Miracles' "Shop Around" are examples. In such songs, also, the bridge is typically short—most often just eight measures—and often occurs twice in the song.

In later (verse-chorus) songs, bridges become decidedly rarer (a more common means of providing contrast is with an instrumental section). Among songs that do have bridges, little can be said by way of generalization. Bridges often de-emphasize tonic harmony, but by no means always; the bridge of the Righteous Brothers' "You've Lost That Lovin' Feeling" does nothing but repeat the progression I–IV–V–IV. The final harmony of the bridge most often seems to be V, as in Otis Redding's "(Sittin' On) The Dock of the Bay" and the Cars' "You Might Think"; in some cases this chord serves a "retransitional" function, reasserting the main key after a move away. (In "You Might Think," for example, the bridge tonicizes vi.) Ending on V is certainly not obligatory, however: in Elton John's "Someone Saved My Life Tonight," the bridge ends on V/V; in Tom Petty and the Heartbreakers' "Refugee" it ends on ♭VII. Bridges in verse-chorus songs most often lead to a third verse or straight to the final chorus; they may also move to an instrumental, as in "Refugee" and Bruce Springsteen's "Born to Run." Endrinal (2011) explores the various tonal and formal functions of bridges; he recommends calling them "interverses," to avoid the "transitional" connotations of the word "bridge."

Prechorus

Many VCUs divide cleanly into just two sections—a verse and a chorus—with no suggestion of further divisions. But other VCUs seem to fall into three distinct parts; in that case, we typically call the second part a prechorus. There are many judgment calls here: How do we decide whether the middle part of the VCU is actually a separate section, as opposed to being part of the verse or the chorus? One factor is simply length: it would seem like a stretch to call something a prechorus if it is less than four measures long. Presumably, also, the middle part has to be contrasting in some way with what precedes and follows; otherwise we would not even be tempted to treat it as a separate section. Here, harmony is often crucial: in particular, in cases where the verse and chorus are centered on tonic harmony (as is usually the case), the prechorus often emphasizes non-tonic harmony. In this respect, the prechorus is similar in function to the bridge, providing a kind of harmonic "departure"—but within the VCU, rather than the song as a whole. Summach (2011) suggests that the prechorus may have grown out of the "departure" segment of the earlier "SRDC" pattern; for example, the third four-measure phrase in Example 8.2 might be regarded as an early prechorus.

Summach notes an additional important consideration in labeling prechoruses, which he calls "completeness." In particular, positing a prechorus implies some degree of completeness in the *previous* section—the verse. Two examples are illustrative. In Madonna's "Like a Virgin" (Example 8.7), one might be tempted to call measures 13–18 a prechorus, but I suggest that they are not. It is true that they introduce some elements of contrast with the previous section—sustained keyboard chords and a more syncopated drumbeat (note the upbeat cymbal crashes before mm. 14 and 16)—and tonic harmony is avoided. But consider the previous section: It is 12 measures long, with three four-measure phrases forming an ABA phrase structure that makes us expect another B; the melody ends (on the word "blue") on a metrically weak point and continues into the next phrase with barely

Example 8.7. Madonna, "Like a Virgin"

any break. Thus there is no sense of completeness at the end of measure 12. A six-measure phrase follows (marked "C" on the example), arriving on a satisfying V chord in measure 17 (perhaps one could call it a half-cadence) as the melody lands on the downbeat with the word "new"—rhyming with the previous three phrases (through/you/blue), which reinforces the connection with them. In this case, then, the middle portion of the VCU is best regarded as part of the verse. (Being six measures in length, the middle portion creates a hypermetrical irregularity at the end of the verse, as is quite common; another example of this was given in section 4.4.) By contrast, consider Green Day's "Longview" (Example 8.8). Here, the first part of the VCU feels much more like a self-sufficient unit: it has a regular 16-measure phrase structure, and the melody ends on the final downbeat (with the word "key"). In this case, then, labeling the following passage as a prechorus seems much more justifiable.

Another characteristic of prechoruses, noted by both de Clercq and Summach, is that they are *transitional* in nature. When we speak of a section being "transitional" in common-practice theory, we usually mean that it takes us from one key to another. Presumably prechoruses are not usually transitional in this sense, since the verse and chorus are most often in the same key. This does happen occasionally, though. In Oasis's "Wonderwall" (Example 8.9), the progression of the prechorus could be seen as forming a

Example 8.8. Green Day, "Longview." The verse and prechorus occur twice before the first chorus; the second verse-prechorus pair is shown here.

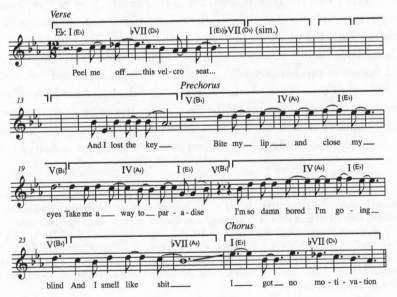

Example 8.9. Oasis, "Wonderwall" 🔊

Prechorus		**Chorus**
And all the roads...	... how	Because maybe ...

```
    D  E  F#m   D  E  F#m    D  E   A    Bsus4        D  F#m  A  F#m
F#: bVI bVII i  bVI bVII i   bVI bVII bIII  IVsus4  |  |
               A: IV  V | I  | IIsus4  |         | IV vi | I  vi |
```

smooth transition from the F# flat-side tonality of the verse to the A major tonality of the chorus—though the strange B chord at the end (with a fourth and no third) casts some doubt on this. The prechorus of Bon Jovi's "Livin' on a Prayer" functions in a similar way (the verse and chorus were shown earlier in Example 8.4C).

More often, prechoruses are transitional in other respects. As noted in the previous section, choruses typically feature a higher level of energy or activity than verses—in terms of vocal register, instrumental texture, and implied loudness. Prechoruses often reflect an intermediate level of energy between the preceding and following sections; in this way, in Summach's words, they serve to "build momentum" going into the chorus. Diana Ross and the Supremes' "Love Child" is an especially clear example (Example 8.10). (In this case, remarkably, the prechorus *begins* the song, followed by a chorus; a complete verse-prechorus-chorus sequence then follows, shown in the example.) Note how the vocal line gradually builds from the register of the verse, centering on E, to that of the chorus, centering on the A above.

Upon further thought, though, the idea of prechoruses as transitional is not so simple. In "Love Child," the syllabic density of the prechorus is higher than that of either the verse or the chorus. (The same is true of "Longview," though not by much.) High syllabic density is a rather typical feature of prechoruses: Michael Jackson's "Billie Jean" and Bon Jovi's "Livin' on a Prayer" are two other songs we have discussed in which syllabic density is higher in the prechorus than either the verse or the chorus.[11] If we think of syllabic density as an aspect of rhythmic activity, it surely is an energy-increasing factor, making prechoruses higher in energy level

---

11. We have also said that syllabic density tends to be higher in verses than in choruses; however, that contrast tends to be less marked in songs with prechoruses. Syllabic density values for the four songs considered in this paragraph (see note 7 of this chapter): "Love Child": V = 6.0, P = 7.5, C = 3.625; "Longview": V = 3.1875, P = 3.5, C = 3.25; "Billie Jean": V = 4.5, P = 6.0, C = 3.25; "Livin' on a Prayer": V = 2.625, P = 5.0, C = 3.25. (In "Longview" I consider just the second verse-prechorus pair preceding the first chorus; in "Billie Jean" I consider just the second of the two verses that precede the first prechorus.)

Example 8.10. Diana Ross and the Supremes, "Love Child"

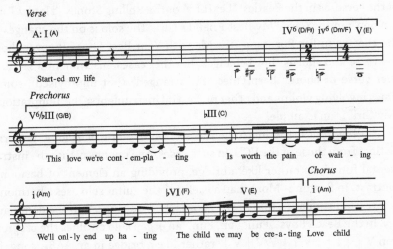

than choruses in this respect—though this is usually outweighed by other factors (vocal register, instrumental texture) that make the chorus more energetic. Here it is useful to invoke the idea of complexity, introduced in section 7.3. I would say the increased syllabic density in prechoruses is best viewed as a strategy to increase *complexity* rather than energy. The idea of prechoruses as harmonic "departures," de-emphasizing tonic harmony—which is observed in both "Longview" and "Love Child"—fits in with this as well. Another characteristic of prechoruses relates to what we might call the "primary grouping level." While melodic grouping is hierarchical, as we have seen, one level of grouping tends to be most salient (due to breaks in the melody and sometimes to patterns of repetition as well), and this level often seems to be faster (shorter) in prechoruses. In "Longview," for example, we move from (mostly) four-measure groups in the verse to two-measure groups in the prechorus; "Billie Jean" is similar in this regard (Example 4.6). This could also perhaps be seen as an increase in complexity; shorter groups seem to suggest a higher level of rhythmic activity, even if the actual note density does not increase. I will say more about prechoruses and complexity in section 9.3.

Solo and instrumental

Following the second VCU in a verse-chorus form, the most common formal move is to an instrumental section. Most often, this is an improvisatory solo; the guitar is the instrument of choice, though sax, harmonica, and keyboards are also seen. In most cases, the solo is on the chord changes of the verse, as in the Beatles' "Let It Be" or the Rolling Stones' "Honky Tonk Women"; in the Cars' "My Best Friend's Girl," the solo is on the changes of the chorus; in Pat Benatar's "Hit Me with Your Best Shot," it covers both the verse and chorus chord changes. In other cases, instrumental sections over verse or chorus harmonies are "arranged" (not improvised), sometimes involving violins and other orchestral instruments: The Temptations' "My Girl" is an example.

In other songs, the instrumental section explores harmonic patterns distinct from those of the VCU. In such cases, one might say that the instrumental functions rather like a bridge, providing an element of harmonic contrast. In Boston's "More than a Feeling," the guitar solo uses a harmonic progression similar to that of the chorus, but transposed to the dominant key. In the Beach Boys' "Fun, Fun, Fun," an organ solo outlines the progression V | | I | | V | | V/V | V |, rather like a bridge in an AABA song. In the Red Hot Chili Peppers' "Give It Away," the strange, backwards-sounding guitar solo occurs over a prolonged dominant harmony, providing contrast with the verses and choruses (which are essentially just tonic harmony).

Intro and link

Nearly every song begins with an instrumental introduction. Very often, the intro simply presents the "main progression" of the song—a progression occurring in multiple sections—if there is one (see section 3.4). If the song contains a riff—a signature instrumental melody or chordal pattern—this often starts the song. Some songs start with just the drum pattern (several examples were given in section 6.3). In many cases, there is a textural buildup in which a single instrument starts the song and others are added, sometimes in several stages. The Beatles' "Day Tripper" opens with the riff heard on guitar alone; the second iteration adds the bass; the third and fourth add tambourine and rhythm guitar; and the fifth adds the drums. Spicer (2004) and Attas (2013) discuss this strategy and offer further examples.

A less widely used but useful term is "link." This refers to a short instrumental interlude between sections. It refers particularly to the passage between the first chorus and the second verse, though it may be applied elsewhere as well. Typically the link uses material from the intro—most often, the main progression or riff of the song. This parallelism creates a kind of cyclic pattern: intro-verse-chorus-link-verse-chorus. (One could actually label the link as a second iteration of the intro, but this would go against the usual understanding of "intro"!) Because of this, the link is perceptually important as the beginning of the second cycle of the pattern; for the first time, the listener is hearing material that they have heard before (and they can now expect to hear repeated material for the next minute or so). It is therefore a point of relaxation for the listener. For this reason, also, it makes sense to think of each VCU as including the preceding instrumental passage—either the intro or the link. Some complexities arise here, though, especially the possibility of overlap between one VCU and the next; we will return to this in section 9.1.

Outro and coda

We can categorize the endings of songs in two basic ways. First of all, do they actually end at a determinate point, or do they fade out? This is surely an important factor in our experience of the song: a determinate ending provides a sense of closure, while a fadeout makes it seem like the song could go on forever. Cutting across this distinction is the question of the material at the very end of the song. A great many songs end with chorus material, in one way or another: the chorus may repeat over a fadeout (the Ronettes' "Be My Baby"); the final phrase of it may repeat over a fadeout (Elvis Presley's "Jailhouse Rock"); or the chorus may bring the song to a determinate end, often with the final phrase repeated one or two extra times (the Beatles' "I Want to Hold Your Hand"). In such cases, there is no need to posit an additional section at the end of the song.

In many other cases, though, songs end with non-chorus material. Most often this happens over a fadeout; such a passage is often called an "outro." Outros can take many forms. The most common kind of outro is a repeated vocal phrase over a simple chord progression. Often, this progression is the main progression of the song, as in Elton John's "Saturday Night's Alright for Fighting" and the Police's "Message in a Bottle." In some cases the outro features quasi-improvisatory material in the vocal, offering the singer an opportunity to show their skills: Marvin Gaye's "I Heard It Through the Grapevine," Aretha Franklin's "Respect," and the Rolling Stones' "Satisfaction" are examples. (In some such cases, the outro could be regarded as a variant of chorus material.) In other cases, the outro is a progression not formerly encountered in the song; the Beatles' "Hey Jude" is perhaps the most famous example, with its I | ♭VII | IV | I | progression repeated many times. Instrumental outros are common, such as the guitar solos at the end of the Eagles' "Hotel California" and Pink Floyd's "Comfortably Numb." Sometimes, an instrumental outro cycles over a progression or riff introduced in the intro and/or link; John Cougar Mellencamp's "Hurts So Good" and Aerosmith's "Walk This Way" are illustrative. (Again, one could sometimes make a case for putting the same label on all three sections.) In such cases, the intro/link/outro material can be an important unifying element of the song.

Occasionally a song ends with material that is not part of the chorus and that actually *ends* (rather than fading out). In classical music, a distinctive section at the end of a piece is called a "coda," and that term seems appropriate here as well. Some codas seem self-consciously classical; the five chords at the end the Who's "Won't Get Fooled Again" bring to mind the end of a Beethoven symphony. A number of Beatles songs have codas, usually bringing back material from earlier in the song; "She Loves You," "Can't Buy Me Love," and "Let It Be" are examples.

8.5 AMBIGUOUS AND UNUSUAL CASES

The identification of form can be one of the most interesting parts of rock analysis. As we have seen, our understanding of rock form categories engages with a variety of musical dimensions: rhythm, harmony, melody, texture, phrase structure. Analyzing the form of a song gets us thinking about all of these dimensions. Often, all of the evidence points to a single analysis. In many cases, though, the cues are in conflict, suggesting two (or more) different interpretations. Such formal ambiguities may arise not only in applying labels to sections, but also in determining what the sections are—what is a section and what is not. We have already considered several kinds of ambiguities that may arise in formal analysis: "chorus or refrain" in section 8.1, "verse or chorus" in section 8.3, "prechorus or not" in section 8.4. While the songs examined above all seem to me to favor one analysis or the other, other songs may leave us truly torn between two interpretations. In other cases, a song may not fall neatly into any conventional form at all. Such cases might make us wonder if there is any extramusical factor—something in the lyrics, perhaps—that might have motivated the unconventional formal treatment. In what follows we consider several examples of ambiguous and exceptional formal structures.

We begin with a song that we have examined several times before, the Beatles' "She Loves You" (Example 8.11). Imagine how we might understand the form of this song on our first hearing of it. After the eight-measure introduction, we hear a 16-measure section that clearly divides into two; the two halves are neutrally labeled A and B. Though the second half goes slightly higher in register than the first, and contains the title phrase, it

Example 8.11. The Beatles, "She Loves You"

Intro	A	B	A	B	C	A	B	C	Coda
She loves you yeah yeah yeah ...	You think you've lost your love ...	She said she loves you...	She said you hurt her so...		She loves you yeah yeah yeah	You know it's up to you ...			Yeah yeah yeah ...
vi I I II I I IV I II I I	i I vi I iii I V I i I vi I iii I V I	I I I vi I I ii°6 I I V I I			vi I I II I I ii°6 I V I II I I				I I I vi I I IV I I I I

is not especially "chorus-like" in other respects; but if we think of it as a refrain, rather than a chorus, we would not expect strong differentiation between the two halves. The AB pair then repeats; on the second iteration, the lyrics of the B section repeat those of the first B. Now it really seems like a refrain; in addition, the mere fact that the song has started with two iterations of a 16-measure section strongly suggests that we are hearing a VRU. Oddly, though, the section ends on V rather than I, which is atypical. The following eight measures (labeled C) then introduce more backing vocals (or at least the added reverb creates that effect), extensive text repetition within the section, and a clear cadential move to I—all hallmarks of a chorus. So far, then, we have ABABC; the song continues with a further AB and then another C, which ends the song (apart from the short coda). This seems to confirm the C section as a chorus; it could hardly be a bridge, since it ends with a strongly cadential gesture and also ends the song. It is significant that "She Loves You" appeared in 1963, a point of transition between the verse-refrain and verse-chorus models; the song seems ambivalent between them, though it ultimately favors the verse-chorus model. Note also how crucial harmony is here: if the B ended on tonic and the C on dominant (imagine swapping the last two measures of the two sections), the song would seem like a rather typical verse-refrain-bridge form, with the ABs as the VRU and the Cs as the bridge (though a final VRU would be needed at the end). An interesting added wrinkle is the "She loves you" (D–E–G) and "Yeah yeah yeah" (G–F♯–E) motives, which appear in various guises in the B section, the C section, the intro, and the coda; but these do not fundamentally change my analysis, as far as I can see. For a more detailed analysis of this complex and fascinating song, see Everett (1999).

In "She Loves You," we have a section that is somewhat chorus-like, presented twice (in alternation with verse-like material), followed by a section that is *really* chorus-like. If the first candidate doesn't quite provide the chorus experience we were looking for, the second one provides full satisfaction. Another twist on this strategy is shown in Example 8.12—Naked Eyes' "Always Something There to Remind Me" (written two decades earlier by Burt Bacharach and Hal Leonard). The verse is unusual in that it begins with an irregular five-measure phrase; this is followed by a repeat which is

Example 8.12. Naked Eyes, "Always Something There to Remind Me" 🔊

Intro	V	C1	V	C1	C2	Instr	V	C1	C2	C1
	I walk along...	Always something...	When shadows fall...		I was born to love you...		If you should find...			(fade)
I I♭VII I vi I V I (2x)	I I I IIV I ii° I 1--7-→♭7--6--♭6 I I I IIV I I 1--7-→♭7--6 IV I I6 I ii7 I 4 ---3 ---2	I IIV II I I 1 ----------- (2x)			iii I vi I IIV I V III I I I	iii I vi I I IV I V I I I♭VII I vi I V I (2x)			

extended by three measures, making an eight-measure unit that nonetheless feels irregular in the context of the first phrase. (Note how the three-measure extension also extends the descending bass line begun by the first phrase.) The next section provides a perfectly respectable chorus, which I have labeled C1; another V–C1 pair follows. At this point we are expecting a bridge, and what we get might be considered one, except for one thing: it reaches a very decisive cadence (which C1 did not). This makes it feel more like a completion of the VCU, rather than a departure from it—like the real chorus of the song (I have labeled it as C2). In some respects, C2 is less chorus-like than C1—note the lower vocal register and the less active percussion—so there is some ambiguity here; for me, though, harmony takes precedence. An instrumental follows, and then another V–C1–C2 sequence. The song then fades out on C1; some might take this as evidence that C1 is the real chorus, but I think it can be understood just as well as an outro.[12] A similar formal structure is found in Paul McCartney and Wings' "My Love." The form of this song could be analyzed as V–C1–V–C1–C2, with the entire structure then repeated. C2 initially seems like a bridge, but cadences strongly in tonic; and in this case, C2 actually ends the song.

A parallel might be drawn here with another unusual formal strategy that has been observed in the rock literature. In some songs, the bulk of the form consists of a fairly conventional verse-chorus or verse-refrain structure, but then a large section of new material is introduced, occurring just once and ending the song (often with a fadeout). The Beatles' "Hey Jude" is one famous example: the final four minutes of the song consist simply of a four-measure melodic phrase repeated over and over. One band that seems

12. In the original recording of the song, sung by Sandie Shaw (a hit in the UK but not in the US), C1 is followed by C2 on every occurrence (except the outro), making clear that the two sections form a two-part chorus. Some might say, then, that Naked Eyes misunderstood the song. I would say, on the contrary, their formal rearrangement of the song adds richness to it—allowing the original formal interpretation, but giving us another way of thinking about it as well.

to specialize in this technique is Journey, in songs such as "Lovin' Touchin' Squeezin'," "Don't Stop Believin'," and "Faithfully." Other songs of this type include the Jackson 5's "I'll Be There" and Chicago's "Beginnings." In each of these cases, the final section of the song is more chorus-like than anything preceding: it features a thicker, more intense texture (usually with backing vocals), and also has more lyric repetition—sometimes just a single syllable ("na" seems to be the favorite for some reason). In some cases, such as "Hey Jude," it also includes the title phrase. Osborn (2013) has examined this formal strategy in depth, focusing on post-2000 progressive rock; he calls it "terminally climactic form." One could simply label the final section of "Hey Jude" (and other examples) as an outro; still, its length and high level of "chorus quality" are noteworthy, making it seem like the energetic peak of the song rather than just a concluding afterthought.[13]

Ambiguities can arise, also, in the analysis of the VCU itself. I mentioned earlier the case where the VCU seems to fall into three sections, in which case we typically call the second part the prechorus. VCUs with even more than three apparent sections can sometimes be found. Def Leppard's "Foolin'" (Example 8.13) begins with a 16-measure section followed by an 8-measure one, both grounded in A Aeolian (the sections are labeled as "A" and "B" in the example). The two sections feel very much like a verse-chorus pair: the second section has a higher vocal register, additional backing vocals, and internal lyric repetition (unusually, the kick-snare alternation also doubles in speed). But what happens next (labeled as "C") calls this analysis into question. A rising bass line supports a rising line in the melody; the harmony hits ♭II twice (B♭ major), which undercuts A as the tonic (note also the unusual first inversion chords). And this leads to another section that is, perhaps, the real chorus ("D" in the example), though the tonal center is D rather than A.[14] The entire large section repeats, making it clear that it is the VCU. The question is how to regard the "B" section: tonally it groups together with "A," but because of its inherent chorus quality, one

13. For Osborn, terminally climactic form requires that the climactic material be new; when the climactic section uses previous material, he suggests calling it "cumulative form," building on the ideas of Spicer (2004). Osborn further argues that in "Don't Stop Believin'," the climactic section "relies largely on recapitulatory material" and that the song is therefore not terminally climactic. Here I disagree; while the climactic section uses the harmonic progression of the verse, the melody is quite new, making it seem like a new section.

14. The end of the chorus—returning to A and overlapping with the second VCU—could be regarded as a very unusual plagal stop cadence (see section 9.2), in which the plagal harmony has been tonicized over the entire previous section. Indeed, one could extend this tonicization back to the "C" section, making the B♭ major chords ♭VI of D rather than ♭II of A.

Example 8.13. Def Leppard, "Foolin'" (first VCU only) 🔊

A	B	C	D	Link
Lady love ...	Is anybody out there...	Oh I just wanna know...	F-F-F-Foolin'...	... a while
A: i│♭VI⁶│ (x8)	i│..♭III♭VII│i│..IV♭III│ i│..♭III♭VII│i │ │ 1-5-♭6-♭7-7-1	♭II│ │♭III│ │ ♭II⁶│ │♭III⁶│ │	D: i│..♭III♭VI│i│..♭III IV│ i│..♭III♭VI│i│..♭III IV│i│ │	A: i│♭VI⁶│

could argue that it groups with "C" and "D" to form a large and complex chorus. Several of Def Leppard's other well-known songs also feature unusually long and complex VCUs, including "Photograph," "Rock of Ages," "Pour Some Sugar on Me," and "Armageddon It."

One of the strongest and most consistent conventions of rock form is that songs tend to start with a section that is presented twice (either a VRU or a VCU)—we might call this the "start-with-two" rule. Any exception to this rule is worth examining closely. The Little River Band's "Lady" is a case in point (Example 8.14). The opening verse begins with eight measures of tonic (an unusual linear motion in the bass descends though ♭$\hat{7}$ to $\hat{6}$ and comes back up again, creating a Mixolydian feel), moving to dominant harmony for four measures (the last of which is missing a beat) and then back to tonic. The following section begins with the same harmonic pattern (I over $\hat{1}$–♭$\hat{7}$–$\hat{6}$–♭$\hat{7}$); we might at first think it is another verse, but the melodic structure is quite different, and it turns out the harmony is different too, forming a blues progression (slightly extended at the end). The Mixolydian bass line is retained under the tonic harmonies of the section, giving it a kind of dreamy quality. Firmly grounded in tonic harmony, and quite self-contained, it is certainly not a prechorus or bridge; it is more like another verse, not a repeat of the first one but an alternative to it (I label it as "V2"). What follows is definitely the chorus, with backing vocals, lower syllabic density, the title phrase, and non-tonic-to-tonic harmonic gestures. So we have a rather unusual, three-part VCU. What is really unusual is that we never get this complete VCU again. The chorus leads into an instrumental based on the harmonies of V2 (the blues progression); then the first part of the VCU, with vocal; then the second chorus, ending the song. So the blues section with vocal occurs only once. This is significant when we consider its lyrics:

A long time ago I had a lady to love
She made me think of things I never thought of
Now she's gone and I'm on my own
A love song has come into my mind
A love song, it was there all the time

Example 8.14. The Little River Band, "Lady" 🔊

V	V2 (?)	C	Instr	V	C	Outro
Look around you...	A long time ago...	So lady...		Look around you...		
I ⎮ ⎮ (x8) 1-♭7-6-♭7 V⎮ ⎮ ⎮ ⎮I⎮ ⎮	I⎮ ⎮ IV ⎮ I ⎮ IV IV⎮ I ⎮ I . IV6 ♭VII⎮I ⎮	IV⎮ I ⎮ IV ⎮ I ⎮ IV⎮ I ⎮ V IV⎮(I)	(harmonies of V2)			I ⎮ 1-♭7-6-♭7 (fade)

We hear of a special time in the past—lost and unrepeatable. (The use of the blues progression adds to its nostalgic effect.) In its internal features, the section resembles a verse, something that is expected to repeat—but it never does. This makes its ephemeral quality all the more poignant. Moments happen, then they're gone and they don't come back: that's what life is *really* like.

Finally, we consider a song that I find particularly remarkable from a formal viewpoint: ABBA's "The Name of the Game" (Example 8.15). The song begins in quite a conventional fashion. The verse, in an F♯ Dorian tonality and based on a repeated four-measure sentence structure (1 + 1 + 2), is followed by a prechorus (higher in register and thicker in texture than the verse, as we would expect, and moving toward the relative major), and then by what seems at first like a rather ordinary chorus (the example begins at this point). The second phrase of the chorus arrives on a hyperdownbeat over tonic harmony (m. 7 of the example). It is at this point that the song goes into completely uncharted territory. The four-measure phrase in measures 7–11 (note the unusual end-accented grouping) weakly tonicizes the dominant key (the V/vi–vi pairs could also be V/ii–ii in the dominant), leading to a V11 chord in measure 11.[15] As noted in section 3.6, V11 is most often used in cadences, usually moving directly to I. The use of the chord here might be described as a *caesura*—a device occasionally seen in classical music in which a phrase or section ends on an unstable dominant harmony (such as V7 or V6/5) followed by a break in the texture.[16] A caesura can create a very special feeling of suspended motion—leaving us hanging in midair as we await the expected tonic harmony. The same is true in this case, but we don't know what to expect beyond that, given the uniqueness of the situation. The following passage does center on tonic harmony, as expected—but what is it? It is not at all like typical chorus material. The melodic range and textural

15. This chord (from the bass up, E–D–A, with some doublings) would more precisely be called a V7sus4; a V11 would have F♯ above the bass. To my mind, though, it is so similar in effect to a V11 that it is justifiable to categorize it as such.

16. Some would define caesura to include *any* textural break after a phrase (with a cadence or without), but I find this more restricted use of the term more useful. An example of a classical caesura is in "Madamina" from Mozart's *Don Giovanni*, m. 29.

Example 8.15. Abba, "The Name of the Game" (chorus)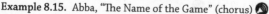

thickness drop greatly; the melody and chord progression present a simple, rather hypnotic sequential pattern, building from $\hat{3}$ up to $\hat{6}$ and then starting at $\hat{3}$ again in measure 16, jumping up to the higher $\hat{1}$, and then tonicizing vi. (This is the second tonicization of vi in the chorus, and remember that this was also the key of the verse.) Again we move to V11 in measure 22, expecting finally a cadential move to I as the title phrase is restated—but now the chord resolves deceptively, tonicizing vi once again and initiating the second VCU. (The end of the second VCU cadences on tonic as expected, and fades out over a repeat of the first part of the chorus.) The return to the title phrase in measure 22 makes it seem as if the entire section is a massive chorus, but it is a chorus with an extraordinarily complex and differentiated internal structure.

Each of the songs that we have analyzed in this section departs from the conventions of rock form in some respect. However, they do so in in fairly mild ways. All of them respect two very basic principles of rock form: first, most of the song is comprised of repetitions of a main repeating section (VCU or VRU); second, if there is a contrasting section, it is followed by a return or at least partial return of the main section (e.g., a chorus).[17] It is not difficult, however, to find rock songs that reject even these principles. Indeed, these include some of the most famous songs in rock, such as the Beach Boys' "Good Vibrations," Crosby, Stills, Nash & Young's "Suite: Judy Blue Eyes," Led Zeppelin's "Stairway to Heaven," and Queen's "Bohemian Rhapsody." In each of these cases, the latter part of the song is comprised of completely new material; there is no repeat of a section heard in the first part (though there are brief references to earlier material at the end of "Stairway" and "Bohemian Rhapsody"). In addition, the contrasts between sections in these songs (in meter, tonality, texture, and thematic material) are much greater than one typically sees in rock. In such songs, it might seem that the norms of rock form are not so much stretched as completely abandoned. I submit, though, that even these songs are not as far removed from rock's formal conventions as they might first appear. In each of these songs except "Stairway," there is a VCU that is presented twice at the beginning of the song, and in some ways these VCUs are quite conventional; note the shift to the relative major in the chorus of "Good Vibrations," and the plagal stop cadence in "Bohemian Rhapsody" (see section 9.2 below). In this way, these songs "touch base" with the conventions of rock form before departing from them. ("Stairway" nods to formal convention in another way, as I will discuss in the next chapter.) There is much more to be said about each of these songs; I leave it to the reader to explore them further. My main point here is that even when a song appears at first to be completely oblivious to rock's formal conventions, closer examination may reveal that it engages with them in subtle and interesting ways.

8.6 QUESTIONS

1. The two versions of "Handy Man" shown in Example 6.1, which we considered with regard to timbre, are also interesting from a formal perspective (this was pointed out to me by Trevor de Clercq). How do the

---

17. Some "terminally climactic" songs might be considered an exception to this, such as "Hey Jude"; but in such cases, as argued earlier, the final section could be regarded simply as an extended outro.

forms of the two versions differ? Could we see this as reflecting a shift from an "AABA" framework to a "verse-chorus" one? (One *harmonic* difference between the two versions is especially important here.)

2. Consider these four songs: Boston's "More Than a Feeling," the Eagles' "New Kid in Town," the Proclaimers' "I'm Gonna Be (500 Miles)," and Bryan Adams's "(Everything I Do) I Do It for You." Each one begins with a traditional formal structure—two VCUs, followed by a contrasting section—but something unusual happens in the third VCU. (In "Everything I Do" there is no third verse, only a chorus.) Discuss. How does this affect the overall shape of the song, tonally/harmonically and also expressively?

3. These songs all contain violations of the "start-with-two" rule: Foreigner, "Feels Like the First Time"; Elvis Costello, "Veronica"; Sheryl Crow, "Soak Up the Sun." Analyze the form of each song. Any thoughts about the reasons (musical or lyrical) why the convention was violated in these particular cases?

4. Some songs are constructed (mostly) from an alternation of two sections (call the first section "A" and the second one "B"), but it is not clear how to analyze them: A and B (respectively) could be verse and chorus, chorus and verse, or VRU and bridge (perhaps among other possibilities). Consider the Turtles' "Happy Together," Jim Croce's "Time in a Bottle," and Supertramp's "Take the Long Way Home." How would you analyze the two sections in each case? Consider all of the characteristic features of verses, choruses, VRUs, and bridges discussed in this chapter, as well as the ways they are typically arranged across the song as a whole.

CHAPTER 9
Strategies

In this chapter, I will examine certain structural patterns that seem to occur in rock with particular frequency. These patterns involve multiple dimensions—melody, harmony, meter, rhythm, phrase structure, and form—and I will refer to them as *strategies*. The term *schema* would also be appropriate; as this term implies, each strategy is defined by a set of features. (Instances of a schema may be more or less typical, sometimes perhaps reflecting some of the features but not all.) I will also attempt to explain, at least to some extent, *why* these strategies are so widely used—what makes them so attractive to rock songwriters and musicians. Explaining the emergence of musical schemata is often difficult; sometimes they may be due simply to historical accident. In part, though, I believe the explanations for these strategies lie in their effects on the listener's experience. I will focus on certain aspects of musical experience in particular: the balance between closure and continuity, trajectories of tension and energy, and emotional connotations of scales and modulations.

9.1 THE VCU BOUNDARY

As noted in section 8.1, nearly every rock song begins with two iterations of the VCU (or VRU, in the case of early rock—though my focus in this section will be on verse-chorus forms). An issue that arises in such songs is how to handle the transition from the first VCU to the second. There are two effects that one might want this transition to achieve: *closure* and *continuity*. At the end of the first VCU, it is desirable to convey a sense of closure and arrival—a sense that a goal has been reached, that the "journey" of the section has been completed. At the same time, it is also desirable to convey a sense of continuity, with one section flowing smoothly into the next—indicating that there is more to come and that it is all part of the same song. To a large extent, closure and continuity are opposite ends of the same spectrum: what enhances closure weakens continuity.[1] So the challenge for the VCU boundary is to find a satisfying middle ground between these goals. In this section, we consider three different strategies for handling the VCU boundary that achieve this purpose in different ways.

Example 9.1 shows passages from three songs. In all three cases, the excerpt shown is the end of the first chorus (the last four-measure phrase) and the beginning of the following verse or link—in other words, the end of the first VCU and the beginning of the second. (Recall that a "link" is a short instrumental passage that occurs between the first chorus and the second verse, and sometimes at other locations as well, most often reusing the introduction material.) In all three examples, the end of the first chorus contains a cadence, by the definition proposed in section 3.6—a move to tonic harmony at the end of the vocal line; this gives them all a sense of tonal closure. In other respects, though, the three cases are quite different.

Consider where the boundary between one VCU and the next falls in each of the three songs. In "Hit Me with Your Best Shot," it seems fairly clear that the second VCU starts right on the beginning of the vocal phrase at the end of the example, "You come on with a come-on." The first chorus ends, presumably, just before that point. The boundary point is further emphasized by a drum fill just before the fifth downbeat and a cymbal crash on the downbeat. In this case, then, there really is no link. (The chorus is built on the same chord progression as the introduction; possibly, then, we could consider the last two measures of the chorus to be a link. But the fact that these measures form the second half of a four-bar hypermeasure groups them more strongly with the chorus. And there is nothing in the accompaniment that marks the third downbeat of the excerpt as a sectional boundary.) Many early (verse-refrain) rock songs show this strategy, with the first refrain leading directly into the second verse; the Beatles' "I Want to Hold Your Hand" is an example.

Example 9.1B is similar to 9.1A in some ways, but also subtly different. The end of the chorus vocal falls on the downbeat of the fourth measure.

1. This could be taken to imply that the balance between closure and continuity is a kind of zero-sum game. This is not a necessary assumption. Closure involves conveying that the VCU is ending; continuity involves conveying that the song as a whole is *not* ending. In theory, it might be possible to enhance one without weakening the other. But this complicates things, so I will keep the "zero-sum game" assumption for now.

Example 9.1. Three strategies for handling the VCU boundary (the end of the first chorus and beginning of the second verse or link)

A. Pat Benatar, "Hit Me with Your Best Shot"

B. John Cougar Mellencamp, "Hurts So Good"

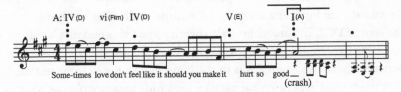

C. Huey Lewis and the News, "The Heart of Rock and Roll"

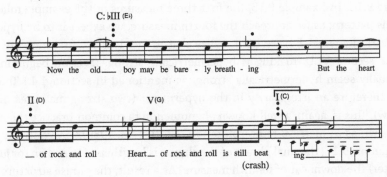

(Clearly, the syllable "good" is an anticipatory syncopation, understood as belonging on the following downbeat.) At this point, the accompaniment returns to the riff from the introduction of the song—and in this case, it is distinctive to the introduction (unlike in Example 9.1A, where the introduction and chorus share the same progression); thus it is clearly understood as a link, beginning the second VCU. Crucially, also, the end of the vocal has a cymbal crash, as one would expect at the beginning of a new section (unlike in Example 9.1A, where no crash occurred at the end of the vocal). So the fourth downbeat is both the end of the first VCU and the beginning of the second. This is what is known as a *grouping overlap*, a well-known phenomenon in common-practice theory (Lerdahl & Jackendoff, 1983).

As noted earlier, the exact location of grouping boundaries can sometimes be difficult to determine, especially with regard to the accompaniment.

Does the second VCU in Example 9.1A begin right at the fifth downbeat, or at the previous eighth-note beat (to include the pickup in the vocal)—or perhaps it includes the pickup beat in the vocal but not in the accompaniment? If the first VCU of Example 9.1B overlaps into the fourth measure, does it contain only the first eighth-note segment of that measure, or the first quarter-note segment, or what? Similar uncertainties about the exact location of section boundaries arise with other examples discussed here. But let us not fuss about such matters; the important point is that the two VCUs overlap in Example 9.1A but not in 9.1B.

Example 9.1C is in some respects similar to Example 9.1B. At the fifth downbeat, the introduction material returns, indicating the beginning of the second VCU. The first chorus also overlaps into this measure, ending the vocal line over tonic harmony, just as in Example 9.1B. The crucial difference between these two examples is in the hypermeter. Recall from section 4.4 that the typical hypermetrical pattern for a four-measure phrase is strong-weak-medium-weak; this is seen in the first four measures of Examples 9.1A and 9.1C. In Example 9.1B, the first three measures of the example follow this pattern; as we approach the fourth measure, we expect it to be hypermetrically weak. But we then realize that in fact it is the first measure of the second VCU, making it hypermetrically strong. (Section beginnings usually seem hypermetrically strong, as mentioned in section 4.4.) There is therefore an irregularity in the hypermeter (two strong measures in a row). This is, again, a well-known phenomenon in common-practice theory, known as a "metrical reinterpretation" (Rothstein, 1989).[2] By contrast, in Example 9.1C, the final phrase of the chorus is lengthened to end on (or just after) the downbeat of its fifth measure. As a result, the phrase structure is irregular, but the hypermeter is not; the five-measure phrase combined with the overlap allows the alternating strong-weak pattern of the hypermeter to continue uninterrupted. We might consider the five-measure phrase an expanded version of an implied four-measure phrase; this view is supported by the fact that the phrase "heart of rock and roll" is repeated. A "recomposition" of the phrase without the expansion is shown in Example 9.2.

Each of these three songs exemplifies a different approach to the handling of the VCU boundary. Each strategy serves in its own way to balance closure and continuity at the end of the first VCU. Example 9.1A is, in a

2. Occasionally, one sees lower-level metrical reinterpretations at sectional boundaries, requiring an actual shift in the bar lines. In the Bobby Fuller Four's "I Fought the Law," the cadential tonic at the end of the chorus occurs on the third beat of the measure, which is then reinterpreted as a downbeat, starting the next VCU. At the end of the chorus in Joan Jett and the Blackhearts' "I Love Rock 'n Roll," beat 4 of the measure is reinterpreted as beat 1, causing an even more radical reinterpretation.

Example 9.2. Recomposition of the VCU boundary of "The Heart of Rock and Roll" 🔊

way, the simplest approach: the first VCU ends and then the second one begins. (The similarity between the chorus progression and the intro provides a subtle element of continuity.) In Example 9.1B, by contrast, the sectional overlap enhances continuity by blurring the formal boundary and helping to bind the two sections together. The overlap also has another effect, however: it makes the cadential tonic hypermetrically strong (in retrospect, anyway). Common-practice theorists have noted that placing a cadential tonic on a hyperdownbeat gives it extra weight and closural force (Schachter, 1980); this is surely true in rock as well. In Example 9.1C, too, the cadential tonic falls on a hyperdownbeat. We can appreciate the effect of this by comparing Example 9.1C to the recomposition in Example 9.2, in which the overlap is removed; in this case, the cadential tonic lands on a weak downbeat, and this makes it seem less emphatic, less forceful. In Example 9.1A, the lack of overlap clarifies the boundary between the VCUs, enhancing closure, but the cadence is hypermetrically weaker (the cadential tonic is strong at the two-measure level but not the four-measure level), giving it less closural force; thus closure and continuity are balanced in another way.

Example 9.3 shows yet one more approach to the VCU boundary (in this case I show the complete eight-measure chorus). This is essentially similar to Example 9.1C: the final four-measure phrase of the chorus is extended to a fifth downbeat, overlapping the second VCU, which brings back the introduction material. But there is an important difference in the accompanying instruments: the bass, drums, and guitar all land on a staccato chord on the fourth downbeat (on "would ya") and then drop out for the rest of the measure, while the vocal continues to overlap into the next measure. This is what I call a "stop," and the cadential gesture as a whole is a "stop cadence" (Temperley, 2011a). As in Example 9.1C, extending the phrase to a fifth measure makes the tonic arrival land on

Example 9.3. Heart, "Barracuda" (chorus)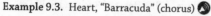

E: ♭VI (C)   i (Em)   ♭VI (C)

You're ly-in' so low in the weeds   I bet you're go-nna am-bush me

i (Em)   ♭VII (D)

You have me   down   down   down____down   on my

IV (A)   i (Em)

knees____   Now   would   ya   Bar-ra-cu-da

a hyperdownbeat. The stop also serves important functions. The momentary loss of harmonic and rhythmic support for the melody creates a kind of tension—a mild surprise—which is then resolved in a satisfying way when the instruments come back in at the following downbeat. But at the same time, I would argue, the stop conveys that a large-scale sectional boundary is taking place (just as a rest within the vocal line typically indicates a boundary between two phrases). As I have suggested, the end of the chorus actually occurs just after the stop, not at the stop itself; but still, the stop might suggest that a large-scale boundary is happening somewhere in the vicinity. In this way, the stop provides an additional cue to sectional closure. The stop also draws our attention to the melody and lyrics at that point, which feature the title phrase of the song (as they typically do in stop cadences).

In the above discussion, I have presented several features that enhance either closure or continuity at the end of the VCU; see Table 9.1. The absence of a feature that favors one side can be taken as a feature on the other side; for example, the absence of a cadence favors continuity. Each of the four examples considered here features some elements of closure and some of continuity. Note that this is not guaranteed. It would be possible, for example, for a VCU to end with a cadence on tonic, followed by a stop (with no overlap in the vocal), followed by the beginning of the second VCU on the next downbeat. In this case, all the cues would favor closure at the expense of continuity. This pattern appears to be practically nonexistent in rock. (David Bowie's "Changes" is perhaps one example.) There are some songs where the chorus ends with a stop and no overlap, but in these cases, the final harmony of the chorus is usually not tonic; AC/DC's "Back in Black"

Table 9.1 FACTORS FAVORING CONTINUITY AND CLOSURE

Closure	Continuity
cadence (especially *hypermetrically strong* cadence)	sectional overlap
stop	similarity between end of chorus and beginning of verse/link

(♭VII—shown in earlier in Example 3.12D), Joe Walsh's "Life's Been Good" (VI), and the Police's "Message in a Bottle" (iv) are examples. In general, then, there seems to be a deliberate effort to strike a balance between continuity and closure.

9.2 THE CADENTIAL IV

In section 3.6, I defined a cadence in rock as a gesture occurring at the end of the VCU (or VRU), in which a move to tonic harmony coincides with the end of the vocal line. I observed also that V and then IV are by far the most common pre-tonic chords in cadences; this is not surprising, since V and IV are the chords that most often precede I in general. It is also not surprising historically, given that V is the usual pre-tonic cadential chord in common-practice music and related styles (e.g., folk, jazz, and Tin Pan Alley), and IV is standard in pre-tonic position in blues cadences (though V is also used). IV–I cadences also occasionally occur in common-practice music, where they are known as "plagal cadences." Our focus in this section is on the cadential use of IV in rock, which is of particular interest.

First let us reconsider Example 9.3. I presented this in the previous section as an example of a stop cadence, in which the vocal line overlaps from the first VCU into the second, with the instruments dropping out just before the second VCU begins, then rejoining the vocal line with tonic harmony. Note that the pre-tonic harmony is IV in this case. Stop cadences with IV in pre-tonic position are extremely common; I call them *plagal stop cadences* (Temperley, 2011a). Table 9.2 shows a list of well-known songs that contain this pattern. It is useful to think of the plagal stop cadence as a kind of schema; the features defining the schema are shown in Example 9.4. Many instances of the schema contain all of these features, but in some cases one or more of the features is missing. For example, one sometimes finds stop cadences with pre-tonic harmonies other than IV. In Survivor's "Eye

Table 9.2 WELL-KNOWN SONGS WITH PLAGAL STOP CADENCES

Title	Artist	Year
Love Me Do	The Beatles	1962
The Way You Do the Things You Do	The Temptations	1964
The Last Time	The Rolling Stones	1965
I Got You (I Feel Good)	James Brown	1965
Back in the USSR	The Beatles	1968
The Weight	The Band	1968
You Can't Always Get What You Want	The Rolling Stones	1969
Tears of a Clown	Smokey Robinson and the Miracles	1970
Bargain	The Who	1971
Won't Get Fooled Again	The Who	1971
Rock and Roll	Led Zeppelin	1971
Rikki Don't Lose That Number	Steely Dan	1974
Golden Years	David Bowie	1975
Magic Man	Heart	1976
Barracuda	Heart	1977
Angel of the Morning	Juice Newton	1981
Everybody Wants You	Billy Squier	1982
Faithfully	Journey	1983
I Want a New Drug	Huey Lewis and the News	1984
(Don't Go Back To) Rockville	R.E.M.	1984
When I Come Around	Green Day	1994
High and Dry	Radiohead	1995
Name	Goo Goo Dolls	1995
Redemption Day	Sheryl Crow	1996
How's It Gonna Be	Third Eye Blind	1997
Blue on Black	Kenny Wayne Shepherd	1997
She's So High	Tal Bachman	1999

Example 9.4. The plagal stop cadence

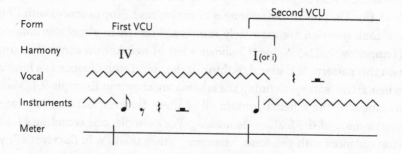

Example 9.5A. Survivor, "Eye of the Tiger" (end of chorus)

Example 9.5B. Elvis Costello, "Chelsea" (end of chorus)

of the Tiger" (Example 9.5A), the pre-tonic harmony is ♭VI; in Whitesnake's "Is This Love" and Metallica's "King Nothing" (Example 7.3), it is ♭II; in Stevie Wonder's "Superstition," it is V; in Queen's "Somebody to Love," it is V11. In another variant of the pattern, the vocal line ends over the stop, with no overlap into the next VCU; this is seen in Elvis Costello's "Chelsea" (Example 9.5B) and Matchbox 20's "3AM" (We will see another instance of this in section 10.5.) Because the vocal line ends over the stop, the chorus as a whole does too (there is no reason to hear it as overlapping into the next measure); thus the effect of this is quite different from that of a typical stop cadence. In yet another variant, the first VCU overlaps into the second with a plagal cadence, but without the stop in the accompaniment; Elton John's "Bennie and the Jets," John Cougar Mellencamp's "Little Pink Houses," and Counting Crows' "Einstein on the Beach" are examples of this.[3]

Example 9.6 offers one more variant on the plagal stop cadence schema. We have all of the essential features: the sectional overlap, the IV–I cadence, and the stop just before the cadential I. But two additional features are unusual. For one thing, the harmonies immediately preceding the cadence could be regarded as a tonicization of ♭III (C), with the ♭VI chord serving

---

3. A few songs in Table 9.1 deserve comment. In the Beatles' "Back in the USSR," the I of the plagal stop cadence is arguably *not* really the beginning of the second VCU; it leads to a IV–♯IV–V "turnaround" which more plausibly marks the VCU boundary. In this case, then, the "sectional overlap" feature of the plagal stop cadence is missing. James Brown's "I Got You (I Feel Good)" is similar in this regard. Another borderline case is the Rolling Stones' "The Last Time"; in this case, the stop is present only in the third chorus, not in the first and second. "I Got You" and Led Zeppelin's "Rock and Roll" are unusual in another respect: the IV–I cadence arises as the last two chords of a blues progression.

Example 9.6. Huey Lewis and the News, "I Want a New Drug" (chorus)

as IV/♭III. The D major chord in the fifth measure then serves an essential tonal function: since it contains F♯, which is incompatible with a tonal center of C, it clearly acts as IV of A, steering the song back toward that key. The second unusual feature is the meter. After the two-measure phrase that begins the chorus ("One that won't make me nervous / Wondering what to do"), one might have expected a second two-measure phrase to answer it. Instead, the second phrase is expanded; as I hear it, the downbeat actually shifts twice, creating two 2/4 measures, as shown in the example. We might first experience the second "you" as beat 3 of a 4/4 measure; but when we realize that the next VCU is starting there, we realize that it is metrically (indeed hypermetrically) strong. (The situation is similar to Example 9.1B—a "metrical reinterpretation.") The metrical irregularities have the effect of delaying the hyperdownbeat, which creates tension and anticipation; the tonicization of ♭III adds to the instability. All this enhances the satisfying effect of the cadential tonic when it finally arrives.

Another, very different, use of IV in a cadential context is shown in Example 9.7A—the end of the first chorus of ABBA's "Fernando." In the third full measure of the example, the chorus seems to come to a strong and quite conventional V–I cadence. The phrase is then repeated, but the V moves to IV instead of to I. Since I is clearly expected at this point, one might regard this as a kind of *deceptive cadence*, similar to the well-known V–vi deceptive cadence in classical music. Example 9.7B shows another instance of the deceptive IV in rock. Like vi in the classical deceptive cadence, IV functions well as a substitute for I, since it contains the tonic scale degree, allowing the melody to resolve to $\hat{1}$ as expected. A classical

Example 9.7A. Abba, "Fernando" (end of chorus)

Example 9.7B. Crosby, Stills & Nash, "Wasted on the Way" (end of chorus)

deceptive cadence is normally followed by a return to V (often via ii or another pre-dominant chord), which then moves to I: for example, ii–V–vi–ii–V–I. By contrast, IV in rock is, itself, perfectly capable of serving as a pre-tonic cadential chord; therefore, after substituting for I, it can complete the cadence by moving to I directly, as it does in Example 9.7B, and arguably 9.7A as well (in that case there is a V between the IV and the I, but it is very brief, and I would argue, inessential).

The deceptive IV is used in rock in a variety of ways. In some cases, the context preceding the deceptive IV (the harmonic progression and sometimes the melody as well) has previously occurred leading to I, which makes the move to IV especially surprising. This is the case in Example 9.7A, as already mentioned; in Example 9.7B, too, IV–V–I has occurred several times before this point, heightening the "deceptive" effect of IV–V–IV. Another instance of this is the Beatles' "Strawberry Fields Forever," where each chorus ends with IV–V–I; at the end of the final chorus, as the title phrase is presented three times, we get IV–V–I, then IV–V–I again, then IV–V–IV. In Alice in Chains' "No Excuses" (Example 9.8A) the first half of each chorus moves ♭VI→♭VII–I; the second half then presents ♭VI→♭VII–IV. (In this case, the IV actually *ends* the VCU.) By contrast, consider the Wallflowers' "One Headlight," shown in Example 9.8B. The VCU ends with a V–IV progression, overlapping into the next VCU. I think we expect a I after the V, and thus the IV is deceptive; but this expectation is only due to our general stylistic expectations for a move to I at the end of the VCU, not to any previous V–I progression within the song.

Example 9.8A. Alice in Chains, "No Excuses" (end of chorus)

Example 9.8B. The Wallflowers, "One Headlight" (end of chorus)

At the beginning of chapter 3, I cited the chorus of the Who's "Bargain" as one of my favorite moments in rock, and promised to explain why. Now, with the aid of the concepts introduced in this section and previous chapters, I will try to make good on my promise. Example 9.9 shows the entire first VCU; let us focus on the chorus first, starting at m. 9 of the example. I submit that the powerful effect of this passage has a lot to do with the IV chord in measure 11 of the example, which functions here in several different ways. First of all, it takes part in a plagal stop cadence, overlapping into the next VCU in the usual way. (Between the downbeat of m. 11 and m. 15, the bass and guitar are mostly inactive, though they restrike the chord at m. 13; a long drum fill starting at the downbeat of m. 12 anticipates the hyperdownbeat.) The chorus is expanded from an expected four measures to six, building up tension going into the cadential resolution. Consider also the harmonies leading up to the IV chord. The progression ♭VI→♭VII is common in rock, most often leading to I or i (as noted in section 3.5, this may be due to the linear logic of the progression); this expectation is strengthened by the melody, which seems to be "zeroing in" on $\hat{1}$ in measure 10. We get the expected melodic resolution, but not the harmonic one; thus the IV chord functions deceptively. But once we hear the

Example 9.9. The Who, "Bargain"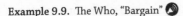

IV chord, another interpretation suggests itself: ♭VI–♭VII–IV in B♭ could be ♭III–IV–I in E♭, a tonicization of IV. This progression too is common (perhaps more common than ♭VI–♭VII–I at the time of this song), seen in songs such as the Beatles' "Sergeant Pepper's Lonely Hearts Club Band" (chorus), Steppenwolf's "Born to Be Wild" (second half of verse), the Jimi Hendrix Experience's "Purple Haze" (verse), and the Who's own "I Can See For Miles" (verse). Thus the IV chord serves three different functions: as a momentary alternative tonic, as a deceptive substitute for I, and as a pre-tonic preparation for I. All of these functions are commonly seen in common-practice music in the approach to a cadence: for example, I–V–vi (deceptive)–V7/IV–IV (tonicization)–V (pre-tonic)–I. The difference is that in this case, the IV chord serves all three functions at once; this, I believe, accounts in part for its momentous impact.

The preceding verse sheds further light on the chorus of "Bargain." It can be seen that it consists of a series of harmonic gestures, each one beginning on i and ending on IV; the gestures form a sentence pattern (2 + 2 + 4) which is then repeated (with different lyrics). The first two short gestures, i–♭VI–♭VII–IV, anticipate the progression of the chorus, though the ♭VII chords are so short that I hear them more as elaborations of an underlying i–♭VI–IV pattern. This i–♭VI–IV progression is perfectly acceptable, but it does not invoke any common harmonic schemata, and we do not quite know what to make of it.[4] All three of the verse's harmonic gestures begin on i and end on IV; while I do not hear any of them as tonicizing IV, they do perhaps raise this possibility in our minds. In the chorus, the ♭VI→♭VII–IV pattern of the verse returns, but now ♭VII is treated as a full-fledged harmony (given a full measure), which makes much more sense out of the progression; it provides a more conventional approach to IV, but at the same time clearly conveys a tonicization of it, as mentioned earlier. The sustained whole-note chords in the accompaniment on the ♭VI and ♭VII draw further attention to the harmony. The melody participates in this narrative as well; while it seems somewhat oblivious to the harmony in the verse, in the chorus it clearly outlines the ♭VII chord, giving it additional emphasis. All this fits perfectly with the lyrics: "To win you, I'd stand naked, stoned, and stabbed," Roger Daltrey sings in the verse; but in the chorus, "I'd call that a bargain / The best I ever had." (Why would he go through all that for his relationship? Because it's so good.) Thus the chorus helps to make sense out of the verse, both musically and lyrically, and the extreme sentiments of the lyrics are matched by their dramatic and powerful musical treatment.

9.3 TENSIONAL CURVES

In section 7.3, I introduced the idea of complexity as an important aspect of musical experience. I noted there that complexity is affected by the sheer density of events—a more active rhythmic texture seems more complex—and also by how expected those events are. I pointed to things such as notes going outside the current scale, progressions avoiding tonic harmony, and irregular meters and phrase structures as causing an increase in complexity, and I suggested that we think of tension as the experiential aspect of complexity.

Many songs seem to maintain a fairly uniform level of tension throughout; the density of events is fairly constant, and nothing very unexpected happens. Other songs feature clear fluctuations in tension, however, and these can greatly affect our experience of the song. Our focus here will be on changes of tension—what we might call *tensional curves*—within the VCU. Bear in mind that tension is not the same as energy—another important aspect of musical experience that we discussed in the last chapter. I suggested there that choruses tend to be higher in energy than verses; we will see that tension often follows a rather different pattern.

4. One could say that the ♭III–IV move in the third gesture (mm. 5-7) anticipates the IV-centered interpretation of the ♭VI→♭VII in the chorus. This connection is difficult to hear, though, due to the different placements of the chords, "weak-strong" in the verse and "strong-weak" in the chorus.

Let us think back to two examples presented in the previous chapter, Madonna's "Like a Virgin" and Green Day's "Longview" (Examples 8.7 and 8.8). The purpose of those two examples was to illustrate the difference between songs containing a prechorus (Example 8.8) and songs in which the middle part of the VCU is simply an extension of the verse (Example 8.7); positing a prechorus is more convincing when the previous section shows some degree of completeness. I noted that a typical feature of prechoruses is a rise in complexity, often manifested in an increase in syllabic density; in the following chorus, syllabic density typically decreases again (and is often even lower than in the verse). (As noted earlier, syllabic density could be regarded as increasing energy as well as complexity. In rock, though, it usually seems to be aligned with other tension-increasing factors.) I noted also that prechoruses often feature a departure from tonic harmony (de-emphasizing it or even avoiding it, especially at hyperdownbeats); this, too, could be regarded as a tension-building device. But now consider Example 8.7. While the passage in measures 13–18 seems more like an extension of the verse than a prechorus, it, too, features the same tension-building devices as Example 8.8: an increase in syllabic density (or at least *note* density, counting the individual notes of the melismas separately) and an avoidance of tonic harmony. Example 8.7 also has another feature not seen in Example 8.8, an irregularity in the hypermeter (and grouping) caused by the six-measure phrase; this too can be seen as causing an increase in tension.

Despite the formal difference between them, then, Examples 8.7 and 8.8 are similar in an important respect: in both cases, the middle part of the VCU provides an increase in complexity and thus tension. The difference between them is simply whether the peak in tension occurs at the end of the verse (leading straight into the chorus) or in a prechorus. Both of these situations occur in numerous songs. Examples of the first type—with a build in tension at the end of an extended verse—include Carly Simon's "You're So Vain," Joan Jett and the Blackhearts' "I Love Rock 'n Roll," Aerosmith's "I Don't Want to Miss a Thing," and Sheryl Crow's "If It Makes You Happy." In such cases, the mere fact that the verse is extended—not merely 8 or 16 measures but something more irregular—is partly what creates the build in tension. Songs of the second type—with a tension-building prechorus—include Diana Ross and the Supremes' "Love Child," Patti Smith's "Because the Night," Michael Jackson's "Billie Jean," and Oasis's "Don't Look Back in Anger." In all of these cases (of both types), a build in tension is created in the middle of the VCU by a rise in syllabic density, de-emphasis of tonic harmony, irregular hypermeter and grouping, or some combination of these. In terms of their tensional curves, we could call these *middle-peaking* VCUs.

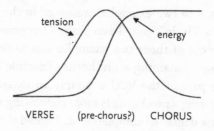

Example 9.10. Tension and energy trajectories for a typical "middle-peaking" VCU

In each of the songs mentioned above, the middle part of the VCU is followed by a fairly conventional chorus, reflecting typical features such as a rise in melodic register, added backing vocals, and thicker instrumental texture. In these respects, the chorus in each of these VCUs can be viewed as the peak in energy, as it typically is, but it is not the peak in tension (see Example 9.10). It is also of interest that in several of the cases with prechoruses, the chorus is in some respects quite similar to the verse; in "Billie Jean" and "Don't Look Back in Anger," the verse and chorus have the same harmonic progression and similar melodic grouping patterns. (One could speak of a kind of ABA pattern in these cases, *within* the VCU.) By repeating elements of the verse, the chorus becomes more predictable; this accentuates the drop in tension in relation to the prechorus. Going back to an issue discussed earlier (section 9.1), the similarity between verse and chorus also helps to enhance continuity between one VCU and the next.

Let us now consider another song already discussed, Huey Lewis and the News' "I Want a New Drug" (Example 9.6). As mentioned in our earlier discussion, this passage, too, has tension-building elements: the tonicization of ♭III, the metrical irregularities, and the "stop" in the instruments. The difference is that in this case, the elements of tension occur in the chorus—indeed, in the second half of the chorus, at the very end of the VCU. This, too, is a pattern seen in other songs; we could call it an *end-peaking* VCU. Other examples of end-peaking VCUs include John Cougar Mellencamp's "Little Pink Houses," Squeeze's "Black Coffee in Bed," and Counting Crows' "Einstein on the Beach." Some other songs with stop cadences could be included in this category as well, such as the Who's "Bargain" and "Won't Get Fooled Again" and Heart's "Barracuda." In all of these cases, the end of the chorus features a prolonged avoidance of tonic harmony, a hypermetrical irregularity, or both. In "Barracuda" (Example 9.3), the cross-rhythm in the melody on "down down down down" (reinforced by an irregular kick-snare alternation—not shown in the example) adds a degree of rhythmic tension as well.

Both middle-peaking and end-peaking trajectories are satisfying in their own way. To my mind, it feels most natural to have a peak of tension in a self-contained musical section somewhere near the middle (certainly this is the case in many common-practice pieces; think of the development section of a sonata movement). On the other hand, having the tensional peak near the end is perhaps more dramatic, perhaps because local tension-releasing factors—the return to tonic harmony (at a hypermetrically strong point) and the restoration of hypermetrical and phrasal regularity—coincide with another more global factor, namely, the return of the beginning of the VCU, which in itself lowers tension due to the predictability of the material.

The idea of tensional curves can also be applied to other phenomena that we have discussed. I noted in section 8.3 that some verses avoid or de-emphasize tonic harmony, such as Prince's "Little Red Corvette." (This is distinct from the case where the verse and chorus are actually in different keys; I discuss this further in section 9.5.) This creates a mild degree of tension, which is then typically resolved by a strong affirmation of tonic in the chorus. (We might speak of plateaus rather than peaks of tension here, if the tension level of each section seems relatively constant.) Other songs reflect the opposite pattern: the verse strongly emphasizes the tonic and the chorus avoids it. In these cases, it is the chorus that creates the higher level of tension. Examples include the Police's "Walking on the Moon" and "Wrapped around Your Finger," AC/DC's "Back in Black," Cream's "Sunshine of Your Love," and Nirvana's "Come as You Are." In such cases the chorus does not usually end the song, though it may (e.g., "Sunshine for Your Love"); unlike in classical music, there is no requirement in rock that a song end with tonic harmony! Yet a third scenario is seen in some chorus-initial songs. I mentioned in section 8.3 that chorus-initial songs often have verses that emphasize non-tonic harmonies. In a chorus-initial song, it is the second chorus that constitutes the first occurrence of repeated material, so this is naturally a moment of relaxation; avoiding tonic harmony in the verse and restoring it in the chorus accentuates this effect.

A final twist on the idea of tensional curves is illustrated by Example 9.11. We might initially analyze this passage (at least I did) as a prechorus. It follows a fairly self-contained verse, and features several tension-building elements: an unusual, syncopated pattern in the bass and drums, suggesting a cross-rhythm; emphasis of non-tonic harmonies; increased syllabic density; and a complex, irregular phrase structure and hypermeter.[5] All these are hallmarks of a middle-peaking VCU. The chorus (which begins

---

5. The section is nine measures long, so there must be an irregularity somewhere. I hear odd-numbered measures as strong through the seventh measure; the eighth measure is initially weak but then reinterpreted as strong.

Example 9.11. Van Halen, "Jump" (prechorus)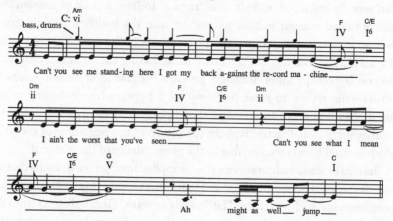

Can't you see me stand-ing here I got my back a-gainst the re-cord ma - chine

I ain't the worst that you've seen___ Can't you see what I mean

Ah___ might as well___ jump___

in the last measure of the example) returns to tonic harmony and to the keyboard riff that supported the verse. As noted by de Clercq (2012), however, there is a formal ambiguity here. What I have called the chorus is really just the word "jump" in the lead vocal (echoed in the backing vocals), and then three repeats of this (with a few additional words, e.g., "go ahead and"), more yelled than sung, at two-measure intervals. We might well think of these vocal phrases as ad-libbed interjections, rather than as a proper chorus. And that suggests an entirely different view: perhaps what I have called the prechorus is actually the chorus (overlapping into the last measure of the example), what I have called the chorus is actually the link beginning the next VCU, and the VCU as a whole is end-peaking rather than middle-peaking. I am slightly playing devil's advocate here—I hear the passage starting at the end of Example 9.11 more as a chorus than as a link—but it has a definite element of "link quality." And perhaps this whole formal ambiguity serves the purpose of continuity, or, one could even say, large-scale sectional overlap—the same passage serves as the end of one VCU and the beginning of the next. Bruce Springsteen's "Born to Run" and Bryan Adams's "Summer of '69" are two other examples of this strategy; in these two cases, I would say, the ambiguous passage is more link than chorus.

9.4 SHAPING A SONG

Much has been said about trajectories of energy and tension within the VCU. But what about an entire song? Normally, a rock song consists mostly of repetitions of the repeating unit (VCU or VRU), or parts of it, and these repetitions are often fairly literal; this tends to limit large-scale fluctuations of tension and energy across the song as a whole. Nevertheless, we do see strategies to create tensional shapes over an entire song. If a song has a bridge, this usually creates a rise in tension, if only because it usually emphasizes non-tonic harmony. This is clearly seen in the standard bridge progressions of AABA songs: a progression such as IV–I–IV–V contains only one tonic harmony, and it usually falls on a (relatively) weak measure (the third measure of an 8-bar structure), thus de-emphasizing it. The non-tonic emphasis in many bridges of verse-chorus songs has a similar effect. The tension is then resolved by the return to the VRU or VCU (or perhaps just the chorus), which restores the emphasis on tonic harmony. In such cases, we might speak of a trajectory of tension spanning the whole song, usually peaking somewhere after the midpoint.

With regard to energy, we often find an increasing trajectory over the course of a song. Often this involves the addition of instruments from one section to the next; this is seen in the Eagles' "Hotel California," described in some detail in section 6.2.[6] In particular, there is often an effort to distinguish the final VCU (or the final chorus) from previous ones: consider the string section added to the third VCU of Simon & Garfunkel's "Bridge over Troubled Water," or the backing vocals in the third VCU of Tom Petty's "Free Fallin'." Sometimes the singer may elaborate the melody of the final chorus or take it to a higher register, as in Stevie Wonder's "Superstition." The final chorus may also be modified to create a stronger sense of closure. Most commonly, this is done by repeating the final phrase, sometimes involving a deceptive cadence; the end of the Beatles' "Strawberry Fields Forever," mentioned earlier, is an example.

Another strategy that builds energy toward the end of a song was discussed in section 8.5: "terminally climactic form." As noted there, some songs end with a section, heard for the first time, that seems in some ways more "chorus-like" than anything previous, with a thick texture, backing vocals, and very limited lyrical content. This creates an energy trajectory for the whole song that resembles that of the typical VCU. Yet another strategy deserving mention is a modulation up a half-step (or more) in the final chorus of the song, sometimes known as a "pump-up" or "truck driver's modulation." Stevie Wonder's "You Are the Sunshine of My Life" is one example; see Griffiths (2015) for others and further discussion. Since higher pitch generally conveys greater energy, this can be seen as a way of slightly boosting the energy level at the end of the song.

6. The form diagrams in Covach & Flory (2015) offer many other nice examples of this.

A rather different strategy for the end of a song is illustrated by "Hotel California." At the beginning of the third verse, the instrumental texture thins out greatly, compared to the previous verses and choruses: a single guitar plays the pattern from the introduction, accompanied only by downbeat notes in the bass and gentle cymbal strokes. The full "orchestral" texture then returns in the second half of the third verse (similar to that of the second verse, shown earlier in Example 6.7). The effect of this is intense and satisfying, perhaps because it reiterates the song's energetic trajectory in a greatly compressed form. De Clercq (2012) notes that this strategy has become rather common in more recent rock. Yet another song-ending strategy is seen in Bon Jovi's "You Give Love a Bad Name." After two VCUs and a guitar solo, we are expecting a chorus, and we get one—but the instruments have dropped out, except for massive, reverberant drum hits on the backbeats; the chorus then repeats with the full ensemble. (Styx's "Renegade" and Joan Jett and the Blackhearts' "I Love Rock 'n Roll" are other examples of this strategy.) This strategy is superficially similar to the previous one, but quite different in its effect: one could speak of a drop of energy in "Hotel California," but hardly in "You Give Love a Bad Name." In the latter case, the absence of harmonic support really makes the texture feel incomplete—creating a kind of tension, perhaps; the return of the full instrumental texture restores normality and gives a feeling of relaxation.

One final strategy, occasionally seen at the end of a song, is illustrated by Example 9.12A, from Led Zeppelin's "Whole Lotta Love." At this point— the end of the third chorus—the tempo is suddenly suspended; we get a vocal phrase, then a brief I chord and a much longer IV, then another vocal phrase—just a very elongated "love"—leading into the return of tonic harmony and the riff, which repeats into the final fadeout. I call this kind of gesture a *grand cadence*. As I define it, a grand cadence is a highly emphasized move to tonic harmony that occurs only once in a song, near the end; in most cases (though not all), there is a fermata (a pause in the tempo) at the pre-tonic harmony.[7] Clearly, a grand cadence functions to establish closure, indicating that the end of the song is at hand—though in its disruptive and surprising effect, it could also be regarded as a tension-building device. In virtually every grand cadence that I have found, the pre-tonic harmony is IV. (There is a clear connection with the plagal stop cadence here: the fermata is analogous to the "stop.") In AC/DC's "Back in Black" and Jefferson Airplane's "Somebody to Love," as in "Whole Lotta Love," a grand cadence follows the final chorus, leading into a fadeout or coda.

---

7. A cadence that simply involves a lengthening of the pre-tonic cadential harmony of the final chorus (as in the Beatles' "She Loves You") is not considered a grand cadence.

Example 9.12A. Led Zeppelin, "Whole Lotta Love" (around 4:03)

Slow and very free tempo

Way down in - side__ Wo - man You__ need it__

Love__

Example 9.12B. Led Zeppelin, "Stairway to Heaven" (around 5:28), guitar part (somewhat simplified)

In the Beatles' "Get Back," the Doobie Brothers' "Long Train Runnin'," and Fleetwood Mac's "Say You Love Me," a grand cadence occurs at the end of the final chorus; in each case, in fact, the IV substitutes for the cadential I (thus functioning deceptively—see section 9.2) and then moves directly to I.

The passage shown in Example 9.12B, from Led Zeppelin's "Stairway to Heaven," could be regarded as a large-scale grand cadence. In keeping with our definition, the cadence occurs only once, near the end of the song; as is typical, the beginning of the cadential IV is emphasized by a fermata. This IV chord is, however, prolonged to a much greater extent than in the other cases mentioned above, lasting some 23 seconds, and it is elaborated by other harmonies. The cadence is somewhat atypical, also, in that there is a substantial section of new material following it; but the expansive character of both the cadence itself and the section that follows seems appropriate, given the large scale of the song as a whole. One could also say that the IV chord is functioning deceptively here; it is approached by a ♭III→♭VII progression that has previously occurred several times, always moving to i.

In general, as we have seen, the energy trajectories for songs—when they are not simply flat—tend to increase toward the end; tension trajectories often exhibit a rise near the end of a song as well, followed by

Example 9.13. Elton John, "Daniel" (end of first verse)

resolution. Not all songs follow these patterns, however. Consider Elton John's "Daniel." The song begins with a rather typical VCU (the verse occurs twice before the chorus, which is not unusual): the chorus ("Daniel my brother") has the customary features of backing vocals and non-tonic-to-tonic harmonic gestures. The verse has one rather unusual feature, though: it ends with a strong cadential gesture, a IV–V–I progression with a melodic move to $\hat{1}$ on a hyperdownbeat (Example 9.13). Elton seems to have realized that this presented an interesting opportunity: a verse that ends with strong cadential closure could convincingly end the song. And indeed it does: the overall form of the song is VVCV$_{inst}$CV. (Notice how the synthesizer melody of the V$_{inst}$ comes back to accompany the vocal in the last verse.) Ending the song with a verse creates an unusual decrease in energy at the end. This has another effect as well. In section 8.3, I suggested that the verse-chorus contrast could be a metaphor for individuality versus unity. This metaphor comes through clearly here: in the verses, the singer laments his brother Daniel's departure and absence ("Daniel is traveling tonight on a plane"), while the chorus is about their relationship ("Daniel my brother, you are older than me"). Ending the song with a verse brings the focus back to the individual, creating a feeling of solitude—or perhaps, loneliness—that is especially acute since it is so unusual at the *end* of a song. The final words say it all: "Oh god it looks like Daniel / Must be the clouds in my eyes."

9.5 SCALAR AND TONAL SHIFT

The final topic we will consider is not so much a specific strategy as a general possibility afforded by rock's musical language, which individual artists have exploited in a variety of interesting ways. This is the possibility of scalar and tonal shift. I will define tonal shift as a shift from one key to another (otherwise known as modulation); scalar shift is a shift of scale within the same key. (As always, "key" simply refers to tonal center. If the tonal center and scale both shift, this is considered a tonal shift.) We will consider both the ways that tonal shift and scalar shift are used, and their implications for the expressive trajectories and meanings of rock songs. Our focus here is on fairly large-scale shifts, in which each tonal center or scale is operative over a whole section or more. (Briefer tonal shifts—tonicizations—were discussed in section 3.6.)

Tonal and scalar shifts can occur in a variety of situations. I mentioned earlier that bridges often emphasize non-tonic harmonies, and this can sometimes involve a real modulation; the bridge of Eric Clapton's "Tears in Heaven" modulates fairly decisively from A to G, then back to A for the remainder of the song. The possibility of modulating up by a half-step or whole-step in the final chorus has also been mentioned. A few songs strongly establish a second key in the prechorus (returning to the main key in the chorus); Fleetwood Mac's "Rhiannon" moves to the relative major, and Talking Heads' "And She Was" moves up by a half-step. My main focus in this section, however, will be on tonal and scalar shifts between verse and chorus; these are especially common, and also reflect some rather interesting and consistent patterns.

I noted in section 8.3 that it is quite common to find tonal shifts between verses and choruses. The most frequently encountered situation is where the chorus is in major mode and the verse is in a different key with the same scale. The popularity of this strategy should not surprise us; in common-practice music, too, the most common modulations are between keys that share the same scale (such as relative major/minor keys—assuming the natural minor scale implied by the minor key signature) or whose scales differ by only one pitch (such as major keys a fifth apart). In rock, shifts between relative-related tonalities, such as between C Ionian and A Aeolian (or a similar "flat-side" scale), are especially frequent: well-known examples include Elton John's "Rocket Man," ABBA's "SOS," Neil Young's "Rockin' in the Free World," U2's "One," and Bon Jovi's "Livin' on a Prayer," discussed earlier. An interesting twist on this strategy is seen in Wild Cherry's "Play That Funky Music." The verse melody is mostly minor-pentatonic (in E) but also emphasizes $\flat\hat{5}$ (B$\flat$), which is $\flat\hat{3}$ of G, the relative major key (see Example 9.14); when the chorus shifts to that key, the melody again uses the minor pentatonic, again emphasizing B$\flat$, which is now $\flat\hat{3}$ (though with hints of $\flat\hat{5}$ in *that* key).[8] The "$\flat\hat{5}=\flat\hat{3}$" connection seems to smooth this rather unusual tonal shift.

Another common situation is where a Mixolydian verse moves to an Ionian chorus with a tonal center a fifth lower (for example, G Mixolydian to C Ionian), again maintaining the same scale. Examples include the Four

8. Could the $\flat\hat{5}$ of G in the chorus (D$\flat$) connect with the rather prominent $\hat{6}$ (C$\sharp$) in the guitar accompaniment of the verse (part of its upper line C$\sharp$–C–B)? Possibly, though I find this connection difficult to hear, perhaps because of the difference in spelling.

Example 9.14. Wild Cherry, "Play That Funky Music"

Tops' "Baby I Need Your Loving," the Animals "We Gotta Get Out of This Place," Elton John's "Don't Let the Sun Go Down on Me," Boston's "More Than a Feeling," Madonna's "Live to Tell," and Divinyls' "I Touch Myself." In some of these cases, one might argue that the verse is in the same major-mode tonality as the chorus but simply emphasizes dominant harmony; there can be a gray area between these two situations.

A general question arises here: Is it always necessary to declare a single main key within a song—as is the assumption in common-practice music (until the late nineteenth century anyway)? I think not. I can think of numerous songs where two tonal centers are established in different sections, and it seems arbitrary to give priority to one or the other. For example, in songs with a relative minor/major shift between the verse and chorus, the two tonalities often seem roughly equally balanced and there seems little point in trying to declare a "winner"; consider "Livin' on a Prayer," for instance (Example 8.4C). In other cases, we may decide that one tonal center takes precedence over the other, perhaps because it is present for longer or is emphasized at important structural positions. One rather common pattern is where the chorus establishes a second tonal center but shifts back to the verse key at the end of the section. John Cougar Mellencamp's "Lonely Ol' Night," shown in Example 3.10B, is an instance of this; others include Simon & Garfunkel's "Mrs. Robinson," Carole King's "It's Too Late," Wild Cherry's "Play That Funky Music," the Police's "Message in a Bottle," Tears for Fears' "Head over Heels," and Metallica's "Nothing Else Matters." In such cases, the verse key is clearly primary, as it occurs at the beginning and end of the VCU; the tonal shift in the chorus serves as a tension-building departure. (Some of these cases might be considered tonicizations rather than modulations.) This could be regarded as a variant of the "end-peaking" strategy discussed in section 9.3.

In some songs, a modulation between verse and chorus involves a change in scale; these are less common, and little can be said about them of a general nature. In the Pointer Sisters' "Jump (For My Love)," a Mixolydian verse moves to a major-mode chorus a whole step higher; in the Police's "Don't Stand So Close to Me," an Aeolian verse moves to an Ionian chorus a fifth higher. Doll (2011) provides other examples. In some cases, modulations with a change of scale can be quite jarring, especially if the two scales have few tones in common. A case in point is Derek and the Dominos' "Layla," which alternates between an E major tonality in the verse and a D Aeolian one in the chorus, retaining just two common tones (E–F♯–G♯–A–B–C♯–D♯ → D–E–F–G–A–B♭–C). The D Aeolian chorus material is used in the intro as well; Example 9.15 shows the transition from the intro to the first verse. This remarkable modulation is made even more striking by the fact that the chorus/intro progression ends with ♭VII/D while the verse begins with a vi/E, creating a chord transition from C major to C♯ minor. This tonal shift creates extreme tension—because it is so unusual—and nicely captures the tormented emotions of a singer about to "go insane."[9] Another distant modulation is in Talk Talk's "It's My Life," which moves from a Mixolydian E♭ in the verse to an Aeolian A tonality in the chorus; these scales have just three notes in common (E♭–F–G–A♭–B♭–C–D♭ → A–B–C–D–E–F–G). The fact that the tonal centers are so far apart (six steps on the line of fifths) no doubt contributes to the disorienting effect.

Scalar shifts—maintaining the same tonic—are sometimes seen between verse and chorus as well. Here again, a shift from a flat-side verse to an Ionian chorus is typical. Hall & Oates's "Kiss on My List" features an Aeolian verse and Ionian chorus (though the verse has touches of $\hat{3}$, and the chorus has touches of ♭$\hat{3}$); the Righteous Brothers' "You've Lost That Lovin' Feeling" has a Mixolydian verse and a mostly Ionian chorus (though the chorus moves to ♭VII at the end). More generally, I would suggest that there is a tendency for the chorus to feature more sharp-side pitch collections than the verse. In the Doors' "Unknown Soldier" and Kiss's "Christine Sixteen," the verse uses ♭$\hat{3}$ while the chorus uses (mostly) $\hat{3}$, but the chorus also employs ♭$\hat{7}$, suggesting Mixolydian mode. See Temperley (2011b) for further examples of scalar shift in rock.

What is the function of tonal and scalar shifts? In the first place, a modulation simply achieves a sense of change or motion from one "place" to another. This can serve a purely musical function—providing an

---

9. While I have tried to keep tension separate from emotion, I would concede that cases of extreme tension such as this can have disturbing effects. In general, though, I would say that scalar and tonal shifts have little effect on tension. One might say that all scalar and tonal shifts cause a slight increase in tension, since they are somewhat uncommon (less common than staying in the same key and scale), but these effects seem fairly mild. The expressive effects of tonal and scalar shifts are better explained in other ways, as discussed below.

Example 9.15. Derek and the Dominos, "Layla" (end of intro and beginning of first verse)

What'll you do when you get lone-ly

especially marked degree of articulation and contrast between sections. Often, however, it serves an expressive function as well and reinforces a shift in the lyrics; songs that modulate between verse and chorus often feature a change in perspective or situation between the two sections. In the Beatles' "Penny Lane," the verse (in B) describes the narrator's childhood experiences of an urban neighborhood; the chorus (in A) brings us back to his current situation, under "blue suburban skies." The final chorus shifts up to B—the key of the verse—unifying past and present in a satisfying way.

We should note, also, the emotional connotations of shifts in scale and tonal center. In particular, as noted earlier, scales that are further in the "flat" direction in relation to the tonic tend to have more negative connotations. This predicts that, for example, a scalar shift from C Aeolian to C Ionian with the same tonal center will be perceived as a "positive" shift; a tonal shift from A Aeolian to C Ionian, maintaining the same scale, will have a similar effect (see Example 8.5). Such valence trajectories are common in rock, often connecting in significant ways with the lyrics. In Don Henley's "The Boys of Summer," the verse (E♭ Aeolian) has the narrator describing the desolate empty beach after the summer and his lover have gone; the chorus (G♭ Ionian) returns to happier days—"I can see you, your brown hair shining in the sun." In Bon Jovi's "Livin' on a Prayer," the E Aeolian verse details the struggles of blue-collar life ("Tommy used to work on the docks, union's been on strike, he's down on his luck"), while the G Ionian chorus reflects hope for a better future ("We're halfway there. . . . Take my hand and we'll make it I swear").

Scalar shifts can be used for expressive purposes as well. Again, this follows the predicted pattern: shifts toward more "sharp-side" scales tend to have positive implications. In the Beatles' "A Hard Day's Night," while the mostly Mixolydian verse-refrain mainly focuses on the drudgery of the "hard day"—"working like a dog"—the major-mode bridge turns to the payoff of the night, when "everything seems to be right." Similarly, in the Rembrandts' "I'll Be There for You" (the theme to the TV series *Friends*), a largely Mixolydian verse describing the hardships of young adulthood ("Your job's a joke, you're broke") contrasts with a comforting major-ish chorus ("I'll be there for you").[10] Another example that I find especially touching is Bob Seger's "Mainstreet," in which an E♭ Mixolydian verse shifts to an E♭ Ionian prechorus, returning to Mixolydian for the brief chorus (or refrain). This shift in scale perfectly expresses the content of the lyrics, especially in the second VCU:

VERSE	In the pool halls, the hustlers and the losers
[Mixolydian]	I used to watch 'em through the glass
	Well I'd stand outside at closing time
	Just to watch her walk on past
PRECHORUS	Unlike all the other ladies, she looked so young and sweet
[Ionian]	As she made her way alone down that empty street
CHORUS	Down on Mainstreet
[Mixolydian]	Down on Mainstreet

While the verse lyric conjures a sleazy atmosphere of strip joints and pool halls, the prechorus focuses on the object of the singer's affection—a single dancer whose beauty and purity set her apart from the rest.

If both shifts in scale and shifts in tonal center can convey a change in emotional valence, then the question arises, what is the expressive difference between them? I would suggest that a shift of scale tends to express a change in perspective about an unchanging situation, whereas a shift of tonal center indicates an actual change of situation. This is based partly on my own gut feelings, but it also finds some support in the lyrics of songs with scalar and tonal shifts. "Mainstreet" changes scale without changing tonal center: the situation is not changing, only the singer's focus (from the seedy strip joints to the beautiful dancer). In "A Hard Day's Night," likewise, the situation does not really change (life is just a constant alternation of day and night), but the focus changes (from the grind of the day to the pleasure of the night); "I'll Be There for You" is similar in this regard. In all of these cases, we find a change of scale rather than tonal center. In "Penny Lane," "The Boys of Summer," and

10. Note my use of the fuzzy descriptions "largely Mixolydian" and "major-ish"; these sections do not actually adhere strictly to diatonic modes. The verse uses the iii chord (with $\hat{7}$), but ♭VII (with ♭$\hat{7}$) is more frequent and prominent; the chorus contrasts with the verse not by emphasizing $\hat{7}$ (which appears minimally if at all—is there a third in the V chord?) but rather by avoiding ♭$\hat{7}$ (except for one ♭VII at the end). Cases such as this point up the inadequacy of conventional scale labels; a more fluid conception of scale-degree distributions (and their line-of-fifths positions), such as that shown in Example 2.13, is really needed to describe these sectional contrasts.

"Livin' on a Prayer," the shift in the lyrics is of a different nature: the verse and the chorus actually reflect different situations (albeit situations that are contemplated from a single vantage point). In these songs, then, a change of tonal center is appropriate. But this is all highly speculative. Further study—and perhaps experimental work—is needed to examine the expressive implications of scalar and tonal shifts, as they are actually experienced.

9.6 QUESTIONS

1. Identify the VCU boundary strategy (at the end of the first chorus) used in each of these four songs: the Hollies, "Long Cool Woman in a Black Dress"; Wild Cherry, "Play That Funky Music"; Escape Club, "Wild Wild West"; Lifehouse, "Hanging by a Moment." Each song uses either the "irregular hypermeter, regular grouping" strategy (like Example 9.1B) or the "expanded phrase, regular hypermeter" strategy (like Example 9.1C).

2. Each of these songs features a middle-peaking VCU: the Doobie Brothers, "China Grove"; the Cars, "Let's Go"; Def Leppard, "Bringing On the Heartbreak"; Janet Jackson, "Runaway." What are the factors (harmony, melodic rhythm, meter/hypermeter, grouping) that create tension in the middle part of the VCU? Would you consider each passage to be an extension of the verse, or a prechorus? (Answers may not be clear-cut.)

3. Tom Petty and the Heartbreakers' "The Waiting" nicely illustrates several strategies discussed in this chapter. Do the verse and chorus have different tonal centers? (Either answer is possible; in either case, the song represents a pattern discussed in the current chapter.) Explain how a tensional peak is created in the middle part of the VCU. The end of the song (the very end of the vocal line) features a distinctive cadence that represents another strategy we have discussed.

4. Consider the verse and chorus in these three songs: the Supremes' "Love Child," Aerosmith's "Janie's Got a Gun" (I consider the chorus to be the "Run away" section), the Police's "Synchronicity 2." In each case, the tonal/harmonic relationship between verse and chorus is the opposite of a more common pattern; explain. Does this relate to the lyrics of the songs in some way?

5. I have argued that syncopation can be a tension-increasing device, and also that the middle part of the VCU (prechorus or extended verse) tends to be a section of increased tension; thus we might expect syncopation to be more prevalent and pronounced in such sections. What do you think? Examine three examples of prechoruses (which could include songs from this chapter and the previous one) to see whether these sections are more syncopated than the previous verse and following chorus.

CHAPTER 10
Analyses

In chapter 1, I distinguished between theory, the study of general principles of a style, and analysis, the study of individual pieces of music. So far, our focus in this book has been on the theory of rock music: the principles of key, harmony, rhythm, melody, instrumentation, and form that characterize the style as a whole. In this chapter, I will try to show how this theoretical framework can contribute to analysis. To a large extent, it does so by drawing our attention to what is normative and unusual in rock songs. In many cases, I believe, what makes a rock song great is the way it plays with the conventions of the style—sometimes adhering to them, sometimes stretching or defying them in creative and surprising ways. I believe that experienced rock listeners understand the conventions of the style—at least at an unconscious level—and are sensitive to the ways that songs follow or depart from them. By focusing on how rock songs play with convention, we can begin to understand how they affect and appeal to people the way they do.

In this chapter, I present six analytical discussions of rock songs. Analysis, as I conceive of it, is the exploration of a piece of music in *all* its aspects and dimensions, paying particular attention to the way that those dimensions work together to create a satisfying and coherent whole. As such, an analysis of a rock song should certainly attend to the lyrics, and this chapter will consider lyrics and text-music connections much more than previous chapters have. Each analytical discussion will focus on some musical dimensions more than others, paying particular attention to features that are in some way original or distinctive. If a particular dimension of a song (say, its phrase structure) is entirely straightforward and typical of the style, there may be little to say about it. However, the way these songs adhere to conventions is also important, and frequently worthy of comment. It is the conventional features of a song that establish its stylistic context, setting up our expectations—therefore allowing the *denial* of expectation; they also help us to orient ourselves to the song's structural framework and to navigate our way through it, with regard to its tonality, form, and other aspects.

While portions of the songs can be heard at the book's website, the reader is encouraged to have full recordings at hand when reading the following analyses.

10.1   MARVIN GAYE, "I HEARD IT THROUGH THE GRAPEVINE" (1968)
By Norman Whitfield and Barrett Strong

Sometimes a single motive can be the generating idea for an entire song; if it is an unusual motive, it can take the song into unique and unexpected places. Such an idea is present, I believe, in "I Heard It through the Grapevine." Composed by two songwriters associated with Motown Records, the song was first recorded by Smokey Robinson and the Miracles in 1966, and was a hit for Gladys Knight & the Pips in 1967; only in 1968 was Marvin Gaye's version released, but it is this one that has stood the test of time. In this analysis, I begin by examining the main motive of the song and the ways it is used; I then discuss some interesting features of the song's form and harmony; finally, I explore some aspects of Gaye's classic vocal performance.

If you know the song, you probably have a rough idea of what I mean by the "main motive," and you are probably roughly right. Defining this motive precisely is not so easy, however, because it appears in a variety of guises. I believe it is something rather abstract: a pattern of *harmonic rhythm*, namely, a move to a harmony on the fourth beat of the measure, held over to the following strong beat (see Example 10.1). Such syncopated harmonic rhythms are quite rare in rock (a few other examples were discussed in section 4.3), and I am hard-pressed to think of another song that features this particular pattern. Most often in this song, the harmony on the downbeat is tonic, followed by a move away from tonic on the third beat (as shown in the example), and back to tonic on the fourth. But even this more specific version occurs in several different harmonic forms. Example 10.2 shows a partial transcription of the first VCU (the introduction, first verse, and chorus); the lower staff shows certain instrumental

Example 10.1. A motive of harmonic rhythm in Marvin Gaye's "I Heard It through the Grapevine"

Example 10.2. Marvin Gaye, "I Heard It through the Grapevine," first VCU

Example 10.2. (Continued)

parts, focusing on instances of the motive. (The form of the song is essentially three iterations of the VCU, with a short instrumental between the second and third.) At the beginning of the introduction, the motive is presented in bare fifths in the electric piano (over a tonic pedal), with just a suggestion of a change of harmony (to bIII) on the third beat. Then the guitar enters (m. 7) with a new pattern, though in the same harmonic rhythm; in this case the non-tonic harmony on the third beat is IV. Just before the vocal enters, an octave leap in the French horn—anticipating similar leaps in the vocal line later in the song—draws extra attention to the fourth beat. In the verse (mm. 11–12 and 15–16), the accompaniment presents a hybrid of the two forms of the motive in the introduction; the electric piano moves to a IV chord, while the bass line moves to $\flat\hat{3}$ (the harmony here is ambiguous). The chorus (mm. 23–24 and 27–28) then presents a variant of this, though with *major* tonic harmony in the strings and backing vocals (on the downbeat anyway)—following the conventional pattern of a "sharp-ward" shift in the chorus. Another variant of the motive, in measures 13–14, has V as the initial harmony; again, the harmonic move on the fourth beat of the measure clearly links this to the other instances of the pattern. In measures 25–26, the motive is present only in the melody (more on this below). One could also hear measures 31–34 as an extended instance of the motive, in which the usual half measure of tonic harmony at the motive's beginning is expanded to two and a half measures (the electric piano and bass have the motive in m. 31, but it is hardly noticed under the backing vocals). The repeated strong-weak $\hat{1}$–$\hat{5}$ gestures in these measures could perhaps be subtle references to the motive as well, setting up its real occurrence in the second half of measure 33 (this connection is indicated by the brackets above the score).

One might wonder whether the fourth-beat chords in the motive are anticipatory syncopations; do we understand them as belonging on the following downbeat? Certainly harmonic patterns can involve anticipatory syncopations (section 4.3); in this case, however, I am skeptical. Anticipatory syncopations at the level of the tactus are very rare, and anticipations of this sheer length—almost half a second—are rare as well. We might look to the text to shed some light; if the fourth beat is an anticipation, we would expect it to carry a stressed syllable. But this is indecisive; the syllables on the fourth-beat chords are sometimes stressed ("'Bout your plans to make me *blue*"), and sometimes not, most notably on the word "grape-vine," where the unstressed syllable "vine" falls on the fourth beat. Rather than viewing the fourth-beat chords as anticipatory syncopations, I suggest we think of them as syncopations in the classical sense—elements that conflict with the underlying meter, creating rhythmic tension and instability.

As can be seen from Example 10.2, there is one passage in the VCU where the motive is notably absent, namely, measures 19–22. Clearly, this passage is the prechorus: it follows a fairly self-contained verse and features a significant departure from tonic harmony (most importantly, on the first measure of the section). The surrounding verse and chorus are quite similar to one another in harmony and melody, so that there is a strong sense of "ABA" within the VCU (a pattern we have observed in other songs as well). The move to vi in measure 19 is a truly memorable moment in the song. Up to this point the harmonic orientation of the song has been strongly flat-side, due to the minor tonic harmony; vi is rarely seen in flat-side environments (see section 3.3). So the harmony is pulled to the sharp side at this point—though the melody resists this, as I will discuss below. The fact that the prechorus avoids the main rhythmic motive of the song makes it satisfying to return to it in measure 23 (and makes up for the fact that the second half of the prechorus is harmonically a bit too similar to the verse and chorus).

So far, my discussion of the motivic and harmonic structure of "Grapevine" has focused on the accompaniment; but the melody also impacts these aspects of the song.[1] Gaye's vocal (shown on the top staff of Example 10.2) is almost entirely within the Dorian mode: all seven degrees are used prominently and frequently. Even when the accompaniment harmony is I, as in the chorus, the vocal uses ♭3̂. (There is one possible use of 3̂, discussed below.) As we have seen, the use of ♭3̂ in the melody over major I is common in rock, but combining ♭3̂ in the lead vocal with 3̂ in the background vocals (in the same octave!), as we find in the chorus, is unusual. To my ears, the ♭3̂ of the vocal takes precedence here, giving the chorus a decidedly flat-side quality. (The effect of the 3̂ in the accompaniment is mainly to give it a fuller sound, and to make the section seem more chorus-like.)

Gaye's handling of the melody in the three prechoruses is especially noteworthy. Let us first consider the lyrics of the prechoruses, which are some of the most poignant in the song. The first one projects a feeling of ironic detachment—as if the singer trying to hide how hurt he really is:

It took me by surprise, I must say, when I found out yesterday

The second one is wistful and, to my mind, especially painful—it wasn't the crime, but rather the cover-up, that hurt the most:

You could have told me yourself that you loved someone else

And the third one is the moment of truth—as he braces himself for the final blow:

Do you plan to let me go for the other guy you loved before?

1. As is often the case, a question arises as to how much of the song's melody is due to the singer and how much to the nominal songwriters. It is known that Gaye often played an active role in creating melodic material (even in songs nominally written by others), sometimes improvising new melodies during recording sessions (Flory, 2010). In this case, it is clear that the basic outlines of the melody were not due to Gaye, since they are present on earlier recordings of the song (especially Smokey Robinson's—the melody of Gladys Knight's version is quite different). But many of the melodic details are unique to Gaye's version; see note 2 of this chapter for one example. A systematic comparison of the various versions of the song would be of interest, but this is beyond our scope.

Example 10.3 shows Gaye's melodies for these three lines. While each one is different, all three emphasize $\hat{6}$—more than any other point in the song: $\hat{6}$ occurs not only at the peaks of the phrases, but prominently near their beginnings as well. (In particular, the octave leap from C4 to C5 in the first VCU nicely complements the leap up from E♭4 to E♭5 in the verse.) The first two use ♭$\hat{3}$, conflicting with the vi chord in the accompaniment; but ♭$\hat{3}$ is avoided on the downbeat, thus allowing the vi chord to come through clearly. In the first prechorus, Gaye moves to ♭$\hat{3}$ directly from $\hat{6}$, creating a tritone interval which itself has a striking, dissonant effect, and highlighting the word "sur-*prise*." This adds an acerbic touch to the major-mode harmonies of the accompaniment, as is appropriate for the lyrics. (It also beautifully encapsulates the Dorian feel of the song, since Dorian is the only mode containing this tritone.) The melody of the third prechorus is rather different; Example 10.4 shows the pitch contour of the first two measures, generated from an isolated vocal recording. This time the mediant note falls right on the downbeat; the note lands close to $\hat{2}$ but then scoops up to a stable segment that is between ♭$\hat{3}$ and $\hat{3}$, sounding more like $\hat{3}$ to my ears (though it could also be considered a blue note). The use of $\hat{3}$ here—its only appearance in the song—is appropriate, as the vocal is moving up to $\hat{5}$ (rather than down to $\hat{1}$, as in the first two VCUs). But in addition to this, a ♭$\hat{3}$ on the downbeat would have obscured the underlying vi chord;

Example 10.3. Marvin Gaye, "I Heard It through the Grapevine," melodies of the prechoruses for the first (A), second (B), and third (C) VCUs

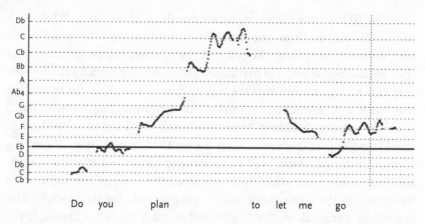

Example 10.4. Pitch contour for the third prechorus of "I Heard It through the Grapevine" (just the first two measures), automatically generated from an isolated vocal recording 🔊

the use of $\hat{3}$ suggests that Gaye sensed the expressive importance of this chord and wanted to let it come through.

Rhythmic aspects of Gaye's vocal are also worthy of attention—in particular, his handling of the main motive. All the occurrences of the motive in the verse and chorus are clearly reinforced by vocal phrases ending strongly on the fourth beat (though, as observed earlier, this syllable is not always stressed). In measure 25, it is only the vocal that conveys the motive; there is no evidence of it in the accompaniment. In the first phrase (mm. 10–11), the fourth beat itself is given an anticipatory syncopation in the vocal; note how every syllable of the phrase is syncopated here. (The "ooh" melisma creates a subtle cross-rhythm that flows neatly into the first stressed syllable, "bet.") In other places, Gaye seems to anticipate the fourth beat harmonically; the $\hat{6}$ on "make *me* blue" (m. 13) seems to prepare the following move to IV. In the prechoruses (mm. 19–22), Gaye avoids the motive, just as the accompaniment does. The only other odd-numbered measure where Gaye withholds the motive is the last phrase of the chorus (m. 29); here Gaye builds up the tension with a more active and dense rhythmic pattern, again highly syncopated, continuing through the following measure to overlap into the next hypermeasure—giving a slight "end peak" to the VCU.[2] (This moment could perhaps be considered a sectional overlap—though mm. 31–34 feel more to me like an extension of the chorus than a link, since they feature new vocal material.) Since (as already noted) the occurrence of the motive

---

2. Withholding the melody in m. 29 seems to have been Gaye's choice. In the Miracles' version, by contrast, the motive is used in the melody at this point.

in measure 31 is covered up by the backing vocals, it is essentially with-held from measure 29 through measure 32, making its return in measure 33 especially effective.

Of course, the impact of Gaye's vocal comes not just from his choices of pitch and rhythm, but also from its timbral aspects. As noted in chapter 6, our limited theoretical tools do not permit much in the way of rigorous analysis of timbre. What we can say is that the vocal of this song presents a wide variety of rich and expressive tone colors. Some syllables have a pure, almost angelic quality (e.g., "you could have *told* me yourself" in the second prechorus); others are strained and raspy, such as "when I *found out*" in the first verse. (One could describe this in terms of "falsetto" versus "modal" register, though this distinction seems more like a continuum in the cur-rent case.) This reflects the tension between the character's facade of cool detachment (one tries to maintain some dignity in such situations) and the raw hurt and anger that he actually feels. As observed in our earlier discussion, analyzing vocal timbre is especially challenging because the spectral content is greatly affected by the vowel being sung; we can control for this by comparing syllables with the same vowel. Example 10.5 shows spectrograms for three syllables with the vowel "oh," all on the same pitch (B♭4): "told" in the second prechorus (this is actually a melisma, C5–B♭4, but only the B♭4 portion is shown), "*oh* I'm just about to" in the first cho-rus, and "know" in the outro ("honey honey I *know*"). In their aural effect, "oh" seems the harshest of the three; "told" is relatively pure, and "know" is in between the two. This is confirmed by the spectrograms. "Oh" has more high-frequency activity than the others; the blurred patch near the top of the spectrogram would seem to indicate noise. "Know" has somewhat less high-frequency content, but more than "told." All three syllables also have a significant degree of vibrato, shown by the wavelike patterns in the spec-trograms; "know" appears to have the most. These comments hardly do

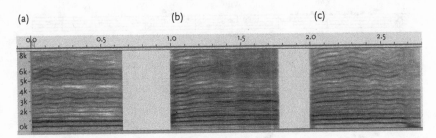

Example 10.5. Spectrograms for three syllables from Marvin Gaye's vocal on "I Heard It through the Grapevine" (all on the pitch Bb4): (A) "You could have *told* me yourself"; (B) "*Oh* I'm just about to"; (C) "Honey honey I *know*" 🔊

justice to Gaye's unforgettable vocal performance; perhaps future research will allow us to penetrate this aspect of the song more deeply.

10.2 ELTON JOHN, "PHILADELPHIA FREEDOM" (1975)
By Elton John and Bernie Taupin

A stand-alone single released at the high point of his career, Elton John's "Philadelphia Freedom" is one of his most successful and enduring songs. While its harmony and melody reflect a number of normative features discussed in previous chapters, they also depart from convention in a number of interesting ways. (A reduced transcription of the first verse and chorus—showing just the pitches, bass notes, and harmonies—is shown in Example 10.6.) A hallmark of Elton's style is its skillful reconciliation of classical and rock harmonic practices (his classical training at London's prestigious Royal Academy of Music served him well in this regard); "Philadelphia Freedom" offers an especially rich illustration of this, as we will see. The structure of the VCU also merits attention, especially its sheer *length*. While a 16-measure verse is not unusual, a chorus of 34 measures is extraordinary; I would challenge the reader to find a longer

Example 10.6. Elton John, "Philadelphia Freedom," showing the harmonies, melodic pitches, and bass notes of the first VCU 🔊

one. (The overall form of the song—just two VCUs followed by an abridged chorus—is somewhat unusual too; perhaps it is partly due to the inordinately long VCU.)

In some respects, the verse is quite typical of the rock style. The first phrase (mm. 9–13) oscillates around $\hat{1}$ (B♭), elaborated with ♭$\hat{3}$ above and $\hat{6}$ below, over major tonic harmony in the accompaniment: this kind of melodic-harmonic construction (combining melodic ♭$\hat{3}$ with harmonic $\hat{3}$) is commonplace, as we have seen (section 2.2). In measures 13–16, the melody again follows convention in its use of mediant mixture—using $\hat{3}$ en route to $\hat{5}$, and ♭$\hat{3}$ coming back down to $\hat{1}$. But the harmonic progression of the phrase, I–II–♭III–II–I, is quite unusual: as noted in section 3.3, the mixing of "sharp-side" (II) and "flat-side" (♭III) triads is uncommon in rock. (Major II is also outside the supermode, though it is not all that uncommon.) The progression could be seen as a kind of harmonic realization of the ♭$\hat{3}$–$\hat{2}$–$\hat{1}$ pattern that occurs repeatedly in the melody (treating each melodic tone as a chordal root)—a creative but logical extension of a conventional practice. (One could also connect it with the introduction, which features the progression IV–♭III–ii–I, though in that case the ii chord is minor.) The melody seems quite oblivious to these chord changes; note especially the downbeat D over the D♭ major chord in measure 14, a striking example of "melodic-harmonic divorce" (section 5.3).

The huge chorus falls into two roughly equal sections, each of which further subdivides into two eight-measure phrases (though the fourth phrase is expanded to ten measures); Example 10.6 shows each phrase on a separate system. Each of the phrases is quite different, making the chorus unusual not only in its length but also in its complexity. The first phrase, again, is quite typical of rock in its pitch organization. The ♭VII6/4 chords could well be regarded simply as linear elaborations of the IV chords on either side; they could also be seen as weakly tonicizing IV. The second eight-measure phrase begins with a rather classical-sounding tonicization of ii (the ♭VII chord in m. 33 could be heard as a ♭VI of ii), followed by the progression ♭VII–VI–♭VI–IV.[3] This progression, again, contains an unusual mixture of sharp-side and flat-side harmonies; it is also tonally ambiguous, undercutting the tonic but not clearly implying any alternative. One could say the half-step motion in the bass (A♭–G–G♭) gives it a kind of logic; unlike

---

3. In a recent seminar, several students argued that mm. 36–37 could be related to the previous tonicization of ii—as ♭VI (or even an augmented sixth) and V. I question this, however. The melody over the G major chord in m. 37 gives no hint that it is functioning as a dominant harmony; and as the beginning of a four-measure phrase, it seems to look forward rather than back.

other linear progressions we have seen, however, this one seems rather isolated from its surroundings—not linearly connected to any structurally important chord. The melody adheres to the progression, in a way, in that the downbeat notes of the VI, ♭VI and IV chords are the fifth of each triad, D–D♭–B♭ (the D♭ and B♭ are anticipatory syncopations, as shown by the diagonal lines). The IV chord that ends the progression also marks the end of the first half of the chorus; perhaps it is not so far-fetched to see it as serving a kind of half-cadential function, unusual in rock—providing partial closure but signaling that more is to come.

Despite its weirdness, the ♭VII–VI–♭VI–IV progression is still more rock than classical (perhaps due to the exclusive use of major root-position triads). And the first two measures of the third phrase—with the melody starting on ♭7̂ and moving to a 6̂-1̂ pentatonic "step," all over tonic harmony—remain firmly in the rock idiom. (From a classical perspective, one might be tempted to label this harmony as V7/IV; but the 6̂-to-1̂ motion over I is not at all classical.) After this, though, the style shifts: the progression in measures 43–47, IV–I6–ii7–I6–V6/5/V–V, is classical to the core. The first five chords could perhaps be viewed as an expanded pre-dominant filled in with I6 chords—the linear bass line (E♭–D–C–D–E) supports this view—though I am reluctant to say that the tonic chords are *subordinate* to the IV and ii7. If anything, the classical allusions become even more obvious in the following measures, with the soaring (almost schmaltzy) violin line over a V7/vi–vi progression.

The third phrase of the chorus also deserves attention with regard to its rhythmic construction (see Example 10.7). The phrase divides into three irregular sub-phrases, 3 + 2 + 3; this breaks up the previously established pattern of four-measure units, which might otherwise have become monotonous. But together, the three units form an eight-measure phrase, preserving regularity at a higher level. Motivic connections—between the

Example 10.7. Elton John, "Philadelphia Freedom," third phrase of chorus (mm. 41–48). Brackets show sub-phrases; dotted brackets show two pairs of motivically related segments.

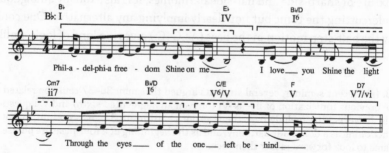

ends of the first and second sub-phrases and within the third sub-phrase (shown in the example)—help to hold the phrase together.

In the fourth phrase, the stylistic shifts between rock and classical become almost head-spinning. The phrase breaks down into two sub-phrases: the first (mm. 49–53) is really a four-measure unit with the final measure expanded into two; the second one (mm. 54–58) could likewise be seen as a four-measure sub-phrase, expanded to overlap into the next VCU, with an additional one-measure expansion of the ii chord. (Such phrase expansions are common in both classical music and rock, as discussed in section 4.4.) After the classical harmony of the third phrase, measures 49–53 bring us back to rock, with a $\flat\hat{3}$–$\hat{2}$–$\hat{1}$ gesture in the melody (mm. 49–50) that connects with the beginning of the verse, and a $\flat$VII6/4–IV progression that recalls the beginning of the chorus. Again, the $\flat$VII6/4 could be seen as an elaboration of the IV; this, coupled with the expansion of the phrase at this point and the suspension of the bass and drums in the accompaniment, gives the IV chord great emphasis. In its dramatic effect, it is a bit like the "grand plagal cadence" discussed earlier (compare with Examples 9.12A and B)—though it occurs at (or near) the end of the VCU rather than at the end of the song, and it does not move *directly* to I.

And then, once again, the song turns classical; the ii–I6–ii6–V6/V–V progression is a common-practice cliché, typically used to approach a half-cadence, recalling the similar harmonic pattern in the third phrase; note once again the linear bass line. (Whether the V really *is* a half-cadence is difficult to say, since this is such a unique context.) In the final few measures, the rock style finally wins out, but with a twist. The moment strongly evokes the schema of the plagal stop cadence (section 9.2): over a "stop" in the accompaniment (though the drums play through it), the vocal line continues and overlaps into the next VCU, coinciding with the cadential move to tonic. The twist is, of course, that the cadence is not IV–I, but rather ii–I. Though ii is an unusual substitute for IV in this context, it is a logical one, sharing two common tones with IV; it also brings to mind the unusual pre-tonic uses of ii (II) in the introduction and in the opening phrase of the verse.

In this song, Elton demonstrates his mastery of both the rock and classical idioms, fusing them together in a unique and satisfying way. Most of the time, as I have suggested, we are clearly in either rock or classical territory (Example 10.8 summarizes these stylistic shifts); yet the transitions between the two are seamless and convincing. Note, especially, how the shifts in harmonic style are sometimes staggered in relation to the eight-measure phrases, providing a kind of cohesion. The unusual instrumentation of the song—a hard-driving rock rhythm section coupled with

Example 10.8. Elton John, "Philadelphia Freedom," chorus, showing harmony (slightly reduced) and shifts between rock and classical harmonic idioms

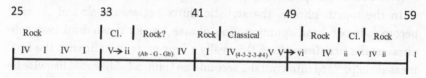

various orchestral instruments (violins, French horn, flute)—seems appropriate in this context. The song also introduces innovative features that are not standard in rock or classical music, but yet seem like logical extensions of the rock idiom—for example, the I–II–♭III–II–I progression in the first phrase and the use of ii in the stop cadence.

I noted earlier that any complete analysis of a song should consider the lyrics and how they relate to the music. In the current case, however, I am stumped; I simply have no idea what the lyrics to this song (written by Elton John's collaborator Bernie Taupin) are trying to say. The beginning of the chorus suggests a patriotic message: "And I live and breathe this Philadelphia freedom / From the day that I was born I waved the flag." But the verses seem to have nothing to do with this. Consider the second verse:

> If you choose to you can live your life alone
> Some people choose the city
> Some others choose the good old family home
> I liked living easy without family ties
> Till the whippoorwill of freedom zapped me right between the eyes

This seems to recount the narrator's transition from an independent, solitary lifestyle to a more interdependent, connected one, and—implicitly— to recommend such a shift to the listener as well: if anything, a rejection of (personal) freedom in favor of commitment and "family ties." What this has to do with Philadelphia or patriotism is unclear. Other lines in the song broach still other, seemingly unrelated, topics: "The less I say the more my work gets done." Given that the lyrics themselves make so little sense, it hardly seems worth puzzling over their connection to the music.[4] This should not be taken as a general criticism of Taupin, whose lyrics include

4. Research into the song's origins sheds little light on the matter. Elton conceived the song as a tribute to the tennis star Billie Jean King, the title being the name of her tennis team (Rosenthal, 2001). But Taupin allegedly said, "I can't write a song about tennis." This tells us that the song is not about tennis, but not much more.

many wonderful (and perfectly intelligible) ones such as "Your Song" and "Goodbye Yellow Brick Road." But it does prove that a great song need not have great lyrics!

10.3 FLEETWOOD MAC, "LANDSLIDE" (1975)

Fleetwood Mac (named after drummer Mick Fleetwood and bassist John McVie) began as a blues-influenced rock band in the late 1960s. The group went through several changes in personnel before McVie and Fleetwood enlisted three singer-songwriters, Lindsey Buckingham, Christine McVie, and Stevie Nicks, a lineup that would bring the band to the highest levels of stardom. "Landslide" is one of Nicks' compositions, from the band's 1975 album *Fleetwood Mac*. It is a simple song in some respects, notably in its instrumentation: just acoustic guitar and some very discreet (almost imperceptible) organ chords in the background. (The basic guitar pattern was shown earlier in Example 6.4B.) But it has some subtle and unusual aspects, and it features a beautiful connection between the music and the lyrics.

Example 10.9 shows the lyrics, melody, and harmony of the first verse. The lyrics are somewhat cryptic (perhaps intentionally so, I will suggest), but this is my best guess: She is taking a walk in the mountains, thinking things through, and trying to decide on her course of action. Her reflection in the snow-covered hills and the landslide that brings it (or her?) down are probably figurative rather than literal: she has a moment of clarity, but this is swept away by the weight of the confused and agitated thoughts in her mind, bringing her back to her uncertain state.

The music of the first verse is uncertain as well. The chord progression of the accompaniment, E♭–B♭6–Cm7–B♭6, uses just the pitches B♭–C–D–E♭–F–G, all within both the E♭ and B♭ major scales and thus fully compatible with

Example 10.9. Fleetwood Mac, "Landslide," first verse

both; the root motions (I–V–vi–V in E♭ or IV–I–ii–I in B♭) do not seem to privilege one key over the other, but the fact that E♭ is hypermetrically strong gives that key an edge. (I have labeled the chords in the key of B♭, but that becomes clear only in retrospect.) The first two melodic phrases trail off oddly, with sharply descending contours; the final note of each phrase is almost mumbled (and hard to hear over the guitar). At this point, perhaps, the singer is focused more on walking than anything else. The melody also clashes with the harmony; outlining a B♭ major triad, it pulls the tonality in that direction, but only weakly given its subdued character. In the third phrase, the melody becomes more forceful (the moment of clarity—"I saw my reflection"), moving to a slightly higher register with more sustained notes, thus asserting the key of B♭ more strongly. But in the fourth phrase it recedes again to the lower register. This phrase has a descending contour similar to the first two and rhymes with them, creating an AABA pattern in the verse; the phrase ends on a G, part of the E♭ major triad, but this coincides with the C minor harmony and thus leaves the tonal ambiguity unresolved.

The uncertainty of the first verse continues into the second verse, but in a different way. The singer's mind is now focused—she knows what she is thinking about—but all she has is questions:

Oh, mirror in the sky, what is love?
Can the child within my heart rise above?
Can I sail through the changing ocean tides?
Can I handle the seasons of my life?

The melody of the first two lines repeats those of the first verse; the third line is similar to that of the first verse, though it goes up to F4 this time, giving further support to B♭ as the tonic. But the fourth line surprises us: instead of returning to the pattern of the first two lines as in the previous verse, it now repeats the third line, hitting its final syllable on the third beat of the measure (instead of on the downbeat as in the first verse). Instead of the AABA form of the first verse, we have a much less conclusive AABB pattern, leaving us expecting another A. We do get a suggestion of that, but it is only half-hearted: the end of the fourth phrase is followed by a long melisma that echoes the first line with a B♭–F–D descent. Thus the second verse is not only tonally ambiguous but feels formally incomplete. The melisma ends with D over the C minor harmony (unlike the end of the first verse which at least gave us a chord tone of C minor), leaving it unresolved in another way as well. At this point, the singer cannot even complete her own incoherent thoughts.

Example 10.10. Fleetwood Mac, "Landslide," first chorus

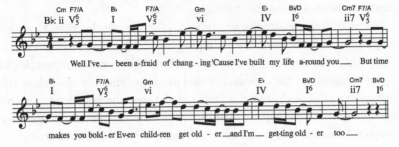

In the chorus (Example 10.10), everything becomes clear—lyrically and musically as well. The singer sees what has been happening in her life and knows what she must do. As soon as we hear that "but" at the beginning of the third line, we know it too: she must—and will—move on from her relationship. Once the decision is made, she is calm and confident. She is even looking ahead now, thinking about her lover's perspective and how she will break the news in a gentle and sympathetic way ("I'm getting older too").

Musically, the crucial moment is the measure just before the chorus (the first measure of Example 10.10). Here the guitar breaks out of the ambiguous harmonic pattern that has occupied it up to that point, moving to an F dominant seventh chord in first inversion ("V6/5" in the example). This introduces A, compatible with the key of B♭ (as $\hat{7}$) but not with E♭ (as $\sharp\hat{4}$). For the first time, then, we have a clear signal of the song's true key. The fact that the chord is in first inversion is significant, not only because it places the disambiguating note A in the bass (making it especially prominent) but in another way as well: inverted chords tend to make the bass line seem more melodic, and thus more intimate, adding poignancy to the harmony as a whole. The rarity of this kind of chordal inversion in rock makes it even more effective.

The strong affirmation of B♭ started by the F6/5 chord continues into the chorus. The four-measure chord progression of the chorus uses the entire B♭ major scale and also (unlike the verse) places B♭ harmony on the hyperdownbeat. The melody arpeggiates the B♭ major triad, with appoggiaturas (accented non–chord tones) preceding each degree of the chord ($\hat{6}$–$\hat{5}$, $\hat{2}$–$\hat{1}$, $\hat{4}$–$\hat{3}$). Rhythmically, too, the fairly regular pattern of syncopations in the melody projects strength and confidence, contrasting with the rather varied and uncertain rhythm of the verse. The third and fourth measures of the chorus recall the verse—the progression E♭–B♭/D–Cm7 resembles the verse progression, and the melody ends on G, as the first verse does; but this is clearly understood in relation to the key of B♭. The second time through the progression, though, these connections with the verse create a smooth transition into the verse that follows.

This next verse features a guitar solo. Like the vocal verses, this verse occupies four iterations of the main progression. But it is structured quite differently, with a four-measure phrase followed by a varied repeat; in this respect it resembles the chorus. The first phrase of the solo also follows the tonal pattern of the chorus: the first part outlines the B♭ major triad while the ending settles on G. The end of the second phrase beautifully reinforces the crucial A of the bass line, and then overlaps into the next chorus to end satisfyingly on the B♭ tonic harmony.

The second chorus is followed by a final verse. Here the words of the first verse are repeated, but with changes in tense (past to present) and perspective (from first person to second person):

> I take my love, take it down
> I climb a mountain and turn around
> And if you see my reflection in the snow-covered hills
> Will the landslide bring you down?

I am not sure what to make of this. Perhaps she is, again, thinking ahead to how her partner will react to the bad news. She is suggesting he do what she did (when I'm confused, I take a walk in the mountains) and wondering, will he see things clearly—and understand *her* perspective—or will he be overwhelmed by a landslide of confusing thoughts and emotions? The third and fourth lines repeat, with a fermata on "hills"—over a B♭ chord, reminding us of the main tonic; then the fourth line repeats one final time, reaching the highest melodic note of the song (G4), and punctuating the final question with a tonally noncommittal C minor harmony.

Overall, I would say, this song is about how a walk in nature can bring clarity of thought. We are walking along, our mind wandering aimlessly, enjoying the scenery, and suddenly it becomes clear to us what is happening in our life and what we must do. (If the lyrics of the verses are a bit cryptic and hard to understand, perhaps this is deliberate—allowing us to experience some of the singer's own confusion.) The musical portrayal of the shift from uncertainty to certainty is as clear as one could wish.

The form of the song is quite unusual: V–V–C–V′–C–V (V′ is the guitar solo), or in more abstract terms (lumping the first two verses together), ABCBA. This form—with A as the verse and B as the chorus—is seen in a few other well-known songs, including the Beatles' "Blackbird," Elton John's "Daniel," and Styx's "Babe." In each of these three songs, though, the verse ends with a strong cadential gesture, which could be said to justify its placement at the end of the song (this was discussed in section 9.4 with regard to "Daniel"). In "Landslide," that is not the case: the verse ends at a point of tonal ambiguity. This makes Nicks's decision to end the song with the verse especially puzzling; it is not a verse that one would normally end a song with. Why did she choose to end the song so inconclusively? By my interpretation, the singer's uncertainty is resolved, and she is now putting herself in her partner's shoes; but one could also choose to see lingering uncertainty in the mind of the singer herself.

10.4   U2, "SUNDAY BLOODY SUNDAY" (1983)
By Bono, the Edge, Adam Clayton, and Larry Mullen

Since their first album in 1980, U2 has been one of the most resilient and hard-working bands in rock. Their artistic path has taken them through a wide range of stylistic identities, earning them continuous success both commercially and critically. But to my mind, they have never (or, I should say, have not yet) surpassed their early work, especially their 1983 album *War* and its first song, "Sunday Bloody Sunday." This song is a statement of protest against the violence in Northern Ireland, taking its name from one especially brutal incident in that struggle. The song has been widely discussed and debated; my analysis here builds on valuable earlier discussions by Fast (2000) and Endrinal (2008). But I believe it is helpful to give greater attention to the ways in which the song interacts with the conventions of the rock style—in particular, *formal* conventions. This will be a recurring theme in the discussion below.

We begin with Larry Mullen's unique drum part in the introduction of the song (Example 10.11A). This could be interpreted as representing either a military march or gunfire; I think it evokes both of these meanings. The military march feel comes from the repetitive pattern of the first four measures, especially the sixteenth-note figures. After that, though, it can be seen that the pattern becomes somewhat irregular; and this is more suggestive of gunshots. Notably, the snare part of the introduction does not do what we expect the snare in a rock song to do, namely, emphasize beats 2 and 4 of the measure. The snare part continues in this vein through the first few measures of the vocal; later on, though (Example 10.11B), Mullen skillfully and discreetly integrates beats 2 and 4 into the pattern, while retaining its original character.

When the vocal enters, we hear the four-measure phrase shown at the beginning of Example 10.12A. Surely we expect this phrase to repeat; it is hardly long enough to be a verse in itself. The phrase that actually follows

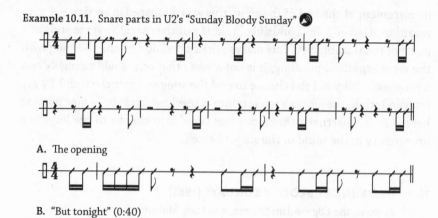

Example 10.11. Snare parts in U2's "Sunday Bloody Sunday"

A. The opening

B. "But tonight" (0:40)

(mm. 5–9 of Example 10.12A) is an unexpected interruption—abrupt and urgent, and contrasting with the first phrase in melodic grouping, harmony, and instrumentation (note the addition of cymbal crashes and sustained violin notes). What follows (mm. 10–13) might seem like a short chorus—note the sparser melodic rhythm and lyric repetition—but later events make clear that it is not. This nine-measure section (mm. 5–13 of the example), which I call X, returns only once in the song, in a completely different context (described further below). Thus, it is a complete anomaly—both in relation to the song and in relation to the conventions of the style: it brings the song into conflict with the "start-with-two" rule that I posited earlier as a strong principle of rock form. I take this violation of convention as deliberate, and the lyrics confirm this: "How long, how long must we sing this song?" The message is clear: No more business as usual, we can't go on like this, the old ways must change. The second occurrence of the X section—in the middle of the second chorus of the song—is similarly unexpected, and surely has the same intent: an effort to wake us up, to shake us out of our stupor.

After the first occurrence of the X section, the initial four-measure melody returns (with different lyrics); this time it is repeated, making it much more like a conventional verse. This is followed by a chorus (Example 10.12B) which is also, in some ways, rather conventional, featuring sparse syllables and internal lyric repetition, as well as background vocals. The chorus falls into two parts (labeled in the example as C1 and C2), with essentially the same melody but quite different harmonic accompaniments.

We noted earlier that there is a strong tradition in rock of opposition between flat-side and sharp-side tonalities within a single song; this most often manifests itself in an alternation between an Aeolian verse and an

Example 10.12. U2, "Sunday Bloody Sunday"

A. First partial verse and "X" section 🔊

B. Chorus 🔊

Ionian (relative-major) chorus, though it appears in other ways as well. "Sunday Bloody Sunday" engages with this convention in a complex and interesting way. The song begins in a clear and unambiguous B♭ Aeolian mode. The beginning of the *X* section (m. 5 of Example 10.12A) briefly tonicizes D♭, the relative major. In the latter part of *X*, the harmony brings the tonality back to B♭; but the melodic line continues to emphasize D♭ and A♭, with the words "But tonight, we can be as one tonight." I see this as highly significant: the singer is withdrawing into his personal relationship (represented by the D♭ major tonality), trying to escape from the pain of the outside world (B♭ Aeolian), but the accompaniment suggests that it cannot be escaped.

In the chorus (Example 10.12B), the opposition between B♭ and D♭ again comes into play. The first part of the chorus (C1) employs the B♭-centered main progression of the song, but the melody once again emphasizes the tonic and dominant degrees of D♭. In the second half of the chorus (C2), the melody repeats its pattern, again suggesting D♭, but now it takes the harmony along with it: the F♭–C♭/E♭–D♭ progression clearly establishes D♭ as tonic (♭III–♭VII6–I). As noted earlier, a shift to the relative major in the chorus is not uncommon, but U2's use of this strategy is noteworthy in two respects. First, using the same melody in two different key contexts is rather unusual in rock. Second, even the D♭ major part of the chorus has a flat-side touch, reflected in the ♭III and ♭VII chords (introducing the ♭$\hat{3}$ and ♭$\hat{7}$ scale-degrees of D♭). (The use of ♭$\hat{3}$ in the accompaniment against $\hat{3}$ in the melody reverses the usual situation.) Again, I see this as expressing the oppressive effect of the violence: Even in an intimate, personal situation, the outside battles intrude, if only in one's private thoughts.

The form of the song as a whole is complex and unique, and I do not have an elegant explanation for it. The first line in the diagram below shows small sections; the second line groups these into larger sections. Ignoring the *X* sections (which I have suggested are *meant* to be disruptive and incongruous), we can discern a loose structure of four VCUs. Each one features verse material followed by chorus material, which includes either both C1 and C2 or just C1. The first four-measure phrase is best regarded as a partial verse, and is shown as V'. The third large verse section consists of a guitar solo (V$_{inst}$), followed by a vocal section ("Wipe your tears away"), labeled as V"; while this is really a new melody, its $\hat{1}$–♭$\hat{7}$–$\hat{5}$ pattern echoes the verse.

V' X V C1 C2 | V C1 X C1 | V$_{inst}$ V" C1 C2 C2 | V C1 |

V   C | V C | V   C | V C |

"Sunday Bloody Sunday" is an outstanding piece of work by virtue of its musical features alone: the unusual form and the skillful interplay between the B♭ and D♭ tonal centers. But what takes it to a higher level is its engagement with the text. We see this in the evocative drum part— mixing military march, gunfire, and backbeat—and in the disruptive *X* sections, challenging the status quo in a musically compelling way. We see it also in the musical depiction of the tension between the personal relationship and the outside world: the D♭ major tonality (representing the personal) is constantly encroached on by negative elements (representing the outside), either the B♭ minor tonality or D♭'s own flat-side degrees. This idea comes through once more at the end of the song, when the verse melody and chorus melody are heard simultaneously—again, an unusual and thoughtful touch. The message is clear, and it is one of U2's guiding principles: That the personal and the political cannot be separated.

10.5 ALANIS MORISSETTE, "YOU OUGHTA KNOW" (1995)

By Alanis Morissette and Glen Ballard

The first single from Morissette's hugely successful album *Jagged Little Pill*, this song is a tirade against an ex-lover. A line from the second verse sets the scene beautifully: "I hate to bug you in the middle of dinner." We can just imagine it: he is out with his new girlfriend at a nice restaurant; she (the singer) happens to walk by and takes the opportunity to confront him; her initial politeness turns to sarcasm, then rage, and finally a kind of cathartic joy. These shifting emotions are clearly reflected in the music, as we will see.

The song is fairly conventional in terms of its large-scale form—V–C–V–C–I–V′–C—but unusual in the construction of the VCU itself. The verse comprises three eight-measure phrases, all built on the same repeating i–IV progression, each one with a different melodic idea.[5] (In the first verse, the first phrase—which begins the song without introduction—is supported only by drums and a few sparse synthesizer sounds; in the second verse, however, this phrase is accompanied by the i–IV progression.) Example 10.13 shows the entire first phrase and part of the second and third. The primary grouping level (indicated by both repetition and breaks in the melody) changes from the two-measure level in the first phrase to the one-measure level in the second; in the third phrase, while the melodic groups are arguably four measures long, a repeated intervallic pattern (shown by a square bracket) is introduced that is only one beat in length. The shortening of repeated patterns, along with the steady increase in syllabic density across the three phrases, creates a gradual increase in both tension and energy, reflecting the singer's rising emotion. The intensities of the syncopations also increase; the displacements of unstressed syllables in the second and third phrases (e.g., "the-a-*ter*," "o-*pen* wide") contribute to the agitated effect.

The expressive trajectory across the three phrases of the verse is also affected by their pitch content. The first phrase uses mainly the emotionally neutral $\hat{1}, \hat{4}$, and $\hat{5}$ degrees, though $\hat{3}$ makes a brief appearance at the end. This captures the singer's restrained, polite demeanor: "I want you to know / That I'm happy for you." The low melodic register also signals

---

5. The lyrics of the third phrase are repeated in the second VCU; one could possibly argue, then, that it is part of the chorus. On the third iteration, though, the lyrics of this phrase are different. And in any case, musically, it seems much more natural to define the following section ("And I'm here") as the chorus: the shift to $\hat{3}$ in the melody, the higher melodic register, and the sparser melodic rhythm are all characteristic chorus features (see section 8.3), and the shift in harmonic progression at that point suggests a sectional boundary as well.

Example 10.13. Alanis Morissette, "You Oughta Know," showing parts of the first verse and chorus. Square brackets indicate units of repetition.

restraint, though the trembling quality of the vocal hints at the emotion boiling beneath the surface. In the second phrase, this emotion bursts through, reflected in the higher register and the more forceful vocal style. The melody of the second phrase evokes what I have called the "Dorian pentatonic"—$\hat{5}$, $\flat\hat{7}$, $\hat{1}$, and $\hat{2}$ (only $\hat{4}$ is absent). Because it lacks both $\hat{3}$ and $\flat\hat{3}$, this scale is expressively ambivalent, though the lyrics have a decidedly sarcastic edge: "Another version of me / Is she perverted like me?" In the third phrase—traversing the entire Dorian mode—the ♭$\hat{3}$ degree makes the narrator's anger clear, as do the lyrics: "And every time you speak her name / Does she know how you told me you'd hold me until you died / But you're still alive."

That last line leads directly into the first line of the chorus: "And I'm here." These words have a double meaning: first, I survived, I made it through our painful breakup; second, I'm here right in front of you, causing you embarrassment. The narrator can take pleasure in both of these meanings—and perhaps, also, from finally having vented her built-up rage in the previous lines. This pleasure is reflected musically as the melody shifts to a triumphant $\hat{3}$ on the opening downbeat of the chorus, accompanied by major tonic harmony in the accompaniment. At this point the harmonic progression shifts to a repeated I–♭VII–♭III–IV pattern. Note that the melody continues to employ $\hat{3}$ as the harmony moves to ♭VII. As noted in section 5.4, this is unusual; it is more common for rock melodies to use ♭$\hat{3}$ over a ♭VII chord. There is something jarring, uncomfortable, out of place, about $\hat{3}$ over ♭VII—not unlike a woman causing a scene in a fancy restaurant. In the third and fourth measures of the chorus, the melody shifts back to ♭$\hat{3}$; the close juxtapositions of $\hat{3}$ and ♭$\hat{3}$ within the melody are also jarring, and expressively bittersweet.

The second four-measure phrase of the chorus repeats the first, but this time the phrase is extended by one measure with the line "You, you, you oughta know." Phrase extensions at the end of the chorus are common, as we have seen—building intensity at this climactic moment. An "end-peaking" trajectory of tension is clearly present here (section 9.3)—reflected in the gradual rhythmic buildup throughout the verse, the phrase extension at the end of the chorus, and the intense alternations between $\hat{3}$ and ♭$\hat{3}$ in the chorus melody. Like "Philadelphia Freedom," the chorus ends with variant of the plagal stop cadence that differs from the typical schema in one important feature. In this case we have a plagal progression, with a stop after the IV, moving to i at the beginning of the second VCU. The twist is that the vocal line ends over the stop; it does not overlap into the next section, as typically occurs in a stop cadence. Indeed, by the definition I proposed earlier, there is no cadence here at all; as a result, the first VCU ends without any sense of resolution.[6]

It is not easy to fit the remainder of the song into the narrative arc described above; formally, it falls back on convention, with a second VCU

6. Actually, the bass slides to a $\hat{1}$ on the final downbeat of the chorus, but because this note is so brief, and lacking harmonic support, it does not convincingly shift the harmony to i.

Example 10.14. Recomposition of the end of the chorus of "You Oughta Know"

of the cross   I bear that you gave to me You you you___ you you ought-a know

followed by an instrumental, an abridged third verse, and two final choruses. The lyrics of the second VCU follow a similar expressive trajectory to the first, with virtually identical music; the only significant difference (already mentioned) is that the i–IV chord progression is now present even in the first phrase of the verse, creating a striking clash between $\hat{3}$ in the melody and the underlying IV chord on the line "I *thought* you should know." In the following instrumental, the guitar maintains the i–IV progression of the verse, but the bass now gravitates around $\hat{4}$ for the whole progression, making the tonic harmony sound more like IVdom9 ($\hat{4}$–$\hat{1}$–$\flat\hat{3}$–$\hat{5}$); the singer riffs rather freely on fragments of the Dorian scale.

The final chorus concludes the same way as the first two, with a stop in the instruments on IV, and the end of the vocal line over the following rest: there the song ends, with the previous IV chord still ringing in our ears. Thus the song as a whole, like the first VCU, ends without a strong sense of closure. Suppose the vocal had continued to the next downbeat and ended over tonic harmony (as in Example 10.14): This would suggest resolution, completion; the scene is over, the singer has stomped out. Instead, because neither the harmony nor the melody is resolved, the whole tirade is likewise left open and unresolved, as if the singer is just standing there, awaiting a response: Well, what do you have to say for yourself? One wonders what he *could* say.

10.6 DESTINY'S CHILD, "JUMPIN' JUMPIN'" (1999)
By Beyoncé, Rufus Elliot, and Chad Knowles

Our final analysis is of a song from 1999—near the end of the historical period that is the focus of this book. Destiny's Child is the female vocal group that launched Beyoncé Knowles's career as one of the most successful stars of the 2000s; "Jumpin' Jumpin'" is from the group's highly successful debut album, *The Writing's on the Wall*. Like the other analyses in this chapter, I will approach the song from the perspective of rock's musical language—the system of conventions presented in earlier chapters. In this case, though, what we will find is not the subtle manipulation and stretching of convention seen in previous discussions, but more radical departures—departures that, in some cases, represent shifting trends in the language itself.

Several things about the song might strike us as surprising from the very beginning. One is its texture. The lead vocal begins the song with no introduction. Accompanying this vocal, at the beginning and almost throughout the song, is a staccato synthesizer line, following the melody an octave above. Also unusual is what is lacking: there is no chordal accompaniment or bass line. Both bass notes and chords appear only here and there throughout the song, as sparse, staccato interjections. The rhythmic feel of the opening is unusual too. The tempo is 88 BPM, fairly slow by the general standards of rock. But the sixteenth-note level is extremely active; the vocal line is nearly all sixteenth notes, something we have very rarely seen up to now. And this persists throughout the song; much of it has a breathless quality, with only very short rests between phrases.

Example 10.15 shows four short segments of the song, labeled "chorus," "T," "verse," and "bridge" ("T" will be explained below). Most of the song is comprised of variants of these four passages. The very sparse texture makes harmonic analysis somewhat difficult, but the example shows the harmonic structure as I hear it. The basic pitch collection of the song is the harmonic minor scale: $\hat{1}$–$\hat{2}$–$\flat\hat{3}$–$\hat{4}$–$\hat{5}$–$\flat\hat{6}$–$\hat{7}$. (The $\flat\hat{7}$ at the end of the first measure of Example 10.15 seems to me to be an "escape tone,"

Example 10.15. Destiny's Child, "Jumpin' Jumpin'"

a type of classical non–chord tone that follows a previous chord tone by step and leaps to another chord tone.) The only harmonies used in the four passages (and indeed in the entire song) are i, V, and ♭VI. All this is highly unusual in the context of rock as a whole: very little rock music uses the harmonic minor scale. Another gesture that I find quite classical is the C♯–B♯ moves on the downbeat of the first measure of the verse (and subsequent measures); I hear this as an appoggiatura, a strong-beat non–chord tone resolving down by step to a chord tone (although the parallel octaves between this inner voice and the bass are *not* classical!).

The form of the song can be represented as follows:

c4 t2 b4 b4 t2 c4 c4 t2 b4 b4 t2 c4 c4 t2 d4 d4 t2 c4 c4 c4 c4 i c4 c4 i
C T V   T C   T V   T C   T Br   T C

The first row shows phrases (with their length in measures); each one is a variant of the passages shown in Example 10.15. The second row shows a larger grouping of these phrases into sections. Note that I have called the first section the chorus and the second section the verse. The main argument for this is that the lyrics of the chorus are unchanging, while those of the verse are different on each occurrence. (The chorus also contains the title phrase and has somewhat lower syllabic density than the other sections.) Starting with the chorus is uncommon but not unprecedented, as discussed in section 8.3. As noted there, chorus-initial songs often feature a verse that departs from tonic harmony, thus functioning somewhat like a bridge, and that is the case here as well: the verses do nothing but prolong V. The actual bridge labeled above uses the same harmonies as previous sections, i and V, in a somewhat irregular pattern; while the melody is slightly different from previous sections, it certainly does not provide the strong contrast that we expect in a rock bridge.

What is most remarkable about the form is the section labeled T, shown in its entirety in Example 10.15; this section occurs after each chorus and also after each verse. I am hard-pressed to think of another song that has the same vocal material occurring in both of these locations.[7] I think of it as kind of a transition—from verse to chorus, and then from chorus to verse. Might we consider the Ts between the Vs and Cs to be prechoruses? (Two measures is rather short for a prechorus, but the slow tempo coupled with the active sixteenth-note level makes this more plausible; a lot can

---

7. Elton John's "Goodbye Yellow Brick Road" is perhaps one—though there the passage seems more closural in function (ending on a strong cadence) rather than transitional.

happen in two measures in this song.) We normally think of a prechorus as building energy, and the T section certainly does that with its rise in register. Prechoruses also tend to create tension, often through emphasis of non-tonic harmony, phrasal irregularity, or high syllabic density. Neither of the first two features is present here—the section is all tonic harmony and rhythmically square—but the syllabic density is indeed higher than in other sections; we also see a quickening of the grouping structure (from one-measure segments in the verse to half-measure segments in the T section), which is also characteristic of prechoruses. Another aspect of the T section also creates tension: the percussion. The traditional backbeat pattern—normally an important cue to the perception of meter in rock—is heard throughout most of the song, but begins to break apart in the beginning of the T section and then disappears, leaving us briefly with no backbeat at all, while a lower drum sound builds energy with a constant sixteenth-note pulse. In the following section (verse or chorus) the regular snare pattern is immediately restored. So despite the T section's tonic harmony and its unusual placement, it has definite elements of "prechorus quality."

Several other aspects of the song deserve mention. There are strikingly few anticipatory syncopations: just one in the chorus (girl with her *friends*) and none in the T section. Syncopations are more prominent in the verse and bridge. Also notable is the harmonization of the chorus melody in "parallel fifths" in the second chorus—with a second line exactly a perfect fifth above the main melody. Beyoncé's improvised flourishes from the third chorus to the end of the song, rhythmically quite free and largely pentatonic, are one of the few strong links with the rock tradition. As for the lyrics, little needs to be said: there is not much deep meaning in them, as far as I can see, but they convey a strong spirit of female independence and empowerment—something that characterizes many of Destiny's Child's songs and Beyoncé's later solo material as well.

The first time I heard this song, I sensed that it was something very fresh and different, and I remember others also having that impression. In this analysis I have tried to show why it has this effect. Some features of the song are truly original and creative: in particular, the staccato synthesizer line doubling the vocal and the transition section that follows each verse and chorus. But a number of its other unconventional features are representative of general trends in rock that began to emerge at about the same time: the slower tempo and dense sixteenth-note vocal style, the use of harmonic minor, and the sparse, linear accompaniment texture. We will say more about these trends in the next chapter.

The six songs listed below will reward careful analytical study. Do a formal analysis of the entire song; transcriptions of certain sections may be appropriate too, as indicated below. (By "transcription" I mean notation of the melody with harmonic symbols.) Consider also the lyrics and their connection to the music. In each case I draw attention to a few notable aspects.

1. The Supremes, "You Can't Hurry Love." This song has an unusual rhythmic feel; consider how syncopation is used, in relation to the tactus level. Transcribe at least the chorus. The melody on the words "can't hurry love" creates a motive that is used in interesting ways. The form is also highly unusual; how does it relate to the narrative of the lyrics?

2. The Beatles, "Eleanor Rigby." This song is interesting from many viewpoints: motive, harmony, phrase structure, instrumentation, and form. Transcribe all three of the repeated sections. How are changes in instrumental texture used to delineate formal sections? (At one point, the accompaniment contains a prominent linear pattern.) The song can be seen as mixing two diatonic modes; which two, and does one have primacy over the other?

3. Joni Mitchell, "Both Sides Now." The song was first recorded by Judy Collins (1967) and only later by Mitchell herself (1969); the two versions offer a fascinating contrast. Begin with Collins's version, transcribing the first VCU. (The harmony is fairly straightforward; the melody has some beautiful moments of independence from it.) Then consider Mitchell's version, in which the harmony is much more ambiguous; how would you analyze it? Do pedals (bass or upper-voice) play a role? Whitesell (2008, 146) prefers Mitchell's version, dismissing Collins's version as a "sugary barrage of primary colors"; do you agree, or does Collins's version bring out the true harmonic potential of Mitchell's matchless melody? Does one version or the other seem better suited to the lyrics? Consider also the structure of the lyrics (shared by both versions), which is unusual; which lyrical segments are repeated across the three VCUs?

4. The Who, "Behind Blue Eyes." The form of the song could be described as ABA′, though the A′ is much shorter than the A. The A falls into two sections (transcribe the first one); are they VCUs? The B section is strongly contrasting in many ways; how so? At certain points in both the A and B sections, there are leanings toward other keys; explain. The IV chord plays a central role throughout the song; at one point, we could say it plays a "reorienting" role, as it does in Example 9.6. Where in the song

do end-accented phrases occur? Does the strong contrast between the A and B sections relate to the lyrics? What do you make of the strange ending?

5. Bonnie Raitt, "I Can't Make You Love Me." Transcribe the melody and harmony of the first verse and chorus. (The second chord of the verse is unusual.) The treatment of tonic harmony is remarkable; how so? At one point there is a subtle but powerful difference between the second VCU and the first. The lyrics of the song take an unusual perspective; does this relate to the music in some way?

6. Pearl Jam, "Better Man." Transcribe the first verse and chorus. Inverted (i.e., non-root-position) chords play an important role; what is the expressive effect of this? How are the verse and chorus different in tonality, or at least tonal clarity? Does this relate to the lyrics in some way? The instrumental texture changes dramatically at a surprising place; explain.

CHAPTER 11
Rock in Broader Context

It has sometimes been noted—usually as a criticism—that the discipline of music theory tends to examine music out of context. We tend to treat pieces of music as "autonomous"—not giving much attention to the social, economic, political, and biographical circumstances in which they were created (Kerman, 1985; McClary, 1987). Certainly, the current study fits this description. I do not regard this as a virtue, but (as explained in chapter 1) I do think it is defensible—that focusing on a rather narrow (and admittedly incomplete) perspective can be useful and productive. I also feel that the sociocultural aspects of music just mentioned, important though they are, are to some extent separable from the purely musical aspects discussed here. I am not sure, for example, that a sociocultural perspective would shed much light on the strategies used in rock for handling the VCU boundary, the factors involved in key identification, the use of syncopation, or the factors involved in choices between $\hat{3}$ and $\flat\hat{3}$—though certainly we should be open to such possibilities.

In one respect, though, I do wish to take a broader perspective in this final chapter of the book, and that is with respect to the *musical* context of rock: the earlier styles from which it grew, the concurrent styles that it has interacted with, and its stylistic evolution in recent years—years in which some might say that it has begun to yield the center stage of American popular music to other genres. This is also a logical place to reexamine the concept of rock itself, as I have defined it. We will consider some stylistic distinctions within rock and changes in the style over the decades, adding some nuance to the rather monolithic view of rock that has been presented so far.

11.1 THE ROOTS OF ROCK

The musical roots of the rock style have been discussed by a number of authors (van der Merwe, 1989; Middleton, 1990; Moore, 2001; Covach & Flory, 2015). Oversimplifying somewhat, we can point to three styles whose influence on rock is thought to have been especially formative: common-practice music, Tin Pan Alley / jazz, and the blues. Each of these requires some comment. By common-practice music, I mean not just eighteenth- and nineteenth-century art music but a much broader range of pre-twentieth-century European (and American) music that shares the same basic principles, such as hymns, Christmas carols, children's songs, folk songs, and marches. Tin Pan Alley refers to early- and mid-twentieth-century American popular song, epitomized by such composers as Cole Porter, George Gershwin, and the team of Richard Rodgers and Lorenz Hart. The inclusion of jazz in this category may seem questionable, but I think this will be justified by the following discussion; what I have in mind is the classic jazz of the 1930s and 1940s, not the more progressive styles (modal jazz and the like) that developed later. Lastly, the blues is often divided into two styles: the "country" or "downhome" blues of the early-twentieth-century American South, and the "urban" blues that developed in the 1940s and 1950s (Titon, 1994; Moore, 2002a). The two styles differ in certain respects; in particular, the twelve-bar harmonic structure that we associate with the blues is much more variable (both harmonically and metrically) in downhome blues than it is in the urban style. My focus here is on the urban style, which is thought to have had more direct influence on rock music.

Before continuing, I should mention two other styles that have been cited as important sources for rock. One is the tradition of African-American religious music known as gospel (Cusic, 2002; Headlam, 2002). Many singers in doo-wop, soul, and funk began as gospel musicians (Sam Cooke, Aretha Franklin, and James Brown are examples), so it is not surprising that it influenced these genres. The most often-cited influence is in the area of vocal style. Gospel singing is often highly ornamented and melismatic in character; elements of the gospel style can be heard in the singers mentioned above, and others such as Percy Sledge ("When a Man Loves a Woman") and Whitney Houston ("I Will Always Love You"). In addition, the close vocal harmony of gospel music clearly influenced doo-wop, which in turn influenced later genres in this regard, from early-1960s girl groups to the Beach Boys and beyond. In terms of harmonic structure, rhythm, and melodic pitch materials, gospel can be seen to combine common-practice elements (simple major-mode harmonic patterns, some use of simple duple meter) with blues elements (some use of minor penta-tonic melody, though the major pentatonic is more common) and may have helped to pass on these elements to rock. The second style that is often mentioned as an influence on rock is country music. I will say more about country below; suffice it to say for now that most elements of early (pre-rock) country can be traced to the common-practice tradition.

The three styles under consideration—common-practice, Tin Pan Alley / jazz, and the blues—were, of course, not independent from one another. Common-practice music was an enormous influence on Tin Pan Alley and jazz; blues elements can be found in jazz and Tin Pan Alley as well; and surely the blues was affected by the common-practice tradition. Still, each of these styles has distinctive features. In what follows, I examine the commonalities between each of these styles and rock. I find strong influ-ences on rock from each of them, in accord with the conclusions of earlier authors. But I would like to be a bit more precise and systematic in identify-ing these influences than previous discussions have been.

Table 11.1 represents each of the four styles—common-practice, Tin Pan Alley / jazz, blues, and rock—with regard to a series of basic musical dimen-sions or features. While I am obviously painting with a very broad brush

Table 11.1 BASIC FEATURES OF COMMON-PRACTICE MUSIC (CPM), TIN PAN ALLEY /JAZZ, THE BLUES, AND ROCK

	CPM	TPA/jazz	Blues	Rock
Extended triadic harmony (9ths, 11ths, 13ths)	Rare	Common	Rare	Rare
Extensive use of chordal inversion	Yes	No	No	No
Close melodic-harmonic coordination	Yes	Yes	No	Somewhat
Preference for "classical" harmonic moves (e.g. desc 5ths)	Yes	Yes	No	Weak
Straight vs. swung tempo	Straight	Swung (mostly)	Swung (in uptempo blues)	Straight (except very early rock)
Hypermetrical irregularity	Often	Rarely	Rarely	Sometimes
Anticipatory syncopation	No	Yes	Yes (but sometimes rhythmically very free)	Yes
Rubato	Yes	No	No	No

here, I believe these generalizations are mostly uncontroversial. There are a number of points to be made about the table. Most broadly, it can be seen that all of the characteristics of rock noted in the table are shared with at least one of the other three styles—consistent with (although certainly not proving) the view that rock primarily grew out of these styles. Anticipatory syncopation comes out of Tin Pan Alley and blues; the prevalence of straight (rather than swung) tempo is presumably of common-practice origin. With regard to the melody-harmony relationship, rock is a fusion of earlier styles, balancing the close melodic-harmonic coordination of the common practice and Tin Pan Alley with the looser approach of the blues; similarly, rock's ambivalence toward classical norms of root motion may also be partly due to blues influence. The scalar character of rock (not shown in the table) may also be seen as a stylistic fusion; as suggested earlier (section 2.2), the "fuzzy" scales of rock melody combine the minor pentatonicism of the blues with a preference for diatonic steps and adherence to the harmony.

One dimension that I find of particular interest is hypermetrical regularity. The very strong norm of 4-, 8-, and 16-measure units in Tin Pan Alley and jazz is well-known, as is the norm of 4-measure and 12-measure phrases in the blues. While this norm is certainly present in common-practice music and rock as well, there are also frequent irregularities in these styles. Even more strikingly, the specific ways that hypermetrical irregularity is used—extended (e.g., five-measure) phrases, overlaps, and metrical reinterpretations (see sections 4.4 and 9.1)—seem very similar between rock and classical music; to my knowledge, these patterns are virtually nonexistent in Tin Pan Alley and the blues. Whether their emergence in rock is due to common-practice influence or whether they developed independently is an open question.

Elsewhere (Temperley, 2004) I have suggested that styles may reflect systematic "trade-offs" between the dimensions in Table 11.1. A case in point is syncopation and rubato (expressive variation in tempo). If a style made extensive use of both rubato and syncopation, the underlying meter might be obscured, so styles tend not to allow both. Classical music allows a high degree of rubato but has little syncopation; jazz has a strict tempo but extensive syncopation; rock is similar to jazz in both respects, so it fits the pattern. I also proposed a trade-off between chordal inversion and extended chords (ninths, thirteenths, and the like). If a style allowed both chordal inversions and extensions, it might be difficult to identify the roots of chords. Classical music makes great use of chordal inversion, but extensions are rare; in jazz, the reverse is true. Interestingly, in rock and the blues, neither chordal inversions nor extensions are common: root-position triads and sevenths are the norm. But the melodic-harmonic independence in blues and rock—unlike classical music and jazz—means that the melody is less informative about the harmony; perhaps this requires the accompaniment to present the harmony more clearly and unambiguously.

One aspect of rock that cannot be convincingly traced to any of these earlier styles is its extensive use of flat-side harmonies: ♭VII, ♭III, and ♭VI. Attributing this to the influence of classical minor seems implausible; as I have shown, rock's "flat side" is quite different from classical minor in other ways, and the ♭VII triad is rarely seen in classical minor (apparent ♭VIIs are usually better explained as V of ♭III). (Minor mode in jazz and Tin Pan Alley is uncommon and is harmonically similar to classical minor.) Wagner (2003) suggests that rock's flat-side harmonies can be viewed as supportive chords (consonantizations) for blues-influenced flat-side melody notes; I think this is part of the explanation but not the whole story. Examining some of the earliest uses of flat-side chords in rock sheds interesting light. The ♭VII chord in Example 11.1A could be explained as emerging from a tonicization of IV—shifting the entire I–IV–I progression down a fifth. Indeed, this ♭VII is arguably IV of IV; but one can imagine how a more independent ♭VII could have grown out of such uses. Del Shannon's "Runaway" (Example 11.1B) uses both ♭VII and ♭VI as part of a i→♭VII→♭VI–V progression, a variant of the "lament bass" pattern that goes back to the Renaissance.[1] Another early appearance of both ♭VI and ♭III is in the Animals' cover of the folk song "House of the Rising Sun" (Example 11.1C); however, the actual folk versions of this song do not use this progression.[2] The ♭VI in the Beatles' "I Saw Her Standing There" (Example 11.1D) seems to me to have no clear historical antecedent; it is a truly original move, a deliberate harmonic surprise (though the fact the ♭VI contains $\hat{1}$—emphasized in the melody—gives it some connection to its context). Perhaps these diverse and (at the time) anomalous uses of flat-side chords planted the seed for the more widespread and conventionalized usages that emerged in the following years.

Another rather distinctive aspect of the rock style is its formal conventions—the VCU and the large-scale formal structures that go with

---

1. The lament bass pattern, $\hat{1}$→♭$\hat{7}$→♭$\hat{6}$–$\hat{5}$, is traditionally harmonized with v6 over the ♭$\hat{7}$ rather than ♭VII. The i→♭VII→♭VI–V progression is used in other styles, notably flamenco. But I suspect that the ♭VII here (and in other early rock songs) is not due to external influence but rather grows out of the general preference in rock for root-position chords.

2. Some early versions of the song, such as Woody Guthrie's, are in major. Other versions, such as Pete Seeger's, are in minor but with different harmonies. The closest to the Animals' version that I can find is Joan Baez's, which uses ♭III and ♭VI, though the latter is in a different location: i→III–V–i→VI–I–V–V. Another early use of ♭III, noted by Rings (2013), is the I→III–IV→III–I riff in the Everly Brothers' "Wake Up Little Susie"— perhaps a harmonic elaboration of a blues melodic gesture.

Example 11.1. Early rock songs with "flat-side" harmonies

A. Buddy Holly and the Crickets, "Not Fade Away"

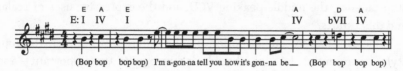

B. Del Shannon, "Runaway"

C. The Animals, "House of the Rising Sun"

D. The Beatles, "I Saw Her Standing There" (chorus)

it. (Form seemed too complex to represent in Table 11.1.) The origin of these conventions seems to have been internal to the development of rock. Covach (2005) suggests, quite plausibly, that the simple-verse form of early rock came out of the blues and that the AABA form prevalent around 1960 grew out of jazz and Tin Pan Alley.[3] Verse-chorus form then seems to have emerged from these forms through a lengthening of the repeating section (and a bifurcation into separate verse and chorus sections), as discussed

---

3. The terms "verse" and "chorus" are used in connection with Tin Pan Alley music, but with a very different meaning (see Covach, 2005, for discussion). As noted by Stephenson (2002), however, there may be a precedent for rock's verse-chorus conventions in earlier music of the common-practice tradition; think of the Christmas carol "We Three Kings," for example.

in section 8.1. Some of the most original aspects of the rock style seem to have developed in connection with verse-chorus form, such as the plagal stop cadence, the middle-peaking VCU, and the expressive uses of scalar and tonal shifts.

Table 11.1 focuses our attention on the differences between the four styles represented, but we should also recognize the important—and even more fundamental—commonalities between them: tonality (defined broadly as organization around a tonal center), meter (primarily duple metrical structures), an underlying twelve-step chromatic scale (notwith-standing some microtonal notes in the blues and perhaps in rock), an essentially triadic harmonic structure, a norm of melody-accompaniment texture, and a norm of regular four-measure phrases (though stretched to varying degrees in different styles).[4] These features set the styles in Table 11.1 apart from many traditional non-Western styles—many of which feature monophonic textures, no harmonic structure, and irregular meters or no meter at all. They also distinguish rock and its stylistic ancestors from much twentieth-century art music—a body of music so diverse that it is difficult to generalize about it, but much of which rejects some or all of the features mentioned above. This of course says nothing about the value of these various styles; it is simply an important set of facts that are surely relevant in organizing and categorizing the world's musics.

11.2 STYLISTIC DISTINCTIONS AND CHANGES WITHIN ROCK

Having compared rock to the styles that preceded it, we now turn to stylistic distinctions within rock itself. I first offer some thoughts about the historical evolution of rock, as a whole, over the period considered in this book (roughly 1955 to 2000).

Several observations have been made about historical changes in rock, but it is useful to bring them together here. In section 4.1, I observed that the *Rolling Stone* corpus shows a noticeable slowing of tempo from the 1950s into the 1960s; average tempo then remains fairly steady until the 1990s, when another slowing occurred. The move into the 1960s also saw a shift from swung tempo to straight tempo. Another shift that we observed was in the area of form: the verse-refrain forms prevalent in the late 1950s and early 1960s gave way to the verse-chorus form that predominated from

---

4. Some might question whether melody-accompaniment texture is the norm in common-practice music—much more complex and contrapuntal textures are often used—but it is certainly one common texture.

then on. A further aspect of historical change that we have not considered is in the area of harmony. In an earlier article, de Clercq and I (2011) showed that the complexity of harmony in the *Rolling Stone* corpus increases markedly between the 1950s and later decades. Example 11.2 shows just one statistic that summarizes this trend: the proportion of harmonies in the corpus that are either *I, IV,* or *V*. (The overall distribution of roots in the corpus was shown earlier in Table 3.1.) It can be seen that this proportion declines markedly after the 1950s and then remains fairly steady after that (though with some further decline in the 1990s). This suggests that 1950s rock mostly adheres to a simple harmonic vocabulary of "primary" triads, while later decades reflect a broader variety of chords. It is noteworthy that in all three of these areas—tempo, harmony, and form—the decisive change seems to be from the 1950s to the 1960s. The small size of the corpus does not permit us to pinpoint the changes much more finely than that, but informal observation suggests that it was largely in the early 1960s that these changes in harmony, tempo, rhythmic feel, and form took place. One might say it was during that time that rock achieved maturity; it then remained stable, in some respects, for several decades after that.

I say "in some respects"—because in other respects, the 1960s witnessed an astonishing explosion of styles. Consider the state of rock in around 1960: we had girl groups like the Shirelles ("Will You Love Me Tomorrow"), the rockabilly of the Everly Brothers ("Cathy's Clown"), early soul groups like the Drifters ("Save the Last Dance for Me")—not much else, and all of these within fairly narrow stylistic range. Compare that to the breadth of styles on the scene in 1970: the heavy metal of Led Zeppelin and Black

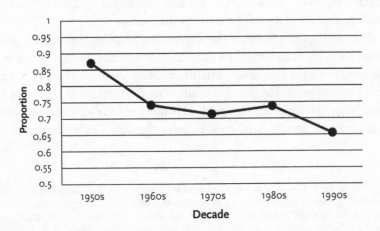

Example 11.2. The proportion of chords in the *Rolling Stone* corpus with roots of *I, IV,* or *V,* broken down by decade

Sabbath, the soft rock of Elton John and James Taylor, the hard-edged soul of Sly and the Family Stone, the dance pop of the Jackson 5, the progressive rock of King Crimson and Pink Floyd—a dazzling stylistic spectrum.

I would argue that the array of styles that developed in the late 1960s largely defined rock's stylistic range for the next three decades. It is easy to lose sight of this, given the many labels that have come and gone over the years: southern rock, glam rock, new wave, contemporary R&B, adult contemporary, alternative, and so on. Such labels often obscure the very strong commonalities that have persisted across rock's history. Yes, we can pretty easily tell the difference between a late-1980s pop song by Madonna or Whitney Houston and a mid-1960s song by the Supremes. But I would argue that this is more due to relatively superficial differences in instrumentation and production (more synthesizers and less reverb in the later songs) than to fundamental differences in musical style. As another example, 1990s songs like Bonnie Raitt's "I Can't Make You Love Me" and Sarah McLachlan's "Angel" were classified as "adult contemporary," but how different are they really from the soft rock of the early 1970s—Carole King's "It's Too Late" or James Taylor's "Fire and Rain"? Yet another example: conventional wisdom has it that a new genre of "alternative" rock developed in the 1990s, represented by bands such as Nirvana, Pearl Jam, Soundgarden, and Green Day. But surely the serious, ambitious music of Pearl Jam has much more in common with Led Zeppelin, and the unpretentious, high-speed music of Green Day has more in common with the Ramones (or, indeed, the Kinks and the early Who), than these two 1990s bands have with each other. In cases such as these, I find the continuities across the decades to be much more striking than the changes.[5] If I am right, then the 1960s not only defined the fundamental features of rock as a whole but also created the stylistic streams that would guide its evolution for the next thirty years.

If we wish to characterize the differences between the various genres within rock, this can largely be done in terms of the musical dimensions discussed in earlier chapters. Pitch organization is certainly a factor. I suggested in chapter 3 that flat-side/sharp-side distinctions in scale and harmony align, to some extent, with stylistic boundaries. Soft rock tends to favor major mode; hard rock is more flat-side (with heavy metal as

---

5. One might make, in a sense, the opposite argument—that differences between *concurrent* genres of rock tend to be exaggerated. Covach (2003) argues that the "new wave" of the late 1970s had much in common with the "corporate rock" that it supposedly rebelled against. But this, too, supports my larger point—that differences between genres of rock, whether within the same time frame or across the decades, can easily be overstated.

an extreme case); soul, funk, and disco tend to be Dorian or pentatonic union, often reflecting the "mixed" practice described in chapter 2 (harmonically major and melodically minor); some blues-influenced hard rock is also mixed. In terms of rhythmic feel, soft rock (including ballads of all kinds) tends to be slow; punk and its offshoots (new wave and some alternative rock) tend to be faster than hard rock (and simpler—heavy metal can sometimes be quite complex and virtuosic); soul, funk, disco, and other dance-oriented pop feature a high level of sixteenth-note activity and complex, multilayered rhythmic textures (like "ABC," discussed in chapter 4). Progressive rock tends toward variety and deliberate unconventionality in all aspects: unusual chord progressions, irregular and shifting meters, and complex, through-composed forms.[6] In terms of instrumental combinations and timbres, too, each style has its distinctive markers: piano and acoustic guitar in soft rock, distorted guitar in hard rock and punk, violins and syncopated rhythm guitar patterns (like Example 6.4A) in disco, synthesizers in 1980s pop. Soul and funk often feature a highly ornamented vocal style, reflecting the gospel influence on these genres.

In other ways, though, the similarities across these styles seem much more striking than the differences. With regard to many of the aspects of rock discussed in this book—principles of tonality (the way that keys are established), formal conventions (verse-chorus differences), patterns of melodic grouping (the norm of "beginning-accented" two- and four-measure groups), uses of anticipatory syncopation, basic principles of drumming (the backbeat and the destabilizing fill before the hyperdownbeat)—I can see little that distinguishes heavy metal from Motown, or alternative rock from disco. I have tried to bring out the generality of these phenomena, and others, by using a range of examples to illustrate them. We have seen, for example, that principles of mediant mixture work much the same way in the Beatles and the Jackson 5, and that the conventions of the prechorus differ little between the Supremes and Green Day. And it is because of commonalities such as these that I believe we are justified in thinking of this broad range of music as comprising a single musical style.

6. Some may feel that the treatment of progressive rock in this book has been insufficient. Certainly it is not commensurate with the large body of analytical work on the subject; this includes the chapters in Holm-Hudson (2002) and many other books, book chapters, and articles as well. But perhaps this is appropriate. Progressive rock, almost by definition, seeks to break away from the conventions of rock—in harmony, meter, form, and timbre—and to develop new approaches to these dimensions; to some extent, then, each piece must be understood on its own terms. This is not to say that rock's stylistic conventions are irrelevant to progressive rock—many analytical studies show that they are not—but they are, perhaps, less important.

While I have emphasized the continuities in rock's history from the mid-sixties to 2000, I certainly would not claim that *no* changes occurred during this period. I have mentioned several—the rise of synthesizer and sequencer technology, changes in production style (e.g., the decrease in reverb), and the decrease in tempo in the 1990s. I wish to point to one further historical shift that I find especially striking and puzzling. Recall that in chapter 2 we defined each melody in the *Rolling Stone* corpus as "major" if $\hat{3}$ occurred more often than $\flat\hat{3}$, and "minor" if $\flat\hat{3}$ occurred more. Considering just the minor songs, it is interesting to examine the frequency of melodic $\hat{6}$ in relation to $\flat\hat{6}$. Grouping both $\hat{6}$ and $\flat\hat{6}$ together as "submediant" degrees, we can define the "submediant ratio" of a song as the proportion of submediant notes that are $\hat{6}$ (as opposed to $\flat\hat{6}$). Roughly speaking, this represents the relative preference for Dorian over Aeolian; Dorian contains $\hat{6}$ (yielding a high submediant ratio), while Aeolian contains $\flat\hat{6}$ (a low submediant ratio). (Minor melodies with a high submediant ratio that include some use of $\hat{3}$ might better be described as using the pentatonic union scale.) The scatterplot in Example 11.3 shows the submediant ratio for all the minor melodies in the *Rolling Stone* corpus (I now extend this to the 2000s, including a corpus of songs from that decade that will be discussed in section 11.4). The pattern is clear and unmistakable: songs from the 1950s and 1960s use $\hat{6}$ almost exclusively; the 1970s, 1980s, and 1990s are a period of transition; and songs from the 2000s overwhelmingly favor $\flat\hat{6}$. This indicates an important shift in the melodic character of rock

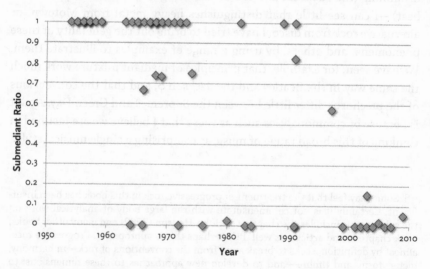

Example 11.3. The submediant ratio (the frequency of $\hat{6}$ as a proportion of $\hat{6} + \flat\hat{6}$) in minor melodies (those in which $\flat\hat{3} > \hat{3}$) in the *Rolling Stone* corpus. Markers with strong shading represent multiple data points.

that is difficult to explain; the expressive connotations of $\hat{6}$ versus $\flat\hat{6}$ may be relevant here. We return to the issue of rock's development in the 2000s in section 11.4.

11.3 INTERACTIONS AND FUSIONS

Rock has interacted with other styles throughout its existence—absorbing their influence and influencing them in turn, and sometimes giving rise to new hybrid genres or "fusions." A few of these stylistic interactions will be discussed here. I cannot treat them in the depth that they deserve, but they seem too important to be left unmentioned.

An important early influence on rock was folk music. Folk became an important part of the American music scene in the late 1950s and early 1960s, represented by acts such as the Weavers; Peter, Paul, and Mary; and Bob Dylan. It has been suggested that the modal element of rock harmony may derive from folk music (Macan, 1997; Biamonte, 2010); but I can find very little modality in the music of the folk groups just mentioned. Folk music does feature a good deal of pentatonic (mostly major pentatonic) melody, which may have influenced rock. More generally, folk music simply reinforced the basic common-practice language that was already in the background of many rock musicians: simple triadic harmony (without the extensions of jazz or the melodic-harmonic independence of the blues) and classical harmonic motions (pre-dominant–dominant–tonic). These elements are prominent in some so-called "folk rock" bands such as the Byrds. Folk music also generated renewed interest in the acoustic guitar, seen in songs such as the Beatles' "Norwegian Wood." Above all, though, the influence of folk on rock is seen in a change in attitude: the idea that rock was more than just frivolous entertainment and could actually be *serious*—in its lyrical content (addressing personal relationships in a mature, thoughtful way, as well as social and political issues) and, by extension, in its musical content as well.

Another important force in American music at around 1960 was Latin and Caribbean music, reflected in a series of fads for genres such as calypso, mambo, cha-cha, and bossa nova. Stewart (2000) has suggested that the influence of these genres—all of which feature a "straight" (i.e., even) rather than "swung" division of the beat—may have contributed to the shift of rock to a straight rhythmic feel at around this time. Some Latin/Caribbean music also features an active sixteenth-note level and complex, multilayered rhythms (consider a song such as Harry Belafonte's "Jump in the Line"); this may have been part of the inspiration for the experiments of James Brown and others along these lines. In 1970s disco, Latin influences became explicit, seen for example in the bossa nova rhythm (3+3+4+3+3) of George McCrae's "Rock Your Baby" and the congas of the Bee Gees' "You Should Be Dancing." The influence of Latin music on rock has become important again in recent years, seen most notably in the explosive success of Santana's album *Supernatural* in 1999. This influence may also account, in part, for the recent rise of harmonic minor in rock, which I discuss in the next section.

The term "fusion" on its own most often indicates mixtures of rock and jazz, and this too has been an important stylistic interaction (Coryell & Friedman, 2000). Fusion can take several forms. In some cases, rock elements can be imported into what is essentially a jazz context. Miles Davis's 1970 album *Bitches Brew*, viewed as a pioneering example of jazz-rock fusion, is in this category; the album uses rock-like drum beats but otherwise features the highly free improvisation characteristic of jazz at the time. In other cases, jazz-rock fusion involves integrating jazz elements into a rock context—most often, harmonic elements. Consider, for example, Steely Dan's "Josie" (the chorus is shown in Example 11.4), which uses complex jazz harmony in what is otherwise a fairly conventional verse-chorus song. Jazz-influenced harmony sometimes also appears in the music of soul and funk artists, such as Stevie Wonder and Earth, Wind & Fire.

So far, we have focused on genres that predated rock and influenced it. In the later decades of rock, we see the rise of new genres that emerged partly from rock's influence. One such genre is electronic dance music (EDM). EDM is largely instrumental, though some genres (such as house) may have vocals; it is largely (often entirely) electronically produced, through synthesis and sometimes sampling; it is often rhythmically complex and extremely repetitive. EDM events feature DJs who mix recordings together in complex and creative ways, thus playing an important role

Example 11.4. Steely Dan, "Josie" (chorus)

in shaping the musical experience. As documented by Butler (2006), EDM grew out of disco in the 1970s, and in the following years it interacted quite closely with rock; some pop music of the 1980s could be considered EDM, such as New Order's "Bizarre Love Triangle." In the 1990s, however, EDM diverged from rock, largely taking over the dance functions that genres of rock had served in earlier decades. Still, Butler shows that many features of rock, especially rhythmic features—anticipatory syncopations and cross-rhythms—are characteristic of EDM as well.

Rap music (or hip-hop) originated in the early 1970s when DJs began speaking over instrumental sections of funk and soul records. Rap steadily increased in importance and popularity throughout the following decades, and many would say that it now eclipses rock in these respects (more on this in the next section). One might wonder why I do not include rap as rock; the simple reason is that the lack of melody (and often of harmony as well) in rap seems to set it apart from all of the genres of rock. Rap does share certain basic features with rock: the basic "backbeat" drum pattern and, in many cases, an alternation of verses (with changing lyrics on each occurrence) and choruses (with unchanging lyrics). In addition, many of the actual drum tracks of rap are sampled from earlier soul, funk, and even hard rock songs. Rap also features anticipatory syncopations, but their complexity (as well as that of rhyme schemes and phrase structures) can far exceed that of most rock (Walser, 1995; Adams, 2009). The fusions between rock and rap are seen most clearly in songs that contain both sung and rapped sections; this includes some of the most successful songs of the 2000s, such as Justin Timberlake's "SexyBack" (with Timbaland), Jay-Z's "Empire State of Mind" (with Alicia Keys), and Rihanna's "Umbrella" (with Jay-Z). An especially interesting kind of fusion between rap and rock is seen in melodies that are definitely pitched but use very limited pitch materials and have the complex and irregular rhythms of rap, such as Usher's "Yeah" (Example 11.5). The influence of rap has also spread to the harder varieties of rock, as seen in bands such as Linkin Park and Rage Against the Machine. I will say more about rock's relationship with rap in the next section.

Finally, we turn to what some might consider the elephant in the room: country music. Country music predates rock, extending back to the 1920s, and has strong roots in the common practice (though with some influence of blues).[7] Early country songs such as Hank Williams's "I'm So

7. The relationship between the blues and early country music (sometimes called "hillbilly music") is a controversial issue. Some authors have argued for strong and pervasive links between the two styles (Hatch & Millward, 1987; Stoia, 2003), but Titon (2002, 16) asserts that relatively few early country artists incorporated blues elements. I find little blues influence in popular country songs of the 1940s and early 1950s.

Example 11.5. Usher, "Yeah"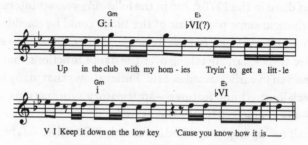

Up in the club with my hom - ies Tryin' to get a litt - le

V I Keep it down on the low key 'Cause you know how it is___

Lonesome I Could Cry," the Carter Singers' "Can the Circle Be Unbroken," and Roy Acuff's "Great Speckled Bird" feature simple major-mode progressions (e.g., I–IV–V–I), close melodic-harmonic coordination, and simple rhythms with only occasional syncopations; this music is almost entirely within the common-practice tradition. This is not to deny the importance of country music as a conduit for this tradition, but I see very little in rock that is due *exclusively* to country's influence.

Country has flourished alongside rock for the entirety of rock's existence. The two have sometimes overlapped in acts such as the Eagles (especially their early music), the Dixie Chicks, and Shania Twain, but they are usually treated as quite distinct styles.[8] And yet, while I am not an expert on country music, it seems to me that the defining musical features of country are very similar to those of rock. We see verse-chorus structures, anticipatory syncopation, backbeat rhythmic patterns, and some use of blues-influenced mediant mixture. Even some quite specific conventions of rock are seen in country; note, for example, the plagal stop cadence in the Marshall Tucker Band's "Heard It in a Love Song." Neal (2000) shows that irregular phrase structures such as metrical reinterpretations and expanded phrases, common in rock, are widely used in country music as well. There are some audible features that set country apart from rock—the use of steel-string guitar, the twangy vocal style—but these would seem to be rather superficial differences, no greater than those found between genres of rock itself.

So, why do I not consider country part of rock music? My answer is simple and unsatisfying: because nobody else does. To include Merle

8. The 200-song *Rolling Stone* corpus used in this study includes just two songs that would definitely be classified as country: one by Hank Williams and one by Patsy Cline. It also includes three songs by Johnny Cash, who seems borderline. Johnny Cash is also the only (arguably) country artist included in the Rock and Roll Hall of Fame. Most books on rock, such as those by Stephenson (2002) and Covach & Flory (2015), say little about country music, except perhaps as an early influence on rock.

Haggard and Garth Brooks in a book ostensibly about "rock" would simply be confusing and misleading. Still, the fundamental commonality between the two styles should be acknowledged. A thorough investigation of this issue, comparing the musical features of rock and country more systematically, would be well worthwhile, but that is another project.

11.4   ROCK AFTER 2000

I made clear in chapter 1 that the main focus of this book would be on rock up to the year 2000—a cutoff that some readers have probably found frustrating. There were several reasons for this decision. From the distance of a couple of decades or more, we can better assess what music has lasting importance and what the significant trends are; admittedly, also, I simply have less knowledge of more recent music. An additional consideration is that, in the opinion of some at least, rock is well past its peak of importance and vitality. One might point to the 500-song *Rolling Stone* list as evidence of this; as noted earlier, the list contains far fewer songs from the later decades—only 20 from the 1990s, and only three from the 2000s (although the survey was only published in 2004). In 2011, Paul Gambaccini, a leading radio personality in the UK, noted the sharp decline in the presence of rock on the popular charts and declared "the end of the rock era"; many other similar statements can be found. Meanwhile, other genres have come to the fore; in particular, hip-hop has greatly increased in both commercial success and critical esteem, arguably surpassing rock in both respects.

Thus, it might be reasonable to view the post-millennial era as the period of rock's decline. Still, it remains an important part of the musical world, and it is interesting to consider what directions it has taken in recent years. In what follows, I offer some observations about this. All of these changes have been gradual, and some of them were already underway in earlier years (I see nothing special about the year 2000). As always, my observations are based largely on informal impressions and analyses of a large number of songs. It seemed desirable to have *some* statistical data, though (partly to allow for comparison with our earlier corpus data), so my student Adam Waller and I created harmonic analyses and melodic transcriptions of a small set of post-millennial songs. The songs were taken from *Rolling Stone*'s list of the "100 Best Songs of the 2000s," spanning the years 2000 to 2009. We examined the top 40 songs on the list; nine of them were hip-hop songs (a significant fact in itself) and were excluded, leaving 31 songs to be analyzed.[9] Obviously, any corpus as small as this will have a large margin of error; the statistical trends I note below are all confirmed by my own intuitions, based on a large number of other songs from the post-2000 era.

We should first acknowledge the huge changes in music technology that have occurred since the 1990s, affecting the production of rock and other musical styles in profound ways. Sequencers (programs for constructing and editing note patterns) combined with synthesizer software now allow the instrumental parts of a song to be created entirely on a computer. Meanwhile, the use of digital sampling—extracting small snippets of a recording for use in another song—has become ubiquitous, especially in rap but also to some extent in rock as well. This complicates the issue of authorship—already complex in rock, as discussed in chapter 1—still further. Patterns of consumption have also changed, as they have throughout rock's history—from singles to LPs to CDs to downloads. The musical effects of all of these developments—especially on structural aspects such as harmony, rhythm, and form—are often difficult to discern. The vast range of music available on the internet has also given rise to a huge variety of genres and subgenres. (In Wikipedia's article on heavy metal, I count 17 subgenres of that genre alone.) Despite all this, I still believe that much of today's popular music can legitimately be described as rock, broadly defined as it is here; indeed, in some ways, the style has remained surprisingly stable through all of these technological upheavals.

Several changes in rock's recent decades relate to tempo and rhythmic feel. It was observed earlier that the 1990s reflect a notable slowing of tempo (see Example 4.3); curiously, the 2000s reverse that trend somewhat, with an average tempo of 108.5 in our corpus, but still show a decline in relation to the 1980s.[10] I suspect this decline in tempo is due to the influence of rap, which tends to feature a dense delivery of syllables, largely at the sixteenth-note level; the slowing of tempo may have arisen to facilitate this. (It may also be due to the rise of electronic dance music, discussed in the previous section; this largely took over the dance function that rock had served in earlier decades, freeing it from the pressure to stay within a danceable tempo range.) This sixteenth-note style of delivery has spread to sung melodies

9. A number of songs included both rapped and sung sections, so the choice of which songs to exclude was somewhat arbitrary; we included any song that seemed to have more sung melody than rap. One song, Eminem's "Lose Yourself" (2002), is in this set but is also in the earlier 200-song set.

10. Schellenberg & von Scheve (2012), looking at songs on the Billboard Hot 100, find similar trends—a decrease in tempo from the 1980s (104.2) to the 1990s (89.4), and then an increase again in the 2000s (99.9).

Example 11.6. R. Kelly, "Ignition (Remix)"

Now I'm not tryin' to be— rude But hey prett-y girl I'm feel - in' you—

as well, seen for example in Maroon 5's "Harder to Breathe" and Destiny's Child's "Jumpin' Jumpin'" (discussed in the previous chapter); we sometimes even see exploration of the thirty-second-note metrical level, as in R. Kelly's "Ignition (Remix)" (Example 11.6), something rarely seen in the earlier decades of rock.[11] These developments parallel the rise of the sixteenth-note level (and the associated drop in tempo) that occurred in the 1960s.

Also in recent years, we have seen a resurgence of "swing" feel, an uneven (long-short) division of the beat. A swing feel was common in very early rock; in recent music, though, it is not the tactus beat (the quarter note) that is unevenly divided, as in 1950s rock, but rather the level below, the eighth note. This rhythmic feel appeared in the late 1980s and 1990s in songs like Janet Jackson's "Nasty" and Sublime's "What I Got," and has continued in the post-2000 era with songs like Avril Lavigne's "Complicated," Beyoncé's "Single Ladies," and Train's "Soul Sister." There is sometimes a gray area between a swung division of the eighth note and an actual triplet division, such as that shown in Example 4.4B.

Some changes are evident, also, in the area of form. The fadeout, the standard way of ending songs in the 1960s and 1970s, seems to have become markedly less popular in the 2000s. This may be due to the changing conventions of radio: fadeouts were convenient in the early years of rock because they allowed the disc jockey to talk over the end of the song, but this practice is no longer common. A further change is the decline in the improvised solo. In recent rock, the contrasting material after the second VCU is much more likely to be a bridge than a guitar solo. Guitar solos were always much more common in the harder varieties of rock, but even in these genres they seem less frequent now. This may represent rock's increasing stylistic distance from the blues, a trend that I will return to below.[12]

11. The issue of the tactus (discussed in section 4.1) arises again here. In my notation of Example 11.6, I take the kick/snare alternation (the snare represented here by hand claps) to define the tactus; but one could say the melodic grouping and harmonic rhythm suggest a tactus twice as fast.

12. Corpus evidence confirms these trends, though—as always—the fairly small sample size should be kept in mind. In songs from the 1960s, 1970s, and 1980s in the *Rolling Stone* corpus, 59% of the songs have fadeouts; in our corpus of songs from the 2000s, only 36% do. Improvised solos (though there is some subjectivity in identifying these) occur in 35% of the songs from the 1960s, 1970s, and 1980s, but only 16% of songs in the 2000s.

In the realm of harmony, songs based on repeating patterns of two to four chords ("loops") seem as prevalent as ever, if not more so. In particular, we must note the amazing rise of the I–V–vi–IV progression (sometimes in other rotations, producing the "fragile tonic" effect, or with vi as the tonic instead of I). Already popular in the 1990s (as noted in section 3.4), this progression has become practically normative in recent years; listening to the radio, it sometimes seems as if every other song uses it. It is notable that the early and late years of rock seem to have been dominated by stereotyped harmonic patterns (the blues and doo-wop progressions in the early years and I–V–vi–IV in the late years); the middle period—its heyday—saw a much greater variety of harmony. I notice also (though this is hard to quantify) that many recent songs have fairly sparse accompaniment textures, comprising just short linear gestures—almost pointillistic sometimes—in the bass and/or upper voices. Destiny's Child's "Jumpin' Jumpin'," analyzed in the previous chapter, is an excellent example; others include Usher's "Yeah" and Justin Timberlake's "SexyBack." This can make harmonic analysis difficult; indeed, one might question the very existence of a triadic harmonic structure in such songs. Perhaps this trend results from the "computer-based" mode of composition and production that is now widespread.

In a recent corpus study, Schellenberg & von Scheve (2012) classify songs from the 1960s through the 2000s as major or minor (based on whether the tonic triad is major or minor) and find a striking rise in the proportion of minor songs. I believe this is a real and important trend, though I would characterize it somewhat differently. Example 11.7 shows the distribution of melodic and harmonic scale degrees from our 2000s corpus, compared with the distributions from the earlier *Rolling Stone* corpus (shown earlier in Example 2.9). Regarding the melodic distributions, the 2000s corpus shows higher values for $\flat\hat{3}$ in relation to $\hat{3}$ and for $\flat\hat{6}$ in relation to $\hat{6}$; this does, indeed, fit the description of a "major-to-minor" shift reasonably well. As noted earlier, however, even within melodies using $\flat\hat{3}$, we see a dramatic increase in the use of $\flat\hat{6}$ relative to $\hat{6}$; this suggests, perhaps, a shift from a Dorian or pentatonic-union orientation to an Aeolian one. The harmonic scale-degree distribution shows these patterns even more strongly: strikingly, in the 2000s distribution, the $\flat\hat{3}$ degree, less than half as common as $\hat{3}$ in the earlier data, is now *more* common than $\hat{3}$, and $\flat\hat{6}$ has greatly increased in frequency in relation to $\hat{6}$ (though still less common). The fondness for Aeolian mode is readily apparent in the music of bands like Linkin Park, Fall Out Boy, and System of a Down. I have also noticed (though this is not strongly shown by the statistical data) a rise in the use of $\flat$II (and melodic $\flat\hat{2}$) in recent music—reflecting even more extreme exploration of the flat

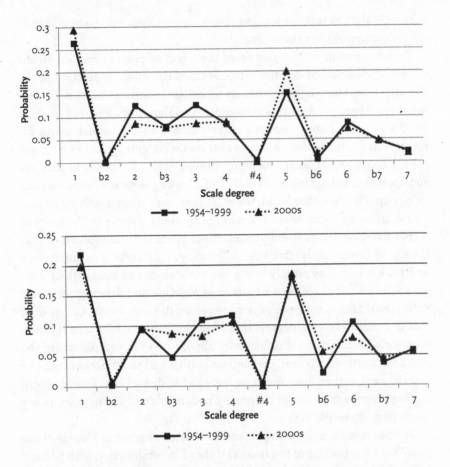

Example 11.7. The distribution of scale-degrees in songs from 1954–1999 and 2000–2009, from melodic transcriptions (above) and harmonic analyses (below).

side. Notably, this is seen not only in the harder genres of rock (where $\flat\hat{2}$ has always had a presence), but also in pop and dance-oriented music—songs such as Britney Spears's "Toxic," the Weeknd's "Can't Feel My Face," and Justin Timberlake's "SexyBack" and "Rock Your Body."

In general, then, I would characterize the recent change in rock's pitch organization as reflecting a flatward shift on the line of fifths. How can we make sense of this? In part, it may reflect a decline in the "mixed" practice common in earlier rock, in which a minor melody is combined with a major accompaniment. This practice seems to be virtually absent in music of the 2000s; when the melody features $\flat\hat{3}$, the accompaniment almost always does so as well. Perhaps this reflects the declining influence of the blues, the original source of the practice. This could partly explain the flatward harmonic shift in recent rock, but it does not account for the similar flat-ward shift in melodies themselves.

Earlier (section 7.1) we discussed the effect of pitch collection on the valence dimension of emotion: if recent popular music is shifting to the flat direction, this suggests that its emotional connotations are becoming more negative. And this calls out for explanation. Perhaps modern youths are less happy than the previous generation, and looking for music that confirms their emotional state (Schellenberg and von Scheve [2012] consider explanations along these lines).[13] Or perhaps they are so happy that things becomes dull, and a bit of gloom is needed to spice things up. On the other hand, the shift may not reflect anything so profound. In many cases, there is nothing especially gloomy in the lyrics of recent flat-side songs (though sometimes there is). I noted earlier that the use of (moderately) flat-side collections (e.g., Dorian) in much disco and funk music may simply bring out the element of mild risk or danger in the situation (often a situation of nightlife and dancing combined with sexual adventure); perhaps more recent flat-side music simply does this to a more extreme degree. In a song like "SexyBack," I take the connotations of the ♭II as mischievous, almost playful—emphasizing the potential perils of a late-night hookup (which add to its excitement in a certain way), rather than anything truly sad or disturbing. There is nothing here comparable to the extremely negative lyrics of Phrygian heavy metal (e.g., Example 7.3).

Further complicating things is another curious harmonic change in the post-2000 era: the rise of the (major) V chord in combination with (minor) i. Roughly speaking, we could think of this as reflecting the "harmonic minor" scale, the standard minor scale in common-practice music. (The harmonic minor scale also contains the $\hat{4}$ and ♭$\hat{6}$ degrees.) Combining i and V is quite rare in earlier rock; by my count, only 12 of the songs (6.0%) in the *Rolling Stone* corpus do so in any significant way. By contrast, 7 of the 31 songs in the 2000s corpus (22.5%) combine i and V. Numerous other examples outside of this small corpus could be cited, such as Maroon 5's "This Love," Britney Spears's "Oops!... I Did It Again," and Bruno Mars's

13. The factor of age is really beyond our scope, but cannot go completely unmentioned if we are trying to explain changes in musical style. Young adults (ages 15 to 25) tend to spend the most money on music (Boorstin, 2004), thus driving music industry trends, and adults of all ages tend to feel most passionately about music they learned in young adulthood (Holbrook & Schindler, 1989). Krumhansl & Zupnick (2013) find that today's young adults are most attached to very recent music, though they also show interest in music of the previous generation, as discussed below.

"Grenade." I suspect this change may reflect the influence of Latin music (salsa and other styles), where the mixing of i and V is common; Santana's "Smooth" and Ricky Martin's "She Bangs" are clearly Latin-influenced songs that have this feature.

Notwithstanding these important changes, perhaps even more striking are the commonalities between post-2000 rock and that of earlier decades. I would suggest that much of the music heard on the radio in recent years could have been heard—perhaps with a few changes in instrumentation and recording techniques—30 or even 40 years earlier. Consider a song like Kelly Clarkson's "Since U Been Gone," one of the biggest hits of the millennium's first decade. This is a veritable showcase of the conventions of the rock style discussed in earlier chapters: Nearly all of the characteristic differences between verses and choruses shown in Table 8.1 are represented ("more internal lyric repetition" is perhaps one exception); we also have conventional features such as a hypermetrically irregular prechorus, another phrase expansion at the end of the chorus, and a variant of the plagal stop cadence (with ii rather than IV—but this kind of tweaking of the schema was often seen in earlier decades as well). Covers of old songs, like Uncle Kracker's version of Dobie Gray's "Drift Away," Christine Aguilera, Lil' Kim, Mýa, and Pink's of LaBelle's "Lady Marmalade," and the Goo Goo Dolls' of Supertramp's "Give a Little Bit," have had great success, while songs like Daft Punk's "Get Lucky" and Mark Ronson's "Uptown Funk" bring to mind 1970s disco and funk. One could say the latter songs are intentionally "retro," and they do have some features that seem more characteristic of the 1970s, especially the rhythm guitar in "Get Lucky." But in most other respects, they fit in quite comfortably with the music of the 2010s; I wonder if younger listeners hear them as alluding to past styles at all.

In the grand scheme of things, the stability of rock over the five decades of its (mature) existence is truly remarkable. Added to this is the fact that many young people today seem to have a great knowledge of older (1970s and 1980s) music and a strong affection for it, as shown by a recent study by Krumhansl & Zupnick (2013). One could say they learned it from their parents (this is in fact Krumhansl & Zupnick's explanation). But did children of the 1970s (I was one, born in 1963) listen to music of the 1940s—Glenn Miller, Count Basie, and Frank Sinatra? Not that I recall! I suspect one reason for this affection for older music among today's youth is that much of the new music they hear is just not that different from it, in terms of the system of conventions needed to understand it. Some might see the stability of rock as a sign of aesthetic decline and stagnation—perhaps resulting from the over-concentration of power in a small number of risk-averse recording companies.[14] Alternatively, one could say—and *I* would say—that the stability of rock shows the fruitfulness of the style, its aesthetic potential; the fact that people still choose to work within the conventions of rock after so many years speaks to the artistic capacity of those conventions, and to their communicative power.

And this brings us to a suitable question to end with—for some, perhaps, the really big question: What is it that makes rock, as a musical style, work so well, for so many people? I promised in chapter 1 to try to shed some light on what makes rock music effective and appealing, and I have tried to do so at various points throughout the book. I believe much of the answer lies in the *expressive* aspects of rock: the way it conveys dimensions of valence, energy, and tension, and changes in these dimensions over the course of a song. Using these dimensions, rock songs can construct complex narratives—albeit of a rather abstract nature—that engage us both cognitively and emotionally. I am not claiming that these are necessary features of *every* successful musical style; to establish this would of course require a much broader investigation. But in the case of rock, at least, I believe these expressive dimensions are crucially important.

Beyond these expressive aspects of rock, though, we can take great pleasure simply in the ways that it manipulates abstract musical structures: melody and harmony, rhythm and meter, phrase structure and form. And this brings me back to a point I have made repeatedly: much of the greatness in individual rock songs—for me and, I think, for many other listeners—lies not in the revolutionary smashing of rules or pushing of frontiers, but in the subtle, incremental, skillful manipulation of conventions. Whether there is anything about the conventions of rock that is particularly conducive to this is an interesting question. Certainly, though, rock is not unique in this regard. Writing about common-practice music, Leonard Meyer expressed similar thoughts:

> Though some composers have both invented new principles and devised new
> means for their realization, creating compositions of the highest aesthetic
> value . . . many of those recognized as great masters have transcended no lim-
> its, promulgated no new principles. Rather they have been inventive strategists,
> imaginative and resourceful in exploiting and extending existing limits. (Meyer,
> 1980, 178)

14. The effect of the recording industry on musical diversity and innovation has been a topic of debate. See Christianen (1995) and Peterson & Berger (1996).

Think of the IV chord in the Who's "Bargain," Marvin Gaye's handling of the prechorus in "I Heard It through the Grapevine," and Stevie Nicks' use of tonal ambiguity in "Landslide." It is moments such as these in rock that first captivated me, and have kept me in the music's grasp ever since. And we can only understand these moments in relation to the musical language of rock as a whole. I hope this book has made a contribution in illuminating rock's framework of conventions, and in showing how the skillful "play" with these conventions can give rise to great music.

11.5 QUESTIONS

1. A musical genre that was popular just before the birth of rock & roll is *jump blues*. Its leading practitioner was Louis Jordan, along with his band the Tympany Five. Jump blues shared many traits with early rock; indeed, Jordan's song "Saturday Night Fish Fry" (1949) has sometimes been called the first rock & roll song. Compare this song with early rock songs like Elvis Presley's "Hound Dog," Chuck Berry's "Johnny B. Goode," and Little Richard's "Tutti Frutti"; what are the similarities and differences?

2. A period that has been somewhat neglected in this study has been the very early 1960s. Covach & Flory (2015) note that this period saw a shift in control over the recording industry from upstart independent labels to established record companies, and they suggest that this led to the incorporation of more conservative stylistic elements (borrowed from Tin Pan Alley and common-practice music) and to the suppression of African-American influences. Compare two songs such as Elvis Presley's "Hound Dog" (1956) and the Shirelles' "Will You Love Me Tomorrow" (1961) (admittedly these songs have been cherry-picked to make the point clearly). In what ways does the latter song show stronger common-practice / Tin Pan Alley influence? Consider aspects such as harmony, melody, rhythm, instrumentation, and form.

3. I mentioned three recent (post-2000) covers of older songs (all from the 1970s): Uncle Kracker's of Dobie Gray's "Drift Away," Christine Aguilera, Lil' Kim, Mýa, and Pink's of LaBelle's "Lady Marmalade," and the Goo Goo Dolls' of Supertramp's "Give a Little Bit." While all three covers retain substantial elements from the originals, there are interesting differences as well; discuss. Do the differences reflect broader trends that we have identified in recent rock music?

4. A number of the most popular songs in the post-2000 era have featured four-chord "loops" that (to my hearing anyway) start on IV. These

include Mariah Carey, "We Belong Together"; Coldplay, "Viva La Vida"; Katy Perry, "Friday Night"; and Taylor Swift, "Bad Blood." What is the exact chord progression in each case? What more general phenomenon does this represent, with regard to the treatment of tonic harmony?

5. Rock has influenced popular music all over the world, often mixing with indigenous styles in interesting ways. Consider Bollywood, the primary popular music genre of modern India. Listen to a few Bollywood songs and consider how the style is similar to or different from rock, with regard to all of the dimensions considered here: tonality/scale, harmony, rhythm/meter, melody, phrase structure, timbre/instrumentation, and form. (This could be a term paper—or another book!)

REFERENCES

Adams, K. 2009. On the metrical techniques of flow in rap music. *Music Theory Online*, 15/5. Retrieved from http://www.mtosmt.org/issues/mto.09.15.5/mto.09.15.5.adams.html.

Aldwell, E., Schachter, C., & Cadwallader, A. 2011. *Harmony and Voice Leading* (4th ed.). Boston: Schirmer.

Attas, R. 2013. Form as process: The buildup introduction in popular music. *Music Theory Spectrum*, 37, 275–96.

Berlyne, D. 1971. *Aesthetics and Psychobiology*. New York: Appleton-Century-Crofts.

Bertin-Mahieux, T., Ellis, D., Whitman, B., & Lamere, P. 2011. The Million Song Dataset. In *Proceedings of the 12th Conference on Music Information Retrieval*, Miami.

Biamonte, N. 2010. Triadic modal and pentatonic patterns in rock music. *Music Theory Spectrum*, 32, 95–110.

Biamonte, N. 2014. Formal functions of metric dissonance in rock music. *Music Theory Online*, 20/2. Retrieved from http://www.mtosmt.org/issues/mto.14.20.2/mto.14.20.2.biamonte.html.

Bigand, E., & Parncutt, R. 1999. Perceiving musical tension in long chord sequences. *Psychological Research*, 62, 237–54.

Björnberg, A. (1985). On Aeolian harmony in contemporary popular music. In A. Moore (ed.), *Critical Essays in Popular Musicology* (275–82). Aldershot, UK: Ashgate.

Boorstin, E. 2004. Music sales in the age of file sharing. Senior thesis, Princeton University.

Bowman, R. 1997. *Soulsville, U.S.A.: The Story of Stax Records*. New York: Schirmer.

Brackett, D. 1994. The politics and practice of "crossover" in American popular music, 1963 to 1965. *The Musical Quarterly*, 78, 774–97.

Brown, M. 1997. "Little Wing": A study in music cognition. In J. Covach & G. Boone (eds.), *Understanding Rock: Essays in Musical Analysis* (155–69). New York: Oxford University Press.

Burgoyne, J. 2011. Stochastic processes and database-driven musicology. Ph.D. Dissertation, McGill University.

Burgoyne, J., Wild, J., & Fujinaga, I. 2011. An expert ground truth set for audio chord recognition and music analysis. In *Proceedings of the 12th International Conference on Music Information Retrieval*, Miami.

Burns, E. 1999. Intervals, scales, and tuning. In D. Deutsch (ed.), *The Psychology of Music* (2nd ed.) (261–64). New York: Academic Press.

Burns, L. 2000. Analytic methodologies for rock music: Harmonic and voice-leading strategies in Tori Amos's "Crucify." In W. Everett (ed.), *Expression in Pop-Rock Music: A Collection of Critical and Analytical Essays* (213–46). New York: Garland.

Burns, L. 2005. Meaning in a popular song: The representation of masochistic desire in Sarah McLachlan's "Ice." In D. Stein (ed.), *Engaging Music: Essays in Musical Analysis* (136–48). New York: Oxford University Press.

Butler, M. 2006. *Unlocking the Groove: Rhythm, Meter, and Musical Design in Electronic Dance Music.* Bloomington: Indiana University Press.

Caplin, W. 1987. The "expanded cadential progression": A category for the analysis of classical form. *Journal of Musicological Research*, 7, 215–57.

Caplin, W. 1998. *Classical Form: A Theory of Formal Functions for the Instrumental Music of Haydn, Mozart, and Beethoven.* New York: Oxford University Press.

Capuzzo, G. 2004. Neo-Riemannian theory and the analysis of pop-rock music. *Music Theory Spectrum*, 26, 177–99.

Christianen, M. 1995. Cycles in symbol production? A new model to explain concentration, diversity and innovation in the music industry. *Popular Music*, 14, 55–93.

Clarke, E. 2005. *Ways of Listening: An Ecological Approach to the Perception of Musical Meaning.* Oxford: Oxford University Press.

Clement, B. 2013. Modal tonicization in rock: The special case of the Lydian scale. *Gamut*, 6/1. Retrieved from http://trace.tennessee.edu/gamut/vol6/iss1/4/.

Coker, W. 1972. *Music and Meaning: A Theoretical Introduction to Musical Aesthetics.* New York: The Free Press.

Conley, J. 1981. Physical correlates of the judged complexity of music by subjects differing in musical background. *British Journal of Psychology*, 72, 451–64.

Conner-Simons, A. 2007. Picking up what they're laying down. *Gelf Magazine.* Retrieved from http://www.gelfmagazine.com/archives/picking_up_what_theyre_laying_down.php.

Coryell, J., & Friedman, L. 2000. *Jazz-Rock Fusion: The People, the Music.* New York: Hal Leonard Corporation.

Covach, J. 1997. Progressive rock, "Close to the Edge," and the boundaries of style. In J. Covach & G. M. Boone (eds.), *Understanding Rock: Essays in Musical Analysis* (3–31). New York: Oxford University Press.

Covach, J. 2003. Pangs of history in late 1970s new-wave rock. In A. Moore (ed.), *Analyzing Popular Music* (173–95). Cambridge, UK: Cambridge University Press.

Covach, J. 2005. Form in rock music: A primer. In D. Stein (ed.), *Engaging Music: Essays in Music Analysis* (65–76). New York: Oxford University Press.

Covach, J., & Boone, G. M. (eds.). 1997. *Understanding Rock: Essays in Musical Analysis.* New York: Oxford University Press.

Covach, J., & Flory, A. 2015. *What's That Sound? An Introduction to Rock and Its History* (4th ed.). New York: W. W. Norton.

Cunningham, M. 1998. *Good Vibrations: A History of Record Production.* London: Sanctuary.

Cusic, D. 2002. The development of gospel music. In A. Moore (ed.), *The Cambridge Companion to Blues and Gospel Music* (44–60). Cambridge, UK: Cambridge University Press.

de Clercq, T. 2012. Sections and successions in successful songs: A prototype approach to form in rock music. Ph.D. Dissertation, University of Rochester.

de Clercq, T. 2016. Measuring a measure: Absolute time as a factor for determining
    bar lengths and meter in pop/rock music. *Music Theory Online*, 22/3. Retrieved
    from http://mtosmt.org/issues/mto.16.22.3/mto.16.22.3.declercq.html.
de Clercq, T., & Temperley, D. 2011. A corpus analysis of rock harmony. *Popular Music*,
    30, 47–70.
DeCurtis, A. (ed.). 1992. *Present Tense: Rock & Roll and Culture*. Durham, NC: Duke
    University Press.
Dettmar, K., & Richey, W. (eds.). 1999. *Reading Rock and Roll: Authenticity,
    Appropriation, Aesthetics*. New York: Columbia University Press.
Dobbins, B. 1994. *A Creative Approach to Jazz Piano Harmony*. Rottenburg,
    Germany: Advance Music.
Doll, C. 2007. Listening to Rock Harmony. Ph.D. Dissertation, Columbia University.
Doll, C. 2009. Transformation in rock harmony: An explanatory strategy. *Gamut*, 2/1.
    Retrieved from http://trace.tennessee.edu/gamut/vol2/iss1/14/.
Doll, C. 2011. Rockin' out: Expressive modulation in verse-chorus form. *Music Theory
    Online*, 17/3. Retrieved from http://www.mtosmt.org/issues/mto.11.17.3/
    mto.11.17.3.doll.html.
Endrinal, C. 2008. Form and style in the music of U2. Ph.D. Dissertation, Florida
    State University.
Endrinal, C. 2011. Burning bridges: Defining the interverse in the music of U2.
    Music Theory Online, 17/3. Retrieved from http://www.mtosmt.org/issues/
    mto.11.17.3/mto.11.17.3.endrinal.html
Evans, P., & Schubert, E. 2008. Relationships between expressed and felt emotions in
    music. *Musicae Scientiae*, 12, 75–99.
Everett, W. 1999. *The Beatles as Musicians: Revolver through the Anthology*.
    New York: Oxford University Press.
Everett, W. 2004. Making sense of rock's tonal systems. *Music Theory Online*, 10/4.
    Retrieved from http://www.mtosmt.org/issues/mto.04.10.4/mto.04.10.4.w_
    everett.html.
Everett, W. (ed.). 2008a. *Expression in Pop-Rock Music: Critical and Analytical Essays*.
    New York: Routledge.
Everett, W. 2008b. Pitch down the middle. In W. Everett (ed.), *Expression in Pop-Rock
    Music: Critical and Analytical Essays* (2nd ed.) (111–74). New York: Routledge.
Everett, W. 2009. *The Foundations of Rock: From "Blue Suede Shoes" to "Suite: Judy Blue
    Eyes."* New York: Oxford University Press.
Farbood, M. 2012. A parametric, temporal model of musical tension. *Music Perception*,
    29, 387–428.
Fast, S. 2000. Music, contexts, and meaning in U2. In W. Everett (ed.), *Expression in
    Pop-Rock Music: Critical and Analytical Essays* (33–57). New York: Routledge.
Flory, A. 2010. Marvin Gaye as vocal composer. In M. Spicer & J. Covach
    (eds.), *Sounding Out Pop: Analytical Essays in Popular Music* (63–98). Ann
    Arbor: University of Michigan Press.
Frane, A. 2017. Swing rhythm in classic drum breaks from hip-hop's breakbeat canon.
    Music Perception, 34, 291–302.
Friberg, A., & Sundström, A. 2002. Swing ratios and ensemble timing in jazz perfor-
    mance: Evidence for a common rhythmic pattern. *Music Perception*, 19, 333–49.
Friedlander, P. 1996. *Rock & Roll: A Social History*. Boulder, CO: Westview Press.
Frith, S. 1981. *Sound Effects: Youth, Leisure, and the Politics of Rock'n'Roll*.
    New York: Pantheon.

Frith, S. 1987. Towards an aesthetic of popular music. In R. Leppert & S. McClary (eds.), *Music and Society: The Politics of Composition, Performance and Reception* (133–49). Cambridge, UK: Cambridge University Press.

Gabrielsson, A., & Lindström, E. 2001. The influence of musical structure on emotional expression. In P. Juslin & J. Sloboda (eds.), *Music and Emotion: Theory and Research* (223–48). Oxford: Oxford University Press.

George-Warren, H., Romanowski, P., Bashe, P. R., & Pareles, J. (2001). *The Rolling Stone Encyclopedia of Rock & Roll.* New York: Touchstone Press.

Gibson, J. 1966. *The Senses Considered as Perceptual Systems.* Boston: Houghton Mifflin.

Gracyk, T. 2001. *I Wanna Be Me: Rock Music and the Politics of Identity.* Philadelphia: Temple University Press.

Grahn, J., & Brett, M. 2007. Rhythm and beat perception in motor areas of the brain. *Journal of Cognitive Neuroscience*, 19, 893–906.

Greenwald, J. 2002. Hip-hop drumming: The rhyme may define, but the groove makes you move. *Black Music Research Journal*, 22, 259–71.

Grey, J. 1977. Multidimensional perceptual scaling of musical timbres. *Journal of the Acoustical Society of America*, 61, 1270–77.

Griffiths, D. 2015. Elevating form and elevating modulation. *Popular Music*, 34, 22–44.

Guitar World. 2009. 50 greatest guitar solos. Retrieved from http://www.guitarworld.com/50-greatest-guitar-solos.

Hatch, D., & Millward, S. 1987. *From Blues to Rock: An Analytical History of Pop Music.* Manchester, UK: Manchester University Press.

Hawkins, S. 1992. Prince: Harmonic analysis of "Anna Stesia." *Popular Music*, 11, 325–35.

Headlam, D. 1997. Blues transformations in the music of Cream. In J. Covach & G. Boone (eds.), *Understanding Rock: Essays in Music Analysis* (59–82). New York: Oxford University Press.

Headlam, D. 2002. Appropriations of blues and gospel in popular music. In A. Moore (ed.), *The Cambridge Companion to Blues and Gospel Music* (158–87). Cambridge, UK: Cambridge University Press.

Heidemann, K. 2016. A system for describing vocal timbre in popular song. *Music Theory Online*, 22/1. Retrieved from http://www.mtosmt.org/issues/mto.16.22.1/mto.16.22.1.heidemann.html.

Hesselink, N. 2014. Rhythmic play, compositional intent and communication in rock music. *Popular Music*, 33, 69–90.

Heyduk, R. 1975. Rated preference for musical compositions as it relates to complexity and exposure frequency. *Perception and Psychophysics*, 17, 84–90.

Holbrook, M., & Schindler, R. 1989. Some exploratory findings on the development of musical tastes. *Journal of Consumer Research*, 16, 119–24.

Holm-Hudson, K. (ed.). 2002. *Progressive Rock Reconsidered.* New York: Routledge.

Huron, D. 2006. *Sweet Anticipation: Music and the Psychology of Expectation.* Cambridge, MA: MIT Press.

Ilie, G., & Thompson, W. 2006. A comparison of acoustic cues in music and speech for three dimensions of affect. *Music Perception*, 23, 319–30.

Iyer, V. 2002. Embodied mind, situated cognition, and expressive microtiming in African-American music. *Music Perception*, 19, 387–414.

Janata, P., Tomic, T., & Haberman, J. 2012. Sensorimotor coupling in music and the psychology of the groove. *Journal of Experimental Psychology: General*, 141, 54–75.

Kastner, M., & Crowder, R. 1990. Perception of the major/minor distinction: IV. Emotional connotations in young children. *Music Perception*, 8, 189–201.

Kearney, M. 2006. *Gender And Rock*. New York: Oxford University Press.

Keightley, K. 2001. Reconsidering rock. In S. Frith, W. Straw, & J. Street (eds.), *The Cambridge Companion to Pop and Rock* (109–42). Cambridge, UK: Cambridge University Press.

Keller, P., & Schubert, E. 2011. Cognitive and affective judgements of syncopated musical themes. *Advances in Cognitive Psychology*, 7, 142–56.

Kerman, J. 1985. *Contemplating Music: Challenges to Musicology*. Cambridge, MA: Harvard University Press.

Koozin, T. 2000. Fumbling towards ecstasy: Voice leading, tonal structure, and the theme of self-realization in the music of Sarah McLachlan. In W. Everett (ed.), *Expression in Pop-Rock Music: Critical and Analytical Essays* (247–66). New York: Routledge.

Krumhansl, C. 1990. *Cognitive Foundations of Musical Pitch*. New York: Oxford University Press.

Krumhansl, C., & Zupnick, J. 2013. Cascading reminiscence bumps in popular music. *Psychological Science*, 24, 2057–68.

Laitz, S. 2012. *The Complete Musician: An Integrated Approach to Tonal Theory, Analysis, and Listening* (3rd ed.). New York: Oxford University Press.

Larkin, C. (ed.). 2003. *The Billboard Illustrated Encyclopedia of Rock*. New York: Billboard Books.

Lerdahl, F., & Jackendoff, R. 1983. *A Generative Theory of Tonal Music*. Cambridge, MA: MIT Press.

Lerdahl, F., & Krumhansl, C. 2007. Modeling tonal tension. *Music Perception*, 24, 329–366.

Levine, M. 1995. *The Jazz Theory Book*. Petaluma, CA: Sher Music.

Levy, R. 2008. Expectation-based syntactic comprehension. *Cognition*, 106, 1126–77.

London, J. 2004. *Hearing in Time: Psychological Aspects of Musical Meter*. New York: Oxford University Press.

London, J. n.d. Metric fake outs. Retrieved from http://people.carleton.edu/~jlondon/.

Macan, E. 1997. *Rocking the Classics: English Progressive Rock and the Counterculture*. New York: Oxford University Press.

Madison, G. 2006. Experiencing groove induced by music: Consistency and phenomenology. *Music Perception*, 24, 201–8.

Madison, G., Gouyon, F., Ullén, F., & Hörnström, K. 2011. Modeling the tendency for music to induce movement in humans: First correlations with low-level audio descriptors across music genres. *Journal of Experimental Psychology: Human Perception and Performance*, 37, 1578–94.

Maher, T., & Berlyne, D. 1982. Verbal and exploratory responses to melodic musical intervals. *Psychology of Music*, 10, 11–27.

Margulis, E. 2005. A model of melodic expectation. *Music Perception*, 22, 663–714.

Margulis, E. 2014. *On Repeat: How Music Plays the Mind*. New York: Oxford University Press.

Mauch, M., Cannam, C., Davies, M., Dixon, S., Harte, C., Kolozali, S., Tidhar, D., & Sandler, M. 2009. OMRAS2 Metadata Project 2009. In *Proceedings of the 10th International Society for Music Information Retrieval*. Kobe, Japan.

McAdams, S. 2013. Musical timbre perception. In D. Deutsch (ed.), *The Psychology of Music* (35–67). Amsterdam: Academic Press.

McClary, S. 1987. The blasphemy of talking politics during Bach year. In R. Leppert & S. McClary (eds.), *Music and Society: The Politics of Composition, Performance, and Reception* (13–62). Cambridge, UK: Cambridge University Press.

Meyer, L. 1956. *Emotion and Meaning in Music*. Chicago: University of Chicago Press.

Meyer, L. 1980. Exploiting limits: Creation, archetypes, and style change. *Daedalus*, 109, 177–205.

Middleton, R. 1972. *Pop Music and the Blues*. London: Victor Gollancz.

Middleton, R. 1990. *Studying Popular Music*. Milton Keynes, UK: Open University Press.

Middleton, R. 2001. Pop, rock and interpretation. In S. Frith, W. Straw, & J. Street (eds.), *The Cambridge Companion to Pop and Rock* (213–25). Cambridge, UK: Cambridge University Press.

Moore, A. 1992. Patterns of harmony. *Popular Music*, 11, 73–106.

Moore, A. 1995. The so-called "flattened seventh" in rock. *Popular Music*, 14, 185–201.

Moore, A. 2001. *Rock: The Primary Text: Developing a Musicology of Rock* (2nd ed.). Aldershot, UK: Ashgate.

Moore, A. 2002a. Authenticity as authentication. *Popular Music*, 21, 209–23.

Moore, A. 2002b. Surveying the field: Our knowledge of blues and gospel music. In A. Moore (ed.), *The Cambridge Companion to Blues and Gospel* (1–12). Cambridge, UK: Cambridge University Press.

Moore, A. 2012. *Song Means: Analysing and Interpreting Recorded Popular Song*. Farnham, UK: Ashgate.

Moorefield, V. 2005. *The Producer as Composer: Shaping the Sounds of Popular Music*. Cambridge, MA: MIT Press.

Neal, J. 2000. Songwriter's signature, artist's imprint: The metric structure of a country song. *Country Music Annual 2000*, 112–140.

Nobile, D. 2011. Form and voice-leading in early Beatles songs. *Music Theory Online*, 17/3. Retrieved from http://www.mtosmt.org/issues/mto.11.17.3/mto.11.17.3.nobile.html.

Nobile, D. 2015. Counterpoint in rock music: Unpacking the "melodic-harmonic divorce." *Music Theory Spectrum*, 37, 189–203.

North, A., & Hargreaves, D. 1995. Subjective complexity, familiarity, and liking for popular music. *Psychomusicology*, 14, 77–93.

Osborn, B. 2013. Subverting the verse-chorus paradigm: Terminally climactic forms in recent rock music. *Music Theory Spectrum*, 35, 23–47.

Osborn, B. 2016. *Everything in Its Right Place: Analyzing Radiohead*. New York: Oxford University Press.

Patel, A. 2008. *Music, Language, and the Brain*. New York: Oxford University Press.

Peterson, R., & Berger, D. 1996. Measuring industry concentration, diversity, and innovation in popular music. *American Sociological Review*, 61, 175–78.

Plasketes, G. (ed.). 2010. *Play It Again: Cover Songs in Popular Music*. Farnham, UK: Ashgate.

Povel, D.-J., & Essens, P. 1985. Perception of temporal patterns. *Music Perception*, 2, 411–40.

Rings, S. 2013. A foreign sound to your ear: Bob Dylan performs "It's Alright, Ma (I'm Only Bleeding)," 1964–2009. *Music Theory Online*, 19. Retrieved from http://www.mtosmt.org/issues/mto.13.19.4/mto.13.19.4.rings.html

Robinson, J. B. 2002. Blue note. In B. Kernfeld (ed.), *The New Grove Dictionary of Jazz* (245–6). New York: Oxford University Press.

Rolling Stone. 2004. The 500 greatest songs of all time. *Rolling Stone*, 963, 65–165.

Rolling Stone. 2011. The 100 best songs of the 2000s. Retrieved from http://www.
    rollingstone.com/music/lists/100-best-songs-of-the-aughts-20110617.
Rolling Stone. 2016. The 100 greatest drummers of all time.
    Retrieved from http://www.rollingstone.com/music/lists/
    100-greatest-drummers-of-all-time-20160331.
Rosenthal, E. 2001. *His Song: The Musical Journey of Elton John*. New York:
    Billboard Books.
Rothstein, W. 1989. *Phrase Rhythm in Tonal Music*. New York: Schirmer.
Russell, J. 1980. A circumplex model of affect. *Journal of Personality and Social
    Psychology*, 39, 1161–1178.
Saffran, J., Aslin, R., & Newport, E. 1996. Statistical learning by 8-month-old infants.
    Science, 274, 1926–28.
Schachter, C. 1980. Rhythm and linear analysis: durational reduction. In F. Salzer
    (ed.), *The Music Forum* (Vol. 5) (197–232). New York: Columbia University
    Press.
Schaffrath, H. 1995. *The Essen Folksong Collection*. D. Huron (ed.). Stanford, CA: Center
    for Computer-Assisted Research in the Humanities.
Schellenberg, G., & von Scheve, C. 2012. Emotional cues in American popular
    music: Five decades of the Top 40. *Psychology of Aesthetics, Creativity, and the
    Arts*, 6, 196–203.
Schoenberg, A. 1969. *Structural Functions of Harmony*. New York: W. W. Norton.
Shepherd, J. 1982. A theoretical model for the sociomusicological analysis of popular
    musics. *Popular Music*, 2, 145–77.
Spicer, M. 2000. Large-scale strategy and compositional design in the early music of
    Genesis. In W. Everett (ed.), *Expression in Pop-Rock Music: Critical and Analytical
    Essays* (77–112). New York: Routledge.
Spicer, M. 2004. (Ac)cumulative form in pop-rock music. *Twentieth-Century Music*,
    1, 29–64.
Spicer, M. 2010. Reggatta de Blanc: Analyzing style in the music of the Police. In
    M. Spicer & J. Covach (eds.), *Sounding Out Pop: Analytical Essays in Popular
    Music* (124–53). Ann Arbor: University of Michigan Press.
Spicer, M. 2017. Fragile, emergent, and absent tonics in pop and rock songs. *Music
    Theory Online*, 22. Retrieved from http://mtosmt.org/issues/mto.17.23.2/
    mto.17.23.2.spicer.html.
Spicer, M., & Covach, J. (eds.). 2010. *Sounding Out Pop: Analytical Essays in Popular
    Music*. Ann Arbor: University of Michigan Press.
Stephan-Robinson, A. 2009. Form in Paul Simon's music. Ph.D. Dissertation,
    University of Rochester.
Stephenson, K. 2002. *What to Listen For in Rock*. New Haven, CT: Yale
    University Press.
Stewart, A. 2000. "Funky Drummer": New Orleans, James Brown and the rhythmic
    transformation of American popular music. *Popular Music*, 19, 293–318.
Stoia, N. 2013. The common stock of schemes in early blues and country music. *Music
    Theory Spectrum*, 35, 194–234.
Summach, J. 2011. The structure, function, and genesis of the prechorus. *Music Theory
    Online*, 17/3. Retrieved from http://www.mtosmt.org/issues/mto.11.17.3/
    mto.11.17.3.summach.html.
Swain, J. P. 1997. *Musical Languages*. New York: W. W. Norton.
Tagg, P. 1982. Analysing popular music: Theory, method, and practice. *Popular Music*,
    2, 37–67.

Tagg, P. 2009. *Everyday tonality: Towards a tonal theory of what most people hear*. New York: Mass Media Music Scholars' Press.

Tallmadge, W. 1984. Blue notes and blue tonality. *The Black Perspective in Music*, 12, 155–65.

Temperley, D. 1999a. The question of purpose in music theory: Description, suggestion, and explanation. *Current Musicology*, 66, 66–85.

Temperley, D. 1999b. Syncopation in rock: A perceptual perspective. *Popular Music*, 18, 19–40.

Temperley, D. 2001. *The Cognition of Basic Musical Structures*. Cambridge, MA: MIT Press.

Temperley, D. 2003. End-accented phrases: An analytical exploration. *Journal of Music Theory*, 47, 125–54.

Temperley, D. 2004. Communicative pressure and the evolution of musical styles. *Music Perception*, 21, 313–37.

Temperley, D. 2007a. The melodic-harmonic "divorce" in rock. *Popular Music*, 26, 323–42.

Temperley, D. 2007b. *Music and Probability*. Cambridge, MA: MIT Press.

Temperley, D. 2009. A statistical analysis of tonal harmony. Retrieved from http://davidtemperley.com/kp-stats/.

Temperley, D. 2011a. The cadential IV in rock. *Music Theory Online*, 17/1. Retrieved from http://www.mtosmt.org/issues/mto.11.17.1/mto.11.17.1.temperley.php.

Temperley, D. 2011b. Scalar shift in rock. *Music Theory Online*, 17/4. Retrieved from http://www.mtosmt.org/issues/mto.11.17.4/mto.11.17.4.temperley.php.

Temperley, D. 2012. Computational models of music cognition. In D. Deutsch (ed.), *The Psychology of Music* (3rd ed). (327–68). Amsterdam: Elsevier.

Temperley, D., & de Clercq, T. 2013. Statistical analysis of harmony and melody in rock music. *Journal of New Music Research*, 42, 187–204.

Temperley, D., Ren, I., & Duan, Z. 2017. Mediant mixture and blue notes in rock: An exploratory study. *Music Theory Online*, 23/1. Retrieved from http://mtosmt.org/issues/mto.17.23.1/mto.17.23.1.temperley.html.

Temperley, D., & Tan, D. 2013. Emotional connotations of diatonic modes. *Music Perception*, 30, 237–57.

Thompson, W. 2014. *Music, Thought, and Feeling: Understanding the Psychology of Music*. New York: Oxford University Press.

Titon, J. 1994. *Early Downhome Blues: A Musical and Cultural Analysis* (2nd ed.). Chapel Hill: University of North Carolina Press.

Titon, J. 2002. Labels: Identifying categories of blues and gospel. In A. Moore (ed.), *The Cambridge Companion to Blues and Gospel* (13–19). Cambridge, UK: Cambridge University Press.

Traut, D. 2005. "Simply Irresistible": Recurring accent patterns as hooks in mainstream 1980s music. *Popular Music*, 24, 57–77.

Tymoczko, D. 2003. Function theories: A statistical approach. *Musurgia*, 10, 35–64. Translated from French at http://dmitri.mycpanel.princeton.edu/files/publications/tonaltheories.pdf.

van der Bliek, R. 2007. The Hendrix chord: Blues, flexible pitch relationships, and self-standing harmony. *Popular Music*, 26, 343–364.

Van der Merwe, P. 1989. *Origins of the Popular Style: The Antecedents of Twentieth-Century Popular Music*. New York: Oxford University Press.

VH1. 2003. *VH1's 100 Greatest Songs of Rock & Roll*. Milwaukee: Hal Leonard.

Vitz, P. 1964. Preferences for rates of information presented by sequences of tones. *Journal of Experimental Psychology*, 68, 176–183.

Wagner, N. 2003. "Domestication" of blue notes in the Beatles' songs. *Music Theory Spectrum*, 25, 353–65.

Walser, R. 1993. *Running with the Devil: Power, Gender, and Madness in Heavy Metal Music*. Middletown, CT: Wesleyan University Press.

Walser, R. 1995. Rhythm, rhyme, and rhetoric in the music of Public Enemy. *Ethnomusicology*, 39, 193–217.

Weisethaunet, H. 2001. Is there such a thing as the "blue note"? *Popular Music*, 20, 99–116.

Whitesell, L. 2008. *The Music of Joni Mitchell*. New York: Oxford University Press.

Witek, M., Clarke, E., Wallentin, M., Kringelbach, M., & Vuust, P. 2014. Syncopation, body-movement and pleasure in groove music. *PLoS ONE*, 9/4. Retrieved from http://journals.plos.org/plosone/article?id=10.1371/journal.pone.0094446.

Zagorski-Thomas, S. 2014. *The Musicology of Record Production*. Cambridge, UK: Cambridge University Press.

Zak, A. 2001. *The Poetics of Rock: Cutting Tracks, Making Records*. Berkeley: University of California Press.

Zbikowski, L. 2004. Modelling the groove: Conceptual structure and popular music. *Journal of the Royal Musical Association*, 129, 272–97.

INDEX OF ARTISTS AND SONGS

Jackson 5, The, 250, 251
  "ABC" (1970), **77**, **103**, **106**, 146, 251
  "Dancing Machine" (1973), **80**
  "I'll Be There" (1970), 177
  "I Want You Back" (1969), 52
Jackson, Janet
  "Nasty" (1986), 66, 259
  "Runaway" (1995), 107, 210
Jackson, Michael
  "Beat It" (1982), 123
  "Billie Jean" (1982), 5, **61**, **74**,
    93, 96, **114**, 139, 158n5, 170,
    197, 198
  "Black or White" (1991), 65
  "Human Nature" (1982), **36**, 70, 164
Jamerson, James, 130
Jane's Addiction, "Jane Says" (1987), 40
Jay-Z, "Empire State of Mind"
    (2009), 255
Jefferson Airplane, "Somebody To Love"
    (1967), 20, 202
Jethro Tull, "Living in the Past"
    (1969), 85
Jett, Joan, and the Blackhearts, "I Love
    Rock 'n Roll" (1981), 186n2, 197,
    202
J. Geils Band, The, "Centerfold"
    (1981), 56n7
Jimi Hendrix Experience, The
  "All Along the Watchtower"
    (1968), **68**, **79**
  "Manic Depression" (1967), 86
  "Purple Haze" (1967), 104n6, 195
  "Voodoo Child (Slight Return)" (1968),
    115, 121
Joel, Billy, 116
  "It's Still Rock and Roll to Me" (1980),
    65, 152
  "Just The Way You Are" (1977), **62**,
    116, 131
  "She's Always a Woman" (1977), 86
John, Elton, 116, 250
  "Bennie and the Jets" (1973), 191
  "Candle in the Wind" (1973), 154
  "Crocodile Rock" (1973), 65
  "Daniel" (1973), **204**, 228–9
  "Don't Let the Sun Go Down on Me"
    (1974), 206
  "Goodbye Yellow Brick Road" (1973),
    60, 225, 238n7

"Philadelphia Freedom" (1975), 220–5,
    220, **222**, **224**
  "Rocket Man" (1972), 205
  "Saturday Night's Alright for Fighting"
    (1973), **95**, **100**, 142, 173
  "Someone Saved My Life Tonight"
    (1975), 65, 167
  "Tiny Dancer" (1971), **131**
  "Your Song" (1970), 5, 52, 142, 225
Jones, Jimmy, "Handy Man" (1959), **110**
Jordan, Louis, and the Tympany
    Five, "Saturday Night Fish Fry"
    (1949), 265
Journey
  "Don't Stop Believin'" (1981), 177
  "Faithfully" (1983), 177
  "Lovin' Touchin' Squeezin'"
    (1979), 177

Kansas, "The Spider" (1977), 116
Kelly, R., "Ignition (Remix)" (2003), **259**
King, Carole, 116
  "It's Too Late" (1971), 43, 206, 250
  "(You Make Me Feel Like) A Natural
    Woman" (1971), 71
  "You've Got a Friend" (1971), **62**
King Crimson, 250
Kinks, The, 250
  "You Really Got Me" (1964), 108
Kinney, Sean, 114, 124
Kiss, "Christine Sixteen" (1977), 207
Knight, Gladys, & the Pips, 212, 216n1
Knowles, Chad, 236
Kramer, Joey, 124

LaBelle, "Lady Marmalade" (1974), 263,
    265
Lavigne, Avril, "Complicated"
    (2002), 259
Led Zeppelin, 81–2, 249, 250
  "Black Dog" (1971), 133
  "Fool in the Rain" (1979), **78**
  "Good Times Bad Times" (1969), 56n7
  "Houses of the Holy" (1975), 91
  "Kashmir" (1975), **71**
  "Living Loving Maid" (1969), **127**
  "No Quarter" (1973), **22**
  "Over the Hills and Far Away"
    (1973), **81**
  "Rock and Roll" (1971), **114**, 191n3

INDEX OF SUBJECTS AND AUTHORS

irregular, 92–3, 96, 107, 144, 196–9,
    222, 245
overlap in, 185–9
unaccented, 91–2
grunge, 5
guitar, 43, 105, 110, 111, 112, 117–123,
    125, 135
effects, 115–6
playing techniques, 117–9
solos, 119–21, 171–2, 228, 259
Guitar World's "50 Greatest Guitar Solos,"
    119n1

hard rock, 20, 52, 141–2, 250–1, 255
Hargreaves, D., 145
harmonic minor scale, 18–19, 23, 41,
    237, 254, 262–3
harmonic rhythm, 80–2, 212–5
harmony (chords)
    common patterns of, 54–7
    extended triadic, 42–3, 244–5, 254
    in common-practice music, 41–2
    inversion in, 43, 130, 227, 244–5
    and meter, 67, 72
    open/closed, 56, 163n10
    principles of progression in, 46–9,
        52–3, 244, 245
    rhythm of. *See* harmonic rhythm
    vocabulary of, 42–6
Hatch, D., 255n7
Hawkins, S., 10
Headlam, D., 54n6, 243
heavy metal, 5, 11, 21, 25, 139–40, 249,
    250, 251, 258, 262
Heidemann, K., 117
Hesselink, N., 68n1
Heyduk, R., 142, 143, 145
hip-hop. *See* rap
Holbrook, M., 262n13
Holm-Hudson, K., 2n2, 251n6
hooktheory.com, 15
Huron, D., 4n6, 98, 144n4
hypermeter, 36–7, 56, 67, 72, 82–4, 107,
    125, 143, 244–5, 263
    and melodic grouping, 90–3
    and tensional curves, 197, 199, 210
    and VCU boundary, 186–7, 210

Ilie, G., 144
information, 143

instrumental (section), 171–2
instrumentation, 109–11, 117–35, 250, 251
    and form, 125, 141, 159, 161–2
    and energy dimension of emotion,
        198, 201–2
instruments,
    brass, 131–2
    harmonica, 131, 171
    sax, 131, 171
    strings, 131, 172
    See also bass guitar, drums, guitar,
        piano, synthesizer
internet, 258
intro, 172–3
Iyer, V., 129, 146

Jackendoff, R., 3, 72, 82, 89, 91, 185
Janata, P., 146
jazz, 7, 42, 43, 49, 55, 68, 73, 129, 146,
    153, 189, 243–7
jump blues, 265

Kastner, M., 138
Kearney, M., 1n1
Keightley, K., 7n10
Keller, P., 144, 146n5
Kerman, J., 242
key-finding, 34–9
key signatures, 17n2
Koozin, T., 37n13
Kostka-Payne corpus, 23n4
Krumhansl, C., 34, 144, 262n13, 263

Laitz, S., 42, 98
lament bass, 246
language (and music), 2–3, 11
Larkin, C., 6n7
Latin/Caribbean music, 253–4, 263
length (of notes), 72
Lerdahl, F., 3, 72, 82, 89, 91, 144, 185
Levine, M., 21n3
Levy, R., 145
Lindström, E., 138, 141, 144
linear patterns, 57–8, 64–5, 130, 222,
    223
line of fifths, 22–3, 27, 28, 30–1, 40, 45,
    48–54, 207, 261
    and form, 164
    and valence dimension of emotion,
        138–41, 147–8, 209n10